“OUR KIND OF MOVIE”

"OUR KIND OF MOVIE" THE FILMS OF ANDY WARHOL

Douglas Crimp

MIT PRESS
CAMBRIDGE, MASSACHUSETTS
LONDON, ENGLAND

MIT Press books may be purchased at special quantity discounts for business or sales promotional use. For information, please email special_sales@mitpress.mit.edu or write to Special Sales Department, The MIT Press, 55 Hayward Street, Cambridge, MA 02142.

This book was set in Helvetica Neue Pro by The MIT Press. Printed and bound in the United States of America.

Library of Congress Cataloging-in-Publication Data

Crimp, Douglas.
"Our kind of movie" : the films of Andy Warhol / Douglas Crimp.
p. cm.
Includes bibliographical references and index.
ISBN 978-0-262-01729-9 (hardcover : alk. paper)
1. Warhol, Andy, 1928–1987—Criticism and interpretation.
I. Warhol, Andy, 1928–1987. II. Title.
PN1998.3.W366C75 2012
700.92—dc23
2011034255

10 9 8 7 6 5 4 3 2 1

WE DIDN'T THINK OF OUR MOVIES AS UNDERGROUND OR COMMERCIAL OR ART OR PORN; THEY WERE A LITTLE OF ALL OF THOSE, BUT ULTIMATELY THEY WERE JUST "OUR KIND OF MOVIE."

ANDY WARHOL

CONTENTS

PREFACE

I conceived this book as a book, not as the collection of essays it turned out to be—a consequence of the occasional way I almost always work. I had set out to write about 1960s New York City queer culture, the culture in which I happily immersed myself when I came to the city after college toward the end of that decade. It was to be an archaeology of a world for which I use the shorthand designation "the back room at Max's," because the room at the back of Max's Kansas City, an art bar on lower Park Avenue near Union Square, was where I mixed with denizens of the underground film and off-off-Broadway theater scene. Once I got down to writing, though, things took their own course. First, the topic quickly changed to Andy Warhol's films. I projected a book about a milieu that was meant to include Warhol and the Factory, certainly, but also a wide range of other underground filmmakers such as Jack Smith, the Kuchar brothers, Ron Rice, and José Rodriguez Soltero, together with the Theater of the Ridiculous in its different guises—the Play-House of the Ridiculous and the Ridiculous Theatrical Company.[1] But I began with an essay on Warhol's early film *Blow Job* and in the process discovered the full extent and richness of Warhol's filmmaking, by itself much more than a book could comprehend.

Like most of these essays, the one on *Blow Job*, "Face Value," was written initially as a lecture. In the summer of 1998, I met the future museum curator Adam Budak while he was still studying at the Jagiellonian University in Krakow. He invited me to speak there, and that invitation extended eventually to a tour of various Eastern European venues, including the Center for Contemporary Art in Warsaw, the Adam Mickiewicz University in Poznan, and the Galerie Rudolfinum in Prague. A lecture on *Blow Job* posed some difficulties in still very Catholic and queer-unfriendly Poland. My translator in Warsaw, reproducing my talk successively, seemed to take unusually long to get each paragraph into Polish, longer than the precision of English often necessitates when rendered into another language. The audience grew more and more restive until finally some of them began yelling at the translator. Since I don't speak Polish, I didn't understand what was happening until I was told later by friends: The translator didn't want to use the colloquial expressions for "blow job," "hustler," and so forth; nor, it seems, did he even want to use the clinical equivalents of "fellatio" and "male prostitute." He attempted to talk his way around such unsavory notions altogether. Of course, this completely ruined my plainspoken prose and often made the sense of my talk incomprehensible, so some in the audience who spoke English well enough to know what the trouble was began shouting out the Polish words the translator should have been using.

Thus begins the story of the occasions for which I wrote these essays. The second, "Mario Montez, for Shame," has a double origin. I had been asked to contribute to an essay collection in honor of Eve Kosofsky Sedgwick and thought something on Warhol might be appropriate. Around the same time, Diedrich Diederichsen, Matthias Haase, and Juliane Rebentisch came to visit me and persuade me to participate in a conference called *Cross Gender/Cross Genre* that they were organizing for Steirischer Herbst 99 in Graz. The conference was one of a series of events organized by a group of Berlin-based critics under the rubric *Remake/Re-model: Secret Histories of Art, Pop, Life, and the Avant-garde.*[2] *Remake/Re-model* also included a complete retrospective of the films of Jack Smith and an installation by Mike Kelly comprising, among other things, video interviews with Warhol superstars, members of the Bay Area psychedelic drag group the Cockettes, and various other performance figures from the 1960s and '70s.[3] This seemed the perfect context for a talk on a Warhol film with drag superstar Mario Montez—a longtime favorite of mine—since it was Smith who discovered René Rivera's gifts and gave him the name Mario Montez.[4] *Screen Test No. 2*, like *Blow Job* a film focused solely on a face, was something I'd considered writing about, and since I was also thinking about Sedgwick's ideas about shame and performativity, the topic of shame seemed a natural.

I had sent "Face Value" to Callie Angell, curator of the Warhol Film Project, whom I'd recently met, and she responded with her typical generosity with two pages of meticulous corrections and discussion of interpretive points. When I sent my second essay, Callie was likewise helpful and so enthusiastic about my reading of *Screen Test No. 2* that she asked my permission to send the text to Ronald Tavel in Bangkok. Tavel was the scenarist and off-screen voice in the film. He was also someone whose work I'd known since the late 1960s, when I'd acquired a copy of his novel *Street of Stairs*, one of very few queer novels available in those days. Tavel, too, expressed enthusiasm about "Mario Montez, for Shame," and we began an exchange that would lead eventually to my writing "Coming Together to Stay Apart," about Tavel's collaboration with Warhol. Tavel was hoping to publish his screenplays for the Warhol films, and my essay began as an introduction to that sadly never-realized project.

By the time I completed writing these first three essays, I had arranged to see a fair number of the restored Warhol films. Before beginning this book, I'd had the opportunity to see only a few, and my memory of them was often vague. Here's what I can piece together of what I'd seen: As a college student in New Orleans in 1967, I saw *The Chelsea Girls* during its national theatrical release. I remember seeing *My Hustler* and *Lonesome Cowboys* in the late 1960s after coming to New York, and, more clearly, I remember seeing the early Paul Morrissey films *Flesh*, *Trash*, and *Women in Revolt* at the time they were released. (Although these latter three films were produced by Warhol, they are not credited to him by the Warhol Film Project; certainly they reflect Morrissey's sensibility, not Warhol's.) In 1981, I attended the Genoa Film Festival, where Warhol superstar Ondine showed a number of the Warhol films that he had shrewdly absconded with, and with which he supported himself over the years by showing them at whatever venue invited him. *Vinyl* was the one among these that made the strongest impression. When I began teaching gay studies at Sarah Lawrence College in 1990, *Vinyl* was one film I knew I wanted to show my students, and the college managed to locate a print. The New York Lesbian and Gay Experimental Film Festival (now the Mix Festival) showed *Blow Job*, also in 1990, and I saw it there for the first time. In 1995, New York's Film Forum mounted a twenty-three-film Warhol retrospective.[5] Although I didn't attend those screenings as assiduously as I would now (since I know how rare a treat it still is to be able to see the films in a movie theater), I saw enough of them to know what I was missing—indeed what we'd all been missing in those years between 1972 and 1988 when the films were officially out of circulation.

As I started to write about the films, I also began to see them more systematically, often arranging to view films at the Museum of Modern Art's Celeste Bartos International Film Study Center. Several times, I taught a seminar on Warhol at the University of Rochester and borrowed the films from MoMA's Circulating Film and Video Library to show my students (and myself). During those semesters I was fortunate in the cooperation of the staff of Rochester's George Eastman House in programming some of Warhol's films publicly at their cinematheque, the Dryden Theatre, including the difficult-to-project double-screen films *Outer and Inner Space*, *Lupe*, and *The Chelsea Girls*. On one occasion Patrick Loughney, then Curator of Motion Pictures at Eastman House, arranged to show the five-hour-plus *Sleep*; only one or two students and I stayed through the entire film, but others came for parts of it between their other classes. In 2005, Lynne Cooke, then curator of the Dia Art Foundation in New York, invited me to program Warhol's films at Dia:Beacon to be shown every weekend from Memorial Day to Labor Day in conjunction with the exhibition *Dia's Andy*.[6] This gave me an opportunity to see many more of the films. When I lectured about the films at universities or museums, my hosts would often arrange to screen the film that was my subject. In these various ways, over the years I've managed to see all but a handful of the fifty-five films that have been restored and a fair number of the twenty-eight reels of preserved *Screen Tests* (ten of them on each reel). I've been lucky enough to see *The Chelsea Girls* five times in all—including that first time as a college student in New Orleans, twice at the Dryden Theatre in Rochester, and twice in regular screenings at MoMA. I've seen *Blow Job* and *Screen Test No. 2* countless times and *Horse*, *My Hustler*, *Paul Swan*, and *Hedy* a great many times.

All of this is to say that I didn't write the essays here with extensive knowledge of the films from the beginning; on the contrary, I feel that I have a decent grasp of the full corpus of restored Warhol films only now that I've completed this book. When I set out to write about a film, I would see it, see it again—sometimes again and again—and then I'd write about it. And usually I would see it yet again and make corrections to the essay. This means that I was ignorant of the wider range of Warhol's films when I wrote the first two essays here, and, of course, this has consequences. For example, when I wrote "Face Value," I demurred at Stephen Koch's claim in his book *Stargazer* that *Blow Job* is "a piece of pornographic wit," because, as I write, "in my estimation the film is far too sexy to be regarded as primarily comic"; instead, "it is another film of the same period, *Mario Banana* . . . that does a blow job as comedy." I still think this is right, but it leaves out something crucial: In 1966, Warhol "remade" the silent *Blow Job* with sound as *Eating Too Fast*, a parody—very funny at times—of the earlier film. I knew of the existence of *Eating Too Fast* when I wrote "Face Value," but I hadn't yet seen it.[7] Similarly, when I wrote "Mario Montez, for Shame," I had not yet seen *Screen Test No. 1*, the first film Tavel wrote for Warhol and a film in which the failure to elicit what Tavel deemed an interesting performance from Warhol's erstwhile boyfriend Philip Fagan led to reprising the scenario with Mario Montez for *Screen Test No. 2*. What could I do about these omissions? The obvious answer would be to revise the essays. But essays often have an internal integrity that can be fatally undone by revision. I've chosen a different method (following the good advice of my friend Juliane Rebentisch): an addendum to the first essay, because it seemed necessary; one to the second, because the brief text I initially wrote for *Superstar! A Tribute to Mario Montez* at Columbia University, at the invitation of Frances Negrón-Mutaner, adds a personal note to my appreciation of Montez; and one to the sixth, because I wasn't quite finished with the subject of camp. Apart from this, the essays are essentially what they were when I first composed them.

I have attempted to refine the argument of "Coming Together to Stay Apart" very slightly, but I remain somewhat uneasy about my use of Leo Bersani's work on new forms of relationality. The redeeming occurrence of what was otherwise a largely dispiriting conference on the subject of "gay shame" at the University of Michigan in the spring of 2003 was becoming friends with Leo. (Dispiriting because my hope that a new theorization of shame might further the project of destabilizing crude identity categories in favor of a more nuanced consideration of difference was shattered by the demagogic reassertion of those very categories.) I had known Leo slightly for many years, having had dealings with him in my capacity as editor of *October* beginning in 1979, when my essay "Pictures" appeared in the same issue of the journal as his and Ulysse Dutoit's essay on Assyrian wall reliefs, "The Forms of Violence," and continuing through the publication of his famous essay "Is the Rectum a Grave?" in the special issue of *October* on AIDS that I edited in 1987. It is a measure of my pleasure in our growing friendship that his work on relationality presented itself as key for my discussion of Tavel's collaboration with Warhol. "I take [Michel] Foucault's summoning us to rethink the relational as a political and moral imperative (a precondition of durable social transformation)," Bersani has written of his project.[8] This seemed to me akin to what I was attempting with my readings of Warhol's films. But I have come to feel some uncertainty about my application of Bersani's work. I am no longer sure that we can take either the lack of connection between Tavel's scenario and the film made "from" it or the superstars' narcissistic displays in the Tavel–Warhol films as what Bersani intends in his work on relationality. When I wrote "Coming Together to Stay Apart," Bersani had not yet published many of the essays and books in which he (in some cases with Ulysse Dutoit as coauthor) develops his ideas about what he calls "impersonal narcissism." I depended largely on the book in which he first proposed his project, *Homos*, where he writes, "The most politically disruptive aspect of the homo-ness that I will be exploring in gay desire is a redefinition of sociality so radical that it may appear to require a provisional withdrawal from relationality itself."[9] Such a withdrawal is what I saw as constituting the originality of the Warhol–Tavel collaborations. But whereas I do think a *non*relation (which is nevertheless a coming together) is the condition of those films, Bersani has gone on to propose not a *non*relation but rather a new type of relationality, one that does not mistake itself for—indeed, actively resists becoming—a relation*ship*.

There is a perhaps discernible break between the first three essays here and the ones that follow. The exigencies of my writing for particular occasions partly accounts for this too. When I conceived this book, I simultaneously thought about a related one, a memoir of my first decade in New York City, when I was finding my way as an art critic and exploring the possibilities and pleasures, just then opening up, of gay liberation culture. In 2005 and for a few years thereafter, invitations to lecture or contribute essays offered irresistible opportunities to embark on the memoir, and so from 2004 to 2008 I worked only sporadically on Warhol. When I returned to writing about the films, I knew more of them and knew many of them better, and I had come to a clearer understanding of how Warhol's unfailing formal sense constructs their sexual politics. This became my subject in "Spacious" and "Misfitting Together," which I first presented, respectively, as the Colin de Land Memorial Lecture in New York at the invitation of Silvia Kolbowski, and at the Postwar Queer Underground Cinema conference at Yale University, organized by George Chauncey, Ron Gregg, and Juan Suárez.

The final essay, "Most Beautiful," is a hybrid. During the hiatus between the first three and second three essays here (I don't count "Warhol's Time," which I've written separately, as an epilogue to this collection), I began to pursue a newfound interest in dance film. It started with a course on an artist whose choreography influenced Warhol and whose filmmaking was in turn influenced by Warhol: Yvonne Rainer. (At the same time, reading Rainer's memoir, *Feelings Are Facts: A Life*, was another impetus to start my own.) I first screened Warhol's *Paul Swan* for a course I taught on dance film in the performance studies program at New York University, thanks to an invitation from José

Muños. That same spring of 2009, Susanne Sachsse, Marc Siegel, and Stefanie Schulte Strathaus invited a group of scholars, filmmakers, and artists to Berlin to see all of Jack Smith's films, which had recently been donated to the Arsenal—Institute for Film and Video Art there, and to plan a festival of events related to the films' public screenings the following autumn. I immediately recognized the relationship of Swan to Smith, and determined to write about the two together for my talk at the festival, *Live Film! Jack Smith! Five Flaming Days in a Rented World!* It was also at that festival that I got the chance to meet Mario Montez, whom Siegel had coaxed out of retirement to perform the stage version of the role that Tavel had written for him but that he had until then refused, Juanita in *The Life of Juanita Castro*. It was a momentous event.

These essays on Warhol's films are far from comprehensive in scope. I never intended to write about more than a small number of the films. There are so many of them and they are all so full of interest that it would take a lifetime, and it must be evident that I have other interests and projects. But in any case I felt no responsibility at all to write a comprehensive book on Warhol's films. That was being undertaken, brilliantly, by Callie Angell in *The Films of Andy Warhol Catalogue Raisonné*, the first volume of which, on the *Screen Tests*, was published in 2006. Tragically, before the completion of the far-larger second volume, Callie died in 2010. That was a great loss both to me personally and to scholarship on Warhol's films, of which Callie had been at the forefront for more than two decades. I depended on Callie for so much in my own work on the films. She was always available to respond to my questions with fuller answers than a fellow scholar could reasonably expect. Her knowledge of the films was astounding. Callie was a Sherlock Holmes of researchers. She tracked down every lead and talked to everyone who knew anything about Warhol—a motley crew to be sure, and countless in number—and then she sorted out all the misinformation. One of my cherished anecdotes about her thoroughness involves going with her to Anthology Film Archives to see *Horse*, Warhol's spoof-western made with a real horse that stands in front of the Factory elevator door. The horse's name, funnily enough, was Mighty Bird. Throughout the film's first reel, Tavel, who wrote the scenario, interrupts the action to recite the film's credits from off-camera, saying, for example, "The Sheriff is played by Gregory Battcock," and later, "Mighty Bird, courtesy of the Dawn Animal Agency." Callie leaned over and whispered in my ear, "I called them. They're still talking about the time they rented Andy Warhol a horse." Sometime later when I wrote "Coming Together to Stay Apart," I sent it, as I did everything I wrote about Warhol, to Callie for fact-checking. As was often the case, her corrections saved me from repeating false "facts" I'd picked up in my own research: "Although I know Tavel recalls that the 'Horse' horse was a 'giant black stallion,' I have to say, speaking as a former horse woman, that Mighty Bird looks to me to be just a regular, medium-sized horse, perhaps even a slightly small horse. Of course, any horse in a loft is going to look enormous. But I've ridden many horses much bigger than this one. This horse looks to me something like a cow pony (the kind of horse cowboys ride), which is at the smaller end of the scale for horses." And further, to a specific question, "Yes that is indeed Larry Latreille with the horse [in the middle one of *Horse*'s three reels, where there is no scripted action]. At one point, he even whispers 'kitchy-kitchy koo' to him. Poor tired horse. . . ."

Callie's generosity as a colleague extended even to my students, who e-mailed questions to her and got long, helpful, fact- and anecdote-filled e-mails back. An ever-widening circle of Warhol film–lovers and scholars gathered around Callie. Many are my good friends, and Callie's generous spirit and love of Warhol infected us all as we exchanged our Callie-derived or -inspired Warhol lore. A very incomplete list includes Nicholas Baume, Karen Beckman, Jennifer Doyle, Jonathan Flatley, Amy Herzog, Branden Joseph, Ann Reynolds, Marc Siegel, Juan Suárez, Amy Taubin, and Lynne Tillman. Beyond this Callie Angell circle, and the people I've mentioned in recounting the book's genesis, there are many more friends, colleagues, and students who have assisted and sustained me in countless ways during the period I worked on this project; an incomplete list includes Henry Abelove, Gregg Bordowitz, Johanna Burton, Lynne Cooke, Rosalyn Deutsche, Devin Fore, Martha Gever, Leanne Gilbertson, Tim Griffin, Rachel Haidu, Claire Henry, Dan Humphrey, Damien Jack, Louise Lawler, Richard Meyer, Yoshiaki Mochizuki, Taro Nettleton, Shota Ogawa, Yvonne Rainer, Matt Reynolds, Victor Manuel Rodríguez, Joan Saab, Kaia Silverman, Rachael Timberlake, Carole Vance, David Velasco, Keith Vincent, Sharon Willis, and Janet Wolff. It is through the sustenance of those mentioned here and a great many more that I have managed for so many years to keep my plural relations—any of them—from "deteriorating into a relationship," in Leo Bersani's memorable formulation.

Staff members of four institutions have facilitated my research and this publication: Nora Dimmock, Stephanie Frontz, Katie Kinsky, and Kim Kopatz of the Rush Rhees Library at the University of Rochester; Geralyn Huxley and Greg Pierce of the Andy Warhol Museum in Pittsburgh; Kitty Cleary, Josh Siegel, and Charles Silver of the Museum of Modern Art in New York; and, at MIT Press, my long-term editor Roger Conover, Anar Badalov, Judith Feldmann, and Marge Encomienda. Two research grants from the Susan B. Anthony Institute for Gender and Women's Studies at the University of Rochester helped defray the cost of illustrations. Finally, my trusty research assistant Lucy Mulroney, herself at work on an important study of Warhol's publications, has assisted in innumerable ways.

FACE VALUE

I BEGIN WITH A QUOTATION FROM *STARGAZER*, STEPHEN KOCH'S MONOGRAPH ON ANDY WARHOL'S FILMS FIRST PUBLISHED IN 1973.

For twenty-five years, Koch's book was one of the few available sources of information about Warhol's film career. The films Warhol made between 1963 and 1968—and there are very many of them, more than 100, not counting the nearly 500 *Screen Tests*—were taken out of circulation in the early 1970s and only recently have again become available, thanks to the Whitney Museum of American Art's Andy Warhol Film Project and the Museum of Modern Art's film preservation work. *Stargazer* has always been tantalizing to read, especially when it was virtually impossible to experience firsthand its objects of analysis, but it's been frustrating too. For all its power of description and keen insights, Koch's book can sometimes leave an unpleasant aftertaste. Now that I'm beginning to see the films again, or in most cases for the first time, I'm able to say why. And in saying why, I hope to say something about what it is that makes them such an extraordinary achievement.

So, the quotation. It's about one of Warhol's most famous early silent films, famous for its blunt sexual title:

> *Blow-Job* is something of a portrait film—the portrait of an anonymity. The recipient looks like a once fresh-faced, foursquare Eagle Scout, a veteran of countless archery contests and cookouts, who discovers in the process of becoming the all-American boy some weak psychic nerves that send him helplessly gliding in activities for which no merit badges are awarded, in which he discovers the body he acquired on all those jamborees and tramps in the woods becoming a bit hollow-eyed, just a touch *faisandé*. Whereupon he takes that body to the Big Apple, where he finds it to be a very sellable commodity. Large numbers of Warhol leads began their careers as homosexual hustlers. It seems a pretty safe bet that the star of *Blow-Job* belongs in their company.[1]

The bad aftertaste is left partly by Koch's tone—arch, knowing, condescending—and in this particular paragraph by the charge that "weak psychic nerves" have made this man "helpless" to resist certain sexual activities, activities that will inevitably make him "a bit hollow-eyed, just a touch *faisandé*." There is, of course, that choice of the French adjective to give just the right nuance to the accusation of decadence, an adjective that invokes being hung and gamey rot all at once. It's a word that we—the writer and his sophisticated readers—use conspiratorially against this man, assuming that he won't even comprehend its meaning. Paradoxically, though, the word choice boomerangs right back on the writer, since in the United States no real man resorts to French when he wants to call a guy a fag. Ultimately, the bad aftertaste comes down to what the whole description moves toward: Koch's presumption that this man—*this man whose face is all we see*—is a hustler. As I hope to make clear, nothing about *Blow Job*'s exquisite presentation of the face suggests the opprobrium of Koch's characterization.

These days, when we see Andy Warhol's *Blow Job*, we have no expectation of actually seeing the act of fellatio the film's title announces. We know from its advance reputation what the film *will* show us: for thirty-six minutes, the *face* of a man presumably getting a blow job. Perhaps we know even more: that the film will be silent and slow; it will be projected at silent speed, sixteen (or eighteen) frames per second, as opposed to the twenty-four frames per second at which it was shot.[2] And finally, we might know that every several minutes the film will flicker and flare momentarily into whiteness, where one of its nine 100-foot reels ends and is spliced to the next. All of these things that we know in advance about *Blow Job* conform to what Callie Angell, the late curator of the Warhol Film Project, referred to as the conceptual status of Warhol's early films, "films that can be instantaneously conveyed as ideas without actually being seen." Thus, for example, *Sleep* is "'an eight-hour film of a man sleeping,'" and *Empire* is "'eight hours of the Empire State Building from sunset to sunrise.'" (Neither of these descriptions is in fact correct.) "The simplicity and outrageousness of [these] encapsulated descriptions have all the efficiency of a Pop Art statement like 'a painting of a Campbell's soup can.'" But, Angell goes on to clarify, now that Warhol's early films are once again available to be seen, our experience of them is "significantly at odds with the simplicity of [their] conception."[3]

Of course, *Blow Job cannot* be described as thirty-six minutes of a guy getting a blow job. The shock of its pop concept is double: It's a film of a blow job that for thirty six minutes we do not see. *Blow Job* was made during a period of police surveillance and censorship of underground cinema, which came to a head in New York City with the seizure of Warhol's early film *Andy Warhol Films Jack Smith Filming Normal Love* along with Smith's own *Flaming Creatures* and Jean Genet's *Un chant d'amour.* As Angell has suggested, *Blow Job* was thus conceived as a clever "catch-me-if you-can" rejoinder: "By undermining the sexually explicit come-on of his title with the comic prudery of his framing, Warhol parodied and subverted the expectations of both porno fans and the film censors, leaving both sets of viewers with a shared experience of frustration and disappointment, and implicating both in the same illicit desire."[4]

Much of what is written about the film involves what we do *not* see, the frustration of our desire to see the "action." "It does seem to be a real live blow-job that we're not seeing," writes Koch in *Stargazer.*[5] And, "In *Blow-Job*, the fellated penis is the focus of attention; it's excluded from the frame."[6] He repeats: "The film's real action is taking place very much out of frame." Its "imagined focus of interest [is] twenty inches below the frame, which the face actually on the screen never for a moment lets us forget. Perversely obdurate, the frame absolutely refuses to move toward the midriff, insists upon itself in a thirty-five minute close-up that must be the apotheosis of the 'reaction shot.'"[7] Although Koch, like Angell, feels that understanding Warhol's films as concepts, as Dada gestures, obscures "their sumptuous beauty,"[8] he nevertheless sees *Blow Job* as "a piece of pornographic wit."[9] Now, it may indeed be true that *Blow Job* has witty implications for censors and porn enthusiasts, but in my estimation the film is far too sexy to be regarded as primarily comic. There are occasional snickers at screenings of *Blow Job*, but rarely real laughter, although it provoked a famously funny response at its first showing: Taylor Mead got up after ten minutes and walked out, saying to the assembled crowd as he did so, "I came already." As we shall see, though, it is another film of the same period, *Mario Banana* (which exists in both black-and-white and color versions), that does a blow job as comedy.

What about what we *do* see in *Blow Job*? What about the "sumptuous beauty" that is *in* the frame? What about that face? Certainly, as we look *at* this beautiful young man, we look *for* the signs of his sexual stimulation, which appear as the play of tension and relaxation of the face. His responses are registered in the tightening and loosening of the muscles around the mouth, the clamping shut and opening up of the eyes; but more significantly they are registered in the raising and lowering of the head.

In describing what it is we see when we watch *Blow Job*, it is important to say at the outset that after a very short time, perhaps midway into the second reel, it becomes clear that we will see nothing more than the repetition, with slight variations, of what we've already seen. We will see only the face of a man, in close-up, looking up, looking down, looking forward, sometimes looking to one side or the other. His head is positioned within the frame at some moments a little more toward the right or the left; it is rarely dead center. One possible result of the realization that this is all we will see is that we are freed to look differently. We know that nothing will happen; or to put it better, we know that what defines "happening," what counts as incident, event, even narrative, what we see and notice and think about, is very different in a film like *Blow Job* than in other kinds of films we've seen. So what I will go on to describe is the result of this realization—the realization that we will not see the blow job announced in the title, the blow job that I have every reason to believe is really taking place and is really in some sense the subject of this film.

Andy Warhol, *Blow Job*, 1964. 16mm film, b/w, silent, 41 minutes at 16 fps. Film stills courtesy of The Andy Warhol Museum.

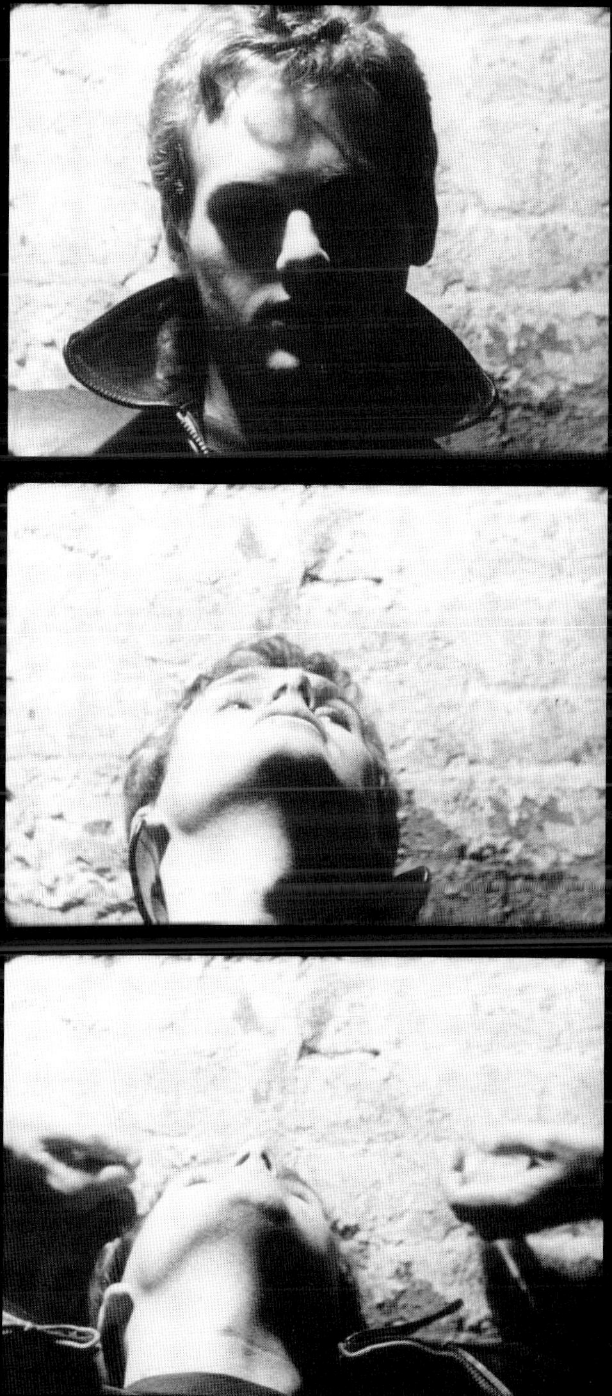

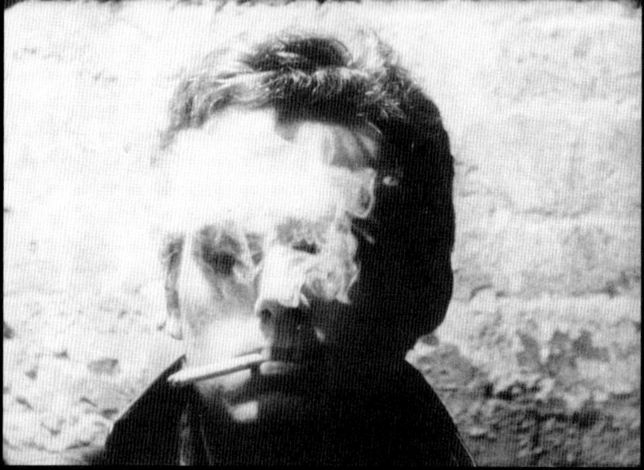

Andy Warhol, *Blow Job*, 1964. 16mm film, b/w, silent, 41 minutes at 16 fps. Film still courtesy of The Andy Warhol Museum.

One could say of this film that it "narrates" a sexual act, and that as such it has a beginning, middle, and end, and even a coda. At the start, the face we see is fairly impassive, the head rather still. Soon enough, though, things begin to happen. The man tilts his head up and down and sometimes thrusts it back against the wall behind him, such that we can see only his taut chin and straining neck with its protruding Adam's apple. His head sometimes jerks to one side or the other (the motion is quick even at silent speed) as his brow furrows and his lips purse or curl. At least once, he licks his lips. Now and then, one or the other of his hands comes into the frame—to scratch his nose, wipe his lips, press against his cheek, or run his fingers through his hair. After seven reels of these minimal occurrences that attune us intimately to this face as it expresses sexual excitation and intermittent lulls, the penultimate reel shows us the face's blissful contortion at the moment of orgasm. Just before we see the decisive spasm, the man's hands spring up behind his head in complete surrender. After coming, he settles back into stasis and impassivity, he scratches his nose, and the reel ends. As the next begins, a few bobs of the head and scrunches of the face suggest the man is zipping up his pants and buckling his belt. He puts a cigarette in his mouth, strikes a match, lights the cigarette, leaves it in place as he inhales, then exhales smoke that momentarily obscures the face. With obvious post-orgasmic satisfaction, he smokes, serenely looks about, wipes his nose and mouth with the back of his hand. He cradles his head in his left arm, then brings his hand to his face and pinches his cheeks together. His mouth forms a few words of silent speech, he leans forward, and the film runs out.

All the while that we have watched this face for what it would communicate of sexual excitement, we will surely have noticed something significant about how we see the face, and how well. The film's lighting illuminates the face not from the position from which we look, but from above. Thus, when the man looks directly at the camera, his eyes are deep in shadow. His face is fully illuminated only when he holds his head back and looks up into the light. If there is any sense of frustration in *Blow Job*, it derives, I think, not from not seeing the sexual act—we really don't expect to—but from not being truly able to see the man's face. No, that's not precisely it. We do see his face, but we see it only when he does not look at us, when, sometimes in rapture, sometimes in tedium, he tilts his head back—and therefore looks away from us. Often he looks directly our way, but we cannot see him looking at us. Warhol's camera captures this face and the sensation it registers, but simultaneously withholds it from us; and he does this through a simple positioning of the light as if by chance, a bare lightbulb hung from the ceiling just above and slightly to the left of the scene. We cannot make eye contact. We cannot look into this man's eyes and detect the vulnerability that his submission to being pleasured surely entails. We cannot take sexual possession of him. We can see his face, but we cannot, as it were, *have* it. This face is not *for us*.

This statement would seem to contradict both of two opposing views of Warhol's films as voyeuristic, on the one hand, and as exhibitionist, on the other. According to Koch, "Even more than it does most movies, voyeurism dominates all Warhol's early films and defines their aesthetic,"[10] while David James argues in *Allegories of Cinema* that this cannot be so, since voyeurism is characterized by "repetitive looking at *unsuspecting* people," whereas Warhol's actors "narcissistically exhibit" themselves for "a camera whose power lies in its threat to look away."[11] Koch qualifies his notion of voyeurism in relation to Warhol's early films by suggesting that "we are held back from the sexual spectacle not by the voyeur's impulse to hide and withdraw, but by the fact that what we see is unreal, is film."[12] In fact, though, the particular ways in which *Blow Job* asserts itself as film—the fixed and absolutely delimiting framing and lighting of the subject, the slowed-down speed—don't so much complicate the experience of voyeurism as cancel it altogether. At the same time, the star of *Blow Job* can hardly be said to exhibit himself. He seems entirely uninterested in the presence of Warhol's camera; he doesn't accommodate himself to it; he doesn't even acknowledge it. As against Koch's charge that Warhol's camera is voyeuristic and James's claim that Warhol's subjects are exhibitionists, I want to claim for *Blow Job* what I will call an ethics of antivoyeuristic looking.

Blow Job is in many respects similar to the *Screen Test* portrait films Warhol began making at just around the time the former film was shot. Like each of the nine segments of *Blow Job*, the *Screen Tests* are black-and-white, silent, 100-foot-reel medium close-ups of faces shot with a stationary camera.[13] Most of the subjects were instructed to keep perfectly still for the duration of the filming so that the filmed portrait would look as nearly as possible like a still photograph. Apart from the sheer variety of countenances, what changes most dramatically is the lighting, which is carefully controlled to produce a wide range of effects. These effects are the filmic equivalent of Warhol's manipulation of photographs in the silkscreen process of his painted portraits, which Jonathan Flatley has argued entail a complex interplay between giving face and effacement, figuration and disfigurement, idealization and erasure, embodiment and abstraction:

> On the one hand, Warhol's portraits have the appearance of being like hypograms, decorative make-up jobs that are unable to "signify" anything in themselves. On the other, the supplementary act of underscoring, *by means of make up*, the features of a face, turns out not to be simple addition, "increase," or improvement but in fact a display of the radical instability of recognizability.... The hypogramic quality of Warhol's portraits quickly slides to the prosopopoetic, inflecting *all* our face recognitions with an uncanny sense of the fictive.... There is no recognition, indeed no face, as it were, *before* the portrait.[14]

Warhol's formal procedures for painting or filming faces have their psychic equivalent in his subjects' self-presentation. Positioned in front of Warhol's camera, each sitter projects a persona, makes of his or her face a mask. As David James explains,

> The camera is a presence in whose regard and against whose silence the sitter must construct himself. As it makes performance inevitable, it constitutes being as performance. The simple activities proffered as the subject of documentation are insufficient fully to engage the sitter and merely establish an alternative area of attention, momentarily allowing self-consciousness to slip away. The sitter oscillates between his activity and awareness of the context in which it is taking place. In *Eat*, for instance, Robert Indiana's eyes focus on the mushroom, then rove around the room seeking to avoid the very place where they must eventually come to rest. The situation is that of psychoanalysis; the camera is the silent analyst who has abandoned the subject to the necessity of his fantastic self-projection.... Alone in the anxiety caused by the knowledge of being observed but denied access to the results of that observation, the subject must construct himself in the mental mirrors of his self-image or his recollection of previous photography.[15]

Although this analysis holds true for many of the *Screen Tests* and other early portrait films such as *Eat* and *Henry Geldzahler*, it works considerably less well for *Blow Job*. In the latter case the simple activity that occupies the man being filmed is not directly documented at all; nevertheless, it is entirely sufficient to engage the subject and keep self-consciousness at bay for the film's duration. His only acknowledgment of the other context—camera and film crew—are the words he forms in the film's final seconds, and it shouldn't surprise us that it is only at that point that he appears to notice them. Indeed, *Blow Job*'s wit might be understood not as a commentary on the porn film but as a lesson in how to produce a really beautiful portrait—better than saying, "Say cheese." Perhaps we need to amend David James's statement that "only if you are unconscious (*Sleep*) or a building (*Empire*) can you be unaware of media attention in Warhol's world" to include getting a blow job.[16]

In fact, no categorical statement will do justice to Warhol's range. Although Warhol's work is extraordinarily coherent in many respects, within that coherence is a very wide variety of experimentation. Take *Kiss*, for example, another portrait-like film made up of 100-foot reels, each of its thirteen segments in this case showing a pair of couples kissing. Although an occasional flicker of awareness of the camera's presence occurs—in a sly smile and a stare at the lens—for the most part the kissing couples are so mutually absorbed that the camera's presence is effectively denied, and in any case the framing of most of the kisses is so close up that we cannot see enough of either kisser to determine anything of self-consciousness. But more interesting in our context is a film that does conform in significant ways to James's description. I have in mind the comic version of *Blow Job*, *Mario Banana*.

Mario Banana is another close-up of a face, this one a bit tighter; the face's position suggests that Mario Montez, the film's star, is prone. Mario wears a low-cut gown, a gaudy necklace, and his Jean Harlow wig, which, as Ronald Tavel, Warhol's resident scriptwriter for the early sound films, remarked, "looks like an ill-skinned white cat."[17] As the reel begins, Mario looks directly at the camera, lowers his eyes in a charade of bashfulness, but just can't help looking right back at the camera. A banana enters the frame. It catches Mario's eye. He casts a knowing look at the camera. The banana moves center screen, toward Mario's mouth, and we see that the banana is held, delicately, by Mario himself, wearing white evening gloves. Mario slowly peels the banana while keeping his eyes glued to the lens. He holds the fruit up, eyes it, licks it, sucks it. The mock fellatio is underway. Mario takes a bite, looks at us, chews salaciously. He licks the banana again, deep-throats it, looks at us, takes another bite. The third time Mario takes the banana in his mouth, he shoves it way in and pulls it out again five times, takes a last bite, and the film runs out. *Mario Banana*: unquestionably "a piece of pornographic wit."

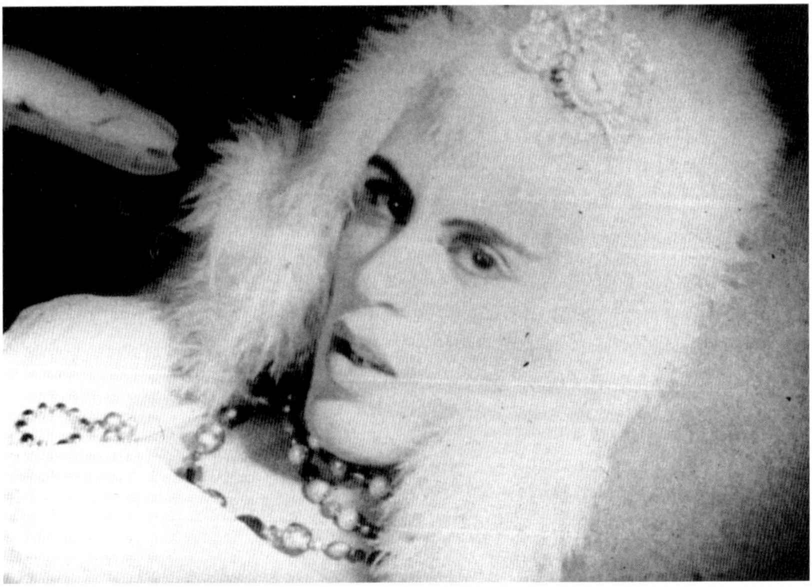

Andy Warhol, *Mario Banana (No. 2)*, 1964. 16mm film, b/w, silent, 4 minutes at 16 fps. Film still courtesy of The Andy Warhol Museum.

Unlike the man in *Blow Job*, Mario is bathed in bright light. His every facial expression is blindingly visible. His eyes look directly into ours. We don't catch him in the act; he beckons to us with his big brown eyes to watch what he can do with that banana. Tavel also wrote, paraphrasing Jack Smith on *Maria* Montez: "Make no mistake about it, Mario Montez believes he is the Queen of the Silver Screen."[18] Mario performs every second of his four-minute role. All persona, Mario is also utterly self-conscious. Indeed, he is self-consciousness personified. Warhol himself suggested what makes Mario's performance so touching: "He adored dressing up like a female glamour queen, yet at the same time he was painfully embarrassed about being in drag (he got offended if you used that word—he called it 'going into costume')."[19] Simultaneously impudent and chagrined, Mario coyly performs his shame of performing, of *what* he's performing, and *as what* he's performing.

David James's astute characterization of Warhol's filmic space as a "theater of self-presentation," where people are "always trying to accommodate themselves to the demands of the camera,"[20] can thus be seen as a paradigm that is tested in different ways by different films. Mario Montez is all accommodation in *Mario Banana*; there is no oscillation between documented activity and awareness of context. Mario's self-consciousness is figured for the camera as a function of the fellatio he performs. By contrast, *Blow Job*'s star makes no accommodation whatsoever. His attention appears fully absorbed by the sensation that is all his face reveals. He doesn't perform at all; he is performed upon.

The difference between the two films is more than this difference between giving and getting, but the meaning of this particular difference in Warhol's world constitutes a portion of its interest, certainly for contemporary queer viewers attempting to reconstruct our histories.[21] Thomas Waugh writes of what he calls Warhol's revision of a "key dynamic" of 1960s gay life, the "queen-hustler paradigm": "If the queen is effeminate, intense, decked out, oral, desirous, and, to use [Parker] Tyler's 1960s word, 'offbeat,' the hustler—or 'trade'—is butch, laid-back, stripped bare, taciturn, ambivalent, and 'straight.' The queen looks, the trade is looked at."[22] In the cases of *Mario Banana* and *Blow Job*, we might add: The queen is fully visible; the hustler is harder to make out.

Now that I, too, have referred to the man in *Blow Job* as a hustler, it is time to come back to my initial objection to Koch's calling him that in *Stargazer*; I do so by once again turning to David James:

> What distinguishes Warhol from his predecessors and successors is his disinterest in moral or narrative inflection; his willingness to allow marginal subcultures entry into the process of documentation is paralleled by paratactical formal structures that make no place for authorial possession of them. Its ingenuousness aside, Warhol's refusal to censor, to censure, or even to create hierarchies bespeaks a toleration, simultaneously ethical and aesthetic, that inheres in all his most characteristic gestures—his collapse of the distinctions between surface and depth, between life and art, between reality and artifice, between high society and the underworld.[23]

I find this portion of James's essay especially significant for tying Warhol's aesthetics to ethics through the disinterest in moralizing and refusal of authorial possession. I do not, however, agree that Warhol's nonjudgmental approach implies toleration, since toleration presupposes precisely the hierarchies Warhol refuses. Toleration is not a two-way street. A dominant culture tolerates a subculture, or doesn't, as it chooses. A subculture has no such choice. As Pier Paolo Pasolini famously wrote, "In relationships with those who are 'different,' intolerance and tolerance are the same thing." [24] An ethical position entails not a toleration of difference but an obligation provoked by the very fact of difference. Warhol's camera makes the fact of difference visible. It is as if Warhol had set about, twenty-five years before the fact, to illustrate Eve Kosofsky Sedgwick's first axiom for an antihomophobic analysis of sexuality in *Epistemology of the Closet*: "People are different from each other." [25] Different people are the intriguing constituents of Warhol's world. "The world fascinates me," he said in an important early interview, "It's so nice, whatever it is. I approve of what everybody does." [26] Warhol does not judge the people in his world. He gives us access to them, to their various shades of beauty, but he does not make them objects of our knowledge. They simply are. The face of the man in *Blow Job* is only a face, a face of a man, a man getting a blow job. That is all. Why then does Koch call him a homosexual hustler, and why do I?

This question returns us to the problem of voyeurism. Koch's response to seeing the face of the man in *Blow Job* is just the opposite of what for James constitutes the aesthetico-ethical stance of Warhol's work: Koch takes possession of him, assumes a knowingness about him, and censures him for what he has construed about him. This man, he avers, has "weak psychic nerves." He falls helplessly into activities without merit. He "takes his body" to the city and offers it as a commodity. He's a rotten piece of meat. Let's compare what Warhol has to say about this man. In *Popism*, he tells a story of asking the actor Charles Rydell to star in the film. Rydell failed to show up because he thought Warhol was putting him on. So, Warhol says, "We wound up using a good-looking kid who happened to be hanging around the Factory that day, and years later I spotted him in a Clint Eastwood movie." [27] John Giorno, Warhol's close associate at the time and the sleeper in *Sleep*, reports, simply enough, "Someone brought to the Factory this young, anonymous actor who was playing Shakespeare in the Park, a beautiful innocent guy who nobody knew and nobody saw again. Andy made *Blow Job* with him, the face of a man getting a blow job and cumming." [28]

As much as I like these characterizations—"a good-looking kid," "a beautiful innocent guy"—I don't want to whitewash the guy in *Blow Job* (who has been identified as DeVerne Bookwalter, a young actor specializing in Shakespeare roles).[29] He may be innocent, but he's no angel. I'm perfectly content to think of him as a guy who's willing to stand in front of a movie camera (and a film crew) while somebody sucks his cock. For that matter, I have no problem with thinking of him as, in Koch's words, "a homosexual hustler," so long as I can call him that without thereby imagining him as an object *for me*. For if, as I am claiming, *Blow Job* constitutes an ethics of antivoyeuristic looking, I cannot *know* this man, where "knowing" means making him an object both of sexual possession and of knowledge. Koch writes of the hustler figure in Warhol's late films, "The hustler, identifying himself as the sexuality of his flesh and nothing more, proposes himself as a wholly passive and will-less being, subject exclusively to the will of others." [30] This may well be true of Joe Dallesandro as represented in Paul Morrissey's films, which share Koch's apparent moralizing even as they exploit a lust for the hustler's hunky body. It is possibly even true of *My Hustler*, one of the first Warhol films Morrissey worked on. But Koch has retroactively applied it to *Blow Job* as well, even while he recognizes that there is a world of difference between the films: "*My Hustler* is a piece of psychological realism. Even today [1973] writing this sentence feels strange. In 1964, one would not have expected ever to write it. It is a structured little piece of film about a probable human situation that is intended to hold the interest of all those people out in movieland. It is a film made at the end of a very long road from *Sleep*." [31]

My Hustler is in some ways typical of the sound films that immediately followed Warhol's silents. These were shot with an Auricon camera that takes 1,200-foot rolls, and many of the films consist of two of these thirty-three-minute reels. The first of these, *Harlot*, is something of a reprise of *Mario Banana*, but this time Montez is joined on Warhol's couch by three other people who watch his shenanigans with bananas. The more significant difference is the addition of a soundtrack. Three men off-screen carry on a conversation that occasionally makes reference to something on the screen. The first reel of *My Hustler* seems as if it was conceived like this, with the camera fixed steadily on Paul America sunbathing on Fire Island. The difference here would have been that the three off-screen voices discuss *only* what is seen on-screen. But this idea is immediately negated by the opening shot, which shows not the hustler but the john. The hustler first appears when the camera pans away from the loquacious queen to catch sight of Paul America walking down to the beach. After dwelling for some time on the hustler's body, a cut returns the viewer to the beach-house deck, after which a series of pans, zooms, and cuts move back and forth between the speakers and the object of their banter.

In an essay deploring the decline of Warhol's films dating from the entry of Morrissey on the scene, Tony Rayns writes, "When Morrissey insisted upon panning the camera from the sex object to the speakers, he not only ruptured the formal integrity of Warhol's methods but also, at a stroke, turned Factory films into vehicles for 'actors.'" [32] At the end of this road, "Morrissey ... introduced a transparent vein of moralism: *Flesh, Trash, Heat* and the horror diptych are chronicles of all the ills that flesh is heir to. These are not only conventionally authored films, but films whose scripting and casting more or less explicitly express an authorial point of view—a mixture, as it happens, of prurience, con-

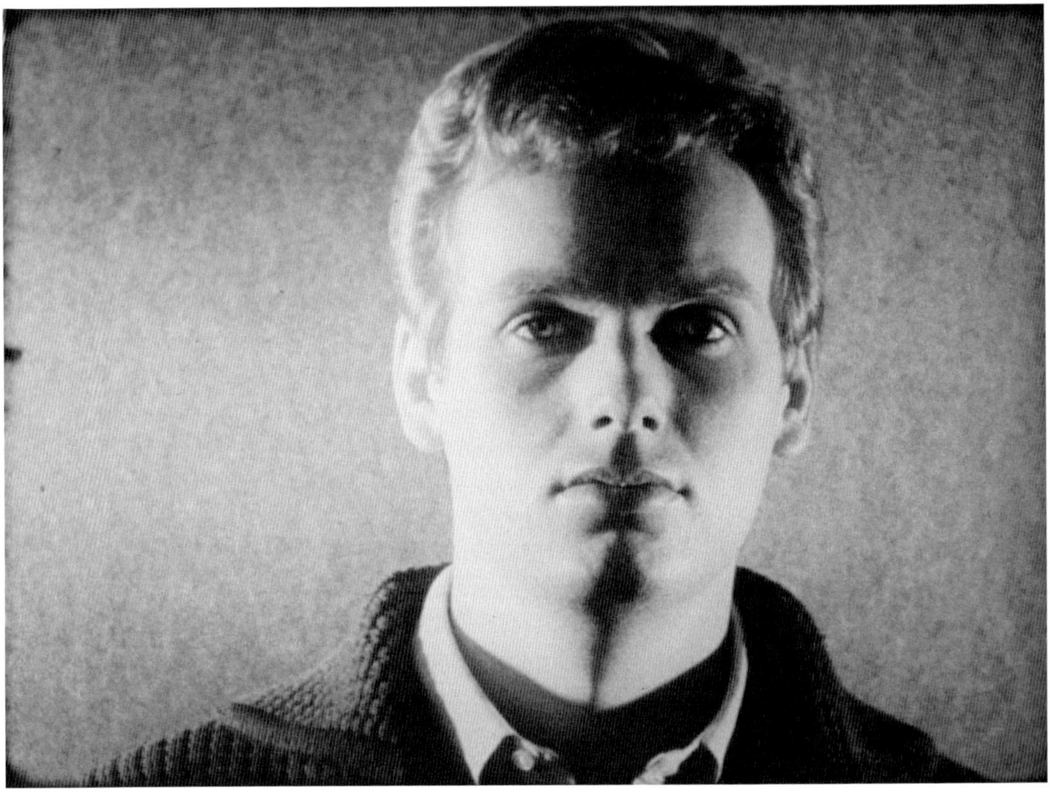

Andy Warhol, *Screen Test: DeVerne Bookwalter*, 1964. 16mm film, b/w, silent, 4 minutes at 16 fps. Film still courtesy of The Andy Warhol Museum.

descension and supercilious contempt."[33] I agree with this assessment of the Morrissey films, but let's return to *My Hustler* to determine what Morrissey has actually done, if indeed Morrissey is to blame.[34] Rayns charges that the change in Warhol's technique signaled by panning up to the beach house makes these films vehicles for actors (he puts "actors" in quotation marks). What I take him to mean is that with *My Hustler* people stop being "themselves" and begin playing roles. But if, in front of Warhol's camera, being oneself is always already performing, what has changed? The answer is a word: "hustler." When Koch writes that this film is a probable human situation, he refers to a story the film schematically plots: A queen has brought a hustler to Fire Island, where he becomes the object of competition between the queen and a fag-hag neighbor and an aging hustler who have dropped by the queen's beach house. Hustler, queen, fag hag, aging hustler: this is what's new about *My Hustler*. It's interesting that "psychological realism" requires that we know characters in such a way as to give them the names of stereotypes. This is the kind of knowledge—a knowledge that is presumptive, knowing; a knowledge of the other for the self; a making of the other into an object for the subject—this is the kind of knowledge that *Blow Job*'s face exceeds.

Since I have spoken of the antivoyeurism of *Blow Job* in relation to ethics, I want to end with a suggestive statement by Emmanuel Levinas; I wish to do no more than juxtapose it with what I've said about Warhol's early film:

> The Other, in the rectitude of his face, is not a character within a context. Ordinarily one is a "character": a professor at the Sorbonne, a Supreme Court justice, son of so-and-so, everything that is in one's passport, the manner of dressing, of presenting oneself. And all signification in the usual sense of the term is relative to such a context: the meaning of something is in its relation to another thing. Here, to the contrary, the face is meaning all by itself. You are you. In this sense one can say that the face is not "seen." It is what cannot become a content, which your thought would embrace; it is uncontainable, it leads you beyond.[35]

ADDENDUM: *EATING TOO FAST*

I sent "Face Value" to Callie Angell, who offered a useful note about Paul Morrissey's role in *My Hustler*:

> I think that the issue of the camera movement in *My Hustler* has been rather distorted. The accepted wisdom is that Warhol had never previously moved his camera, and didn't want to do so until Morrissey convinced him to do so; but, in actuality, there is plenty of camera movement in a number of the films from '63 through '65, leading up to *My Hustler*: *Tarzan and Jane, Batman Dracula, Poor Little Rich Girl, Restaurant, Afternoon*, and—particularly interestingly—in *Space*. I don't disagree with your interpretation of the camera movement in *My Hustler*—and, I think it's true, Warhol was reluctant to make this particular choice in this particular film, actually did shoot another reel with the same action without moving the camera, and always afterwards said he liked the second reel of *My Hustler* (in the bathroom) best. But I think it's somehow wrong to attribute this to—or blame it on—Morrissey. Warhol was perfectly capable of using a moving camera, if he wanted to; he would of course have understood the formal implications of different kinds of camera movement (or non-movement) in minimalist films vs. commercial narratives, and he was responsible for this decision. I think there are many examples of interesting accommodations between Warhol's hard-core aesthetic instincts and his commercial aspirations, of which this may be the first, but I also think one runs the risk of overlooking the scope of Warhol's ambition by describing this shift simply as something he was talked into against his better judgment.
>
> Furthermore, Morrissey has always been the one to draw attention to this moment—perhaps in a retroactive attempt to enhance the significance of his role in the Warhol films? After all, the real "other" person behind *My Hustler* was Chuck Wein, whom Morrissey never talks about.... I know *My Hustler* was deliberately planned as a commercial production, produced by Chuck and Dorothy Dean, and the stylistic differences in it were related to that intent. My gut feeling is that Morrissey was, at that point, a relatively new techie on the Factory scene, and probably not someone with all that much influence on what Andy did.[1]

I was too eager to accept Tony Rayns's views about Morrissey's pernicious influence on *My Hustler*. I'm not a great fan of Morrissey's films; Morrissey seems to me to have cynically attached himself to Warhol and adopted a great many of Warhol's formal strategies only to put them to a very different, even opposite purpose. His conventionally moralistic views about sex, drugs, and all kinds of nonconformism and his often shrill Philistinism about Warhol's artistic achievement make him an easy target for partisans of Warhol's films. But Rayns's argument does, as Angell suggests, also cast Warhol as too easily manipulated and thus reproduces the cliché of Warhol's passivity. I return to *My Hustler* in "Spacious" with a rather different view of it.

When I wrote "Face Value," I knew of the existence of a "sound remake" of *Blow Job* called *Eating Too Fast*, but I hadn't seen it and didn't know much about it. So when I wrote that *Mario Banana* did a blow job as comedy, I was unaware that *Eating Too*

Fast even more explicitly did just that. *Eating Too Fast* was made some two years after *Blow Job* during the period Warhol was making mostly two-reel films, some of which were eventually assembled for *The Chelsea Girls*. As in several films from 1965 and 1966, *Eating Too Fast*'s camera doesn't move in the first reel (until the very end of the reel), then becomes constantly mobile in the second. The film might have been intended for double-screen projection to highlight the contrast between the camerawork in the two reels.[2] Both in framing and in lighting, the first reel's shot is virtually identical to Warhol's *Screen Tests*, and in fact its subject, Gregory Battcock, had sat for a *Screen Test* in 1964. The immediately discernible difference from a *Screen Test* is the presence in *Easting Too Fast* of ambient sound—dogs barking, street traffic—and the film's projection at sound speed. It is hard to know whether the idea of turning this version of a facial response to a blow job into a parody of the original was Warhol's or Battcock's, although I suspect the latter.[3] Battcock knew Warhol's films well, having appeared in *Batman Dracula*, *Soap Opera*, and *Horse*, and written fairly extensively about Warhol's cinema; his essay on *Blow Job* appeared in *Film Culture* the year before *Eating Too Fast* was made. In the "remake," Battcock's studied display of indifference to his sex partner's ministrations is clearly a parodic reading of DeVerne Bookwalter's butch impassivity in *Blow Job*, about which Battcock wrote, "The expressions registering emotion and acknowledgment of the act on the part of the actor are limited and repetitive. They are enacted and re-enacted with the regularity of a formula but they nonetheless suggest, at various times, boredom, mild ecstasy, some interest, interest in something else, aloofness, and awareness of the camera."[4]

Like Bookwalter's, Battcock's detachment is carried to such an extreme as to be interpretable as deliberately sadistic, although the possibility of thus eroticizing Battcock's unresponsiveness is mitigated by the comedy midway through when he answers the telephone and chats nonchalantly with someone called Bob. "I'm not asleep," he says to Bob, and he might just as well be reassuring his fellator. "Oranjebeer is the worst.... Your grandmother died, really?" Battcock continues, then reports to the man slurping away (we hear his slurps) below the camera's range, "Bob's grandmother died." "Oh, too bad," he replies matter-of-factly, as Warhol moves his camera down to capture the back of his head for the first time. The fellator takes a sip of wine and the first reel comes to an end.

The telephone is a plant: Just before it rings, you can hear someone putting it down near Battcock. The conversation bridges the film's two reels, and Battcock's knowing performance includes, at the beginning of the second thirty-three-minute reel, an invitation to Bob to come over: "Yeah, come over in thirty-five minutes, exactly thirty-five minutes." During those remaining minutes, Warhol gets busy with his camera, mostly with zooms in and out and tilt-pans down to the fellator and back up to Battcock. Continuing his self-absorption, at one moment Battcock begins eating an apple. He chews noisily and takes a new bite before he's swallowed the former one, with the result that he chokes. "You shouldn't eat so fast," scolds the voice from below, to which Battcock pays no attention. We never see much more of the fellator than the back of his head with its curly dark hair. That head moves very little, considering what he's supposed to be up to. Perhaps he's returning Battcock's indifference, although toward the end, from the sounds of things, he gets himself off—maybe. There's heavy breathing, but no sure climax, sexually or narratively. And the film runs out.

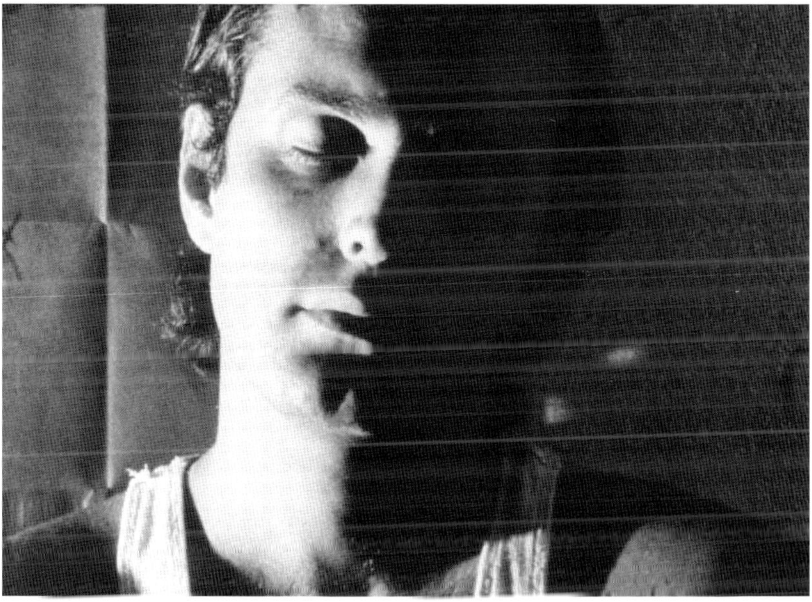

Andy Warhol, *Eating Too Fast*, 1966. 16mm film, b/w, sound, 66 minutes. Film still courtesy of The Andy Warhol Museum.

MARIO MONTEZ,
FOR SHAME

“FROM SHAME TO SHYNESS TO SHINING—AND, INEVITABLY, BACK, AND BACK AGAIN: THE CANDOR AND CULTURAL INCISIVENESS OF THIS ITINERARY SEEM TO MAKE WARHOL AN EXEMPLARY FIGURE FOR A NEW PROJECT, AN URGENT ONE I THINK, OF UNDERSTANDING HOW THE DYSPHORIC AFFECT SHAME FUNCTIONS AS A NEXUS OF PRODUCTION: PRODUCTION, THAT IS, OF MEANING, OF PERSONAL PRESENCE, OF POLITICS, OF PERFORMATIVE AND CRITICAL EFFICACY.”[1]

Eve Kosofsky Sedgwick's intuition, indicated here in one of her essays on queer performativity, might be more unfailing than she knew, since at the time she wrote this sentence she would have seen very little of what most bears it out—Andy Warhol's vast film production from the mid-1960s.[2] I want here to consider one instance of Warhol's mobilization of shame as production and, in doing so, to specify the urgency Sedgwick imagines such a project might entail, an urgency that compels a project of my own.[3] I should qualify "my own" by adding that this project heeds Sedgwick's axiom for antihomophobic inquiry: "People are different from each other." This is, of course, Axiom 1 from the introduction to *Epistemology of the Closet*, but I take it to be much more thoroughly axiomatic for Sedgwick's writing generally and what I've learned most from it: the ethical necessity of developing ever-finer tools for encountering, upholding, and valuing others' differences—or better, differences *and* singularities—nonce-taxonomies, as she wonderfully named such tools. In one of the many moving moments in her work, Sedgwick characterizes this necessity in relation to the "pressure of loss in the AIDS years"—years in which we sadly still live—"that the piercing bouquet of a given friend's particularity be done some justice."[4]

—

"Poor Mario Montez," Warhol writes in *Popism*,

> Poor Mario Montez got his feelings hurt for real in his scene [in *The Chelsea Girls*] where he found two boys in bed together and sang "They Say that Falling in Love Is Wonderful" for them. He was supposed to stay there in the room with them for ten minutes, but the boys on the bed insulted him so badly that he ran out in six and we couldn't persuade him to go back in to finish up. I kept directing him, "You were terrific, Mario. Get back in there—just pretend you forgot something, don't let *them* steal the scene, it's no good without you," etc., etc. But he just wouldn't go back in. He was too upset.[5]

Poor Mario. Even though Andy is full of praise for Mario's talents as a natural comedian, nearly every story he tells about him is a tale of woe:

> Mario was a very sympathetic person, very benign, although he did get furious at me once. We were watching a scene of his in a movie we called *The Fourteen-Year-Old Girl* [also known as *The Shoplifter* and *The Most Beautiful Woman in the World*, the film is now known as *Hedy*], and when he saw that I'd zoomed in and gotten a close-up of his arm with all the thick, dark masculine hair and veins showing, he got very upset and hurt and accused me in a proud Latin way, "I can see you were trying to bring out the worst in me."[6]

—

I call my project, provisionally, "Queer before Gay," because I wish to reclaim aspects of New York City queer culture of the 1960s as a means of countering the recent homogenizing, normalizing, and desexualizing of gay life. In the essay initiating the project, on *Blow Job*, I wanted to contest the facile charge of voyeurism so often leveled at Warhol's camera. It seemed to me important to recognize that there can—indeed must—be ways of making queer differences and singularities visible without always entailing the charge of violation, making them visible in ways that we would call *ethical*. Titling the essay "Face Value" both to suggest that I meant to pay attention to what was *on* the screen (in this case, as in so many others, a face) and to gesture toward Emmanuel Levinas's ethics, I contrast the self-absorption of the subject of *Blow Job* to what seems to me its comic opposite, the utter self-consciousness of Mario Montez as he performs mock fellatio on a banana in *Mario Banana*, a single 100-foot-reel Warhol film of the same year as *Blow Job*. To reiterate: on this subject of Mario's self-consciousness, Warhol wrote, "He adored dressing up like a female glamour queen, yet at the same time he was painfully embarrassed about being in drag (he got offended if you used that word—he called it 'going into costume')."[7]

How certain the violation, then, when Mario was subjected by Warhol in *Screen Test No. 2* to being shamed precisely for his gender illusionism, or perhaps his gender *illusions*. Warhol—with his uncanny ability to conceal dead-on insight in the bland, unknowing remark—writes of that film in a parenthetical aside in *Popism* "*Screen Test* was Ronnie Tavel off-camera interviewing Mario Montez in drag—and finally getting him to admit he's a man."[8] I call this "insight" because, although it doesn't really describe what takes place in the film at all, it nevertheless gets right to the point of what is most affecting, most troubling, most memorable about it—that is, Mario's "exposure"—a word that Warhol used, in its plural form, as the name of his 1979 book of photographs,[9] and the word Stefan Brecht chose to characterize Warhol's filmic method.

Following page

Andy Warhol, *The Chelsea Girls*, 1966. 16mm film, b/w and color, sound, 204 minutes in double screen. Film still courtesy of The Andy Warhol Museum.

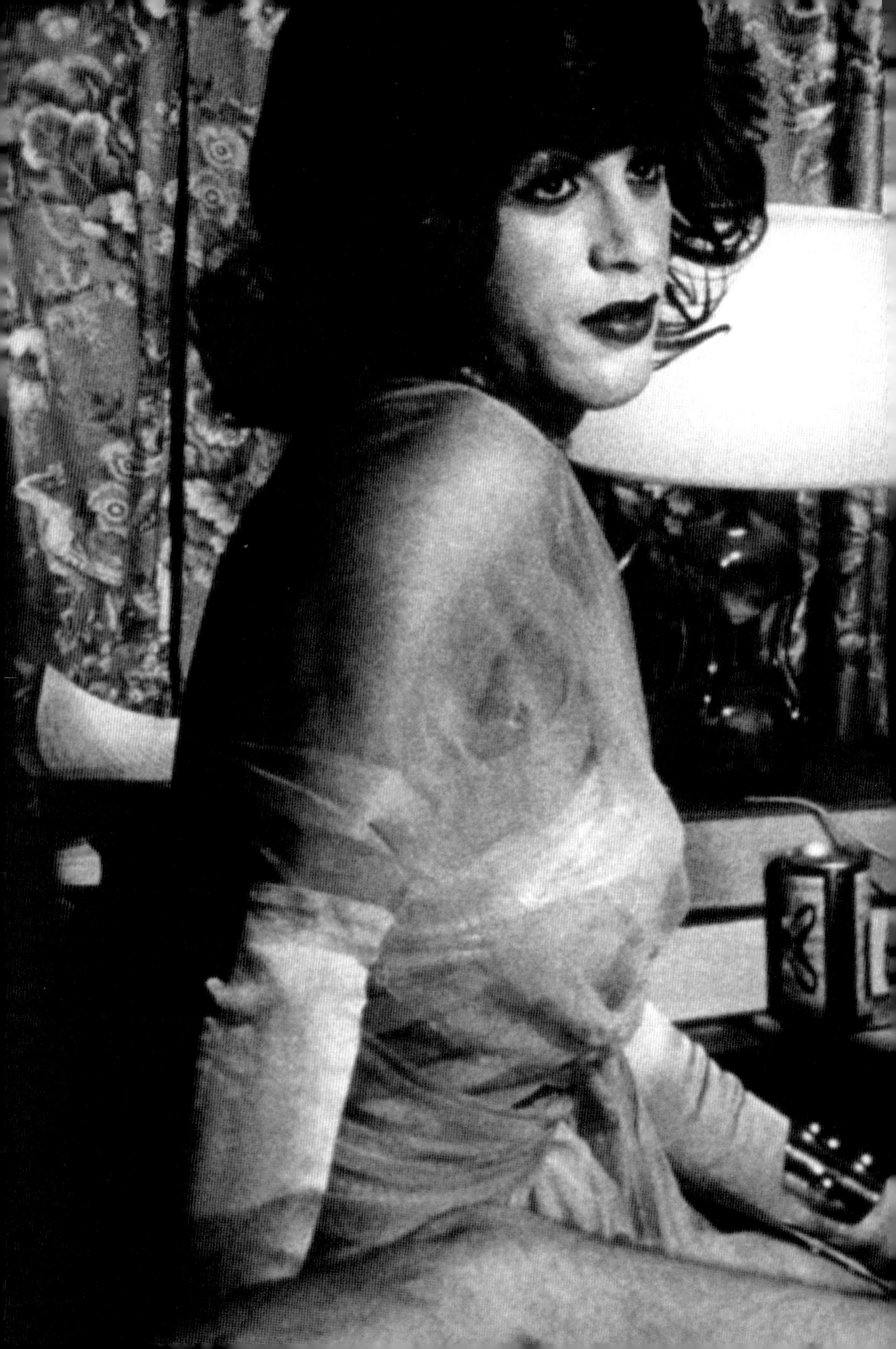

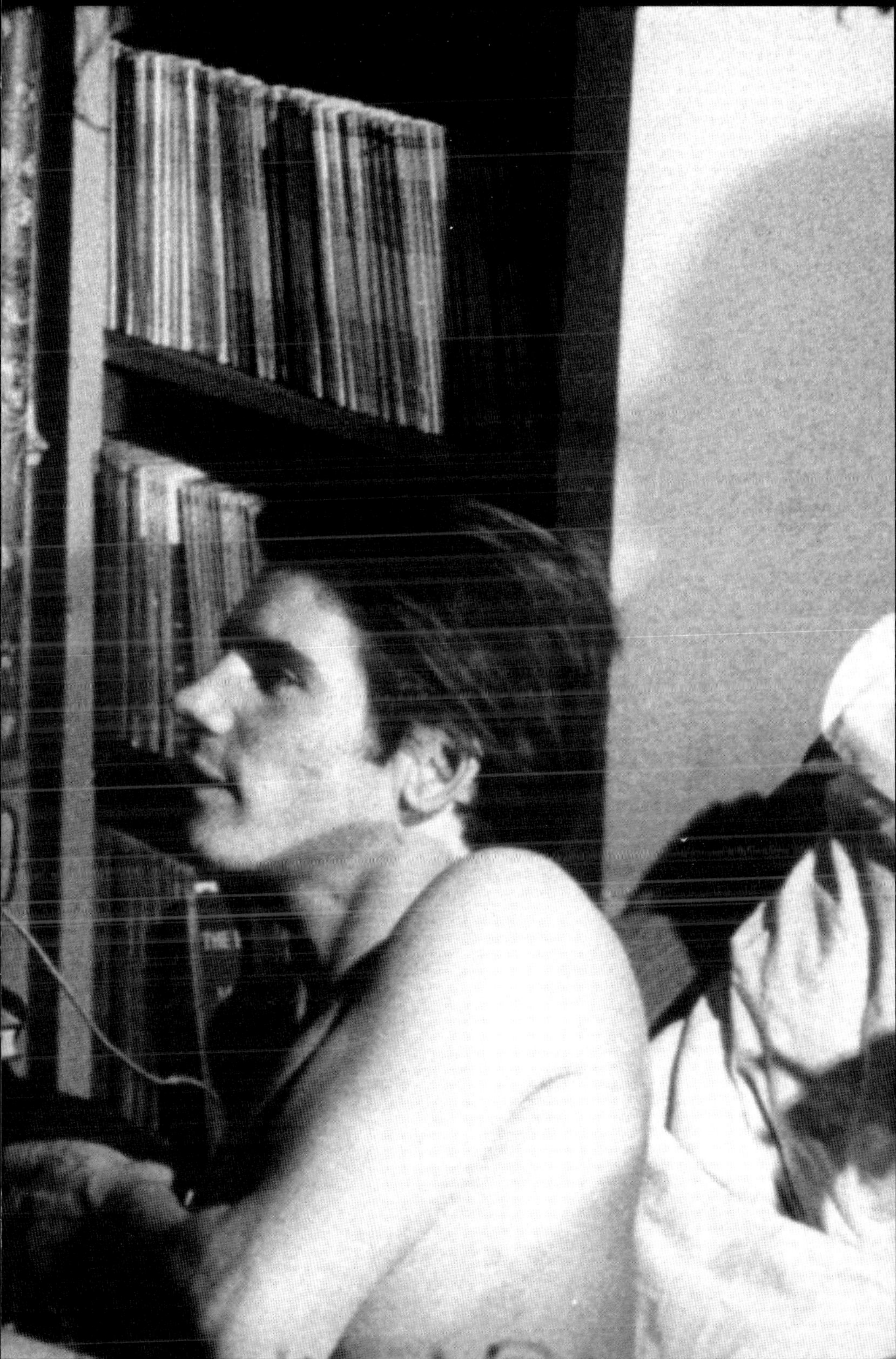

> Warhol around 1965 discovered the addictive ingredient in stars. He found that not only are stars among the industrial commodities whose use-value is a product of consumer phantasy, a phantasy that publicity can addict to a given brand of product,—stars can be made,—but that what addicts the consumer is the quality of stardom itself.... He set out to isolate this ingredient, succeeded, proceeded to market it under the brand name "Superstar,"—Warhol's Superstar. Superstar is star of extraordinary purity: there is nothing in it but glamor, a compound of vanity and arrogance, made from masochist self-contempt by a simple process of illusio-inversion. The commercial advantages of this product originated in its area of manufacture: the raw materials, any self-despising person, were cheap, and the industrial process simple: to make the trash just *know* he or she is a fabulous person envied to adoration. You didn't have to teach them anything. If the customers would take them for a star, they would be a star: if they were a star, the customers would take them for a star; if the customers would take them for a star the customers would be fascinated by them. Exposure would turn the trick. Here again Warhol's true genius for abstraction paid off: he invented a camera-technique that was nothing but exposure, and simply, having made himself the first superstar, utilized the superstar's public sycophancy to himself as advertising for the superstar, gave them exposure by association.[10]

Ostensibly just what its title says it is, *Screen Test No. 2* is the second of Warhol's screen-test films of early 1965 in which Tavel, novelist, founding playwright of ridiculous theater,[11] and Warhol's scenarist from 1964 to 1966, interviews a superstar for a new part (*Screen Test No. 1* stars Philip Fagan, Warhol's lover of the moment, who shared the screen with Mario Montez in *Harlot*, Warhol's first sound film and the first in which Tavel participated).[12] In the case of *Screen Test No. 2*, Mario is ostensibly being tested for the role of Esmeralda in a remake of *The Hunchback of Notre Dame*. He is shown throughout in a slightly out-of-focus close-up on his face, wearing (and often nervously brushing) a cheap, ratty dark wig. He also wears dangling oversize earrings and long white evening gloves. For a long time at the film's beginning, he ties a silk scarf into his wig, using, it seems, the camera's lens as his mirror. After speaking the credits from off-screen, where he remains throughout the film, Tavel begins to intone, insinuate, cajole, prod, demand: "Now, Miss Montez, just relax ... you're a lady of leisure, a grande dame. Please describe to me what you feel like right now." "I feel," Mario begins his reply—and there follows rather too long a pause as he figures out what to say—"I feel like I'm in another world now, a fantasy ... like a kingdom meant to be ruled by me, like I could give orders and suggest ideas."

Poor Mario. *This* kingdom is ruled by Ronald Tavel. It is he who gives orders and suggests ideas. At first, though, he indulges Mario's fantasy. He asks about his career to date, allowing Mario to boast of his debut as Delores Flores in Jack Smith's *Flaming Creatures*, his part as the handmaiden in Ron Rice's *Chumlum*, his starring role as the beautiful blond mermaid in Smith's *Normal Love*, and his small part as the ballet dancer wearing pink tights in the same film. Asked whether the critics were satisfied with his performances, he gives an answer fully worthy of his namesake in Smith's famous paean, "The Perfect Filmic Appositeness of Maria Montez."[13] "It's a funny thing," Mario says with no guile whatsoever, "but no matter what I do, somehow it comes out right, even if it's meant to be a mistake. The most wonderful mistakes that I've done for the screen have turned out the most raging, fabulous performances."[14]

Poor Mario. Now begins his humiliation. Tavel tells Mario to repeat after him, "For many years I have heard your name, but never did it sound so beautiful until I learned that you were a movie producer, Diarrhea." Mario is obliged to say "diarrhea" again and again, with various changes of inflection and emphasis. Then to lip-sync as Tavel says it. "Mouth 'diarrhea' exactly as if it tasted of nectar," Tavel instructs. Mario obeys, blissfully unaware of where this game of pleasing a producer named Diarrhea will lead. He will gamely demonstrate his ecstatic response to "playing spin the bottle"—to masturbating, that is, by shoving a bottle up his ass (remember, though, we see only his face).[15] Mario will ferociously mime biting the head off a live chicken as he obeys Tavel's demand that he pretend he is a female geek. He will show how he'll manage, as Esmeralda, to seduce three different characters—captain, priest, Quasimodo—in *The Hunchback of Notre Dame.* He'll scream in terror and dance a gypsy dance with only his shoulders; he'll pout, sneer, and stick out his tongue; he'll cover the lower half of his face with a veil and show that he can be evil or sad using only his eyes. He'll repeat after Tavel, apparently as an exercise in stressing consonants, "I have just strangled my pet panther. Patricia, my pet panther, I have just strangled her, my poor pet. Yet I am not scratched, just a little fatigued."

Now and again Tavel gives encouragement: "That's fine, Miss Montez, thank you very much." "That was delightful, Miss Montez." "Thank you, Miss Montez, that was beautiful, that was perfect, and I think we are going to sign you on immediately for this role."

"How can I ever thank you?" Mario replies, so delighted as to make it obvious he's still hoodwinked. But the encouragement only sets Mario up for his fall, which comes near the end of the film's second thirty-three-minute reel. Mario has just cheerfully described the furniture in his apartment. Then it comes, as if out of nowhere.

"Now, Miss Montez, will you lift up your skirt?"

"What?" Mario asks, with a stunned look. He's clearly caught completely off-guard.

"And unzipper your fly."

"That's impossible," Mario protests, shaken.

"Miss Montez," Tavel continues, "you've been in this business long enough to know that the furthering of your career often depends on just such a gesture. Taking it out and putting it in, that sums up the movie business. There's nothing to worry about, the camera won't catch a thing. I just want the gesture with your hands. This is very important.

Your contract depends on it." Following confused, helpless, silent stalling, Mario finally gives in, and the humiliation continues: "Look down, look down at it," he's commanded.

"I know what it looks like," is his petulant response.

"Zipper your fly halfway up and leave it sticking out. That's good, that's good, good boy, good boy." When he refers to Mario this way, Tavel isn't calling attention to Mario's "true" gender; far worse than that, he's treating Mario like a dog. "Take a look at it, take a look at it, please. What does it look like?"

Mario half-heartedly fights back, "What's it look like to you?"

"It looks fairly inviting, as good as any," Tavel answers, not with much conviction. "Will you forget about your hair for a moment. Miss Montez, you're not concentrating."

But Mario is defiant: "It's really senseless what you're asking me. I must brush my hair."

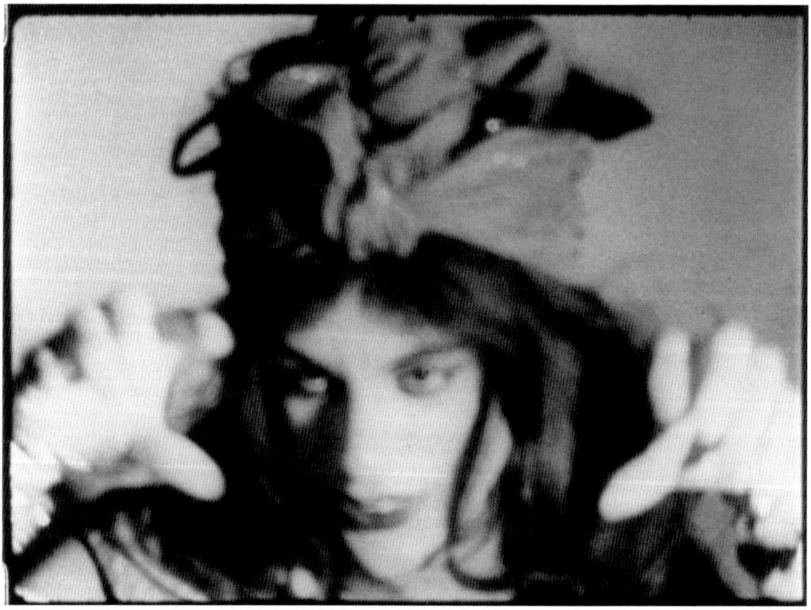

Andy Warhol, *Screen Test No. 2*, 1965. 16mm film, b/w, sound, 66 minutes. Film still courtesy of The Andy Warhol Museum.

Mario seems finally able to put a stop to this couch-casting episode, and we breathe a sigh of relief. But Tavel has still one more ordeal in mind, and it's no doubt all the more painful for Mario because it follows upon the mockery of his cross-dressing. Remember that Warhol writes in *Popism* of Mario's embarrassment about doing drag. He goes on to explain that Mario "used to always say that he knew it was a sin to be in drag—he was Puerto Rican and a very religious Roman Catholic. The only spiritual comfort he allowed himself was the logic that even though God surely didn't *like* him for going into drag, that still, if He really hated him, He would have struck him dead."[16] So, resisted by Mario in making him expose his sex, the ever-inventive Tavel moves on to a new torment. Showing Mario how to take a supplicating pose, with eyes and hands turned heavenward, he instructs him to say, and repeat, and repeat again, "Oh Lord, I commend this spirit into Thy hands." Poor Mario looks alternately bewildered and terrified, as though he feels he might truly be struck dead for such irreverence. Finally, though, Tavel has little time left to taunt his superstar. As Mario begins to acquiesce in giving the camera the cockteaser look Tavel wants, the film runs out. Just how tense the experience of watching a Warhol film can make us is revealed by the release that comes at this moment when the reel comes to an end, a moment always entirely unanticipated but occurring with astonishingly perfect timing.

Many of Warhol's films include similar scenes of cruelty that are met with disbelief on the part of the performers, most famously when Ondine, as the pope in *The Chelsea Girls*, slaps Ronna Paige.[17] "It was so for real," Warhol writes, "that I got upset and had to leave the room—but I made sure I left the camera running."[18] The moment that I'd found most discomfiting, up to seeing Mario's shaming in *Screen Test No.2,* is when Chuck Wein, who's been taunting Edie Sedgwick through the whole of *Beauty No. 2*, but who's rarely a match for her sparkling repartee, suddenly hits the raw nerve of her relationship with her father. She looks more stunned than if she'd been literally hit, like Ronna. It isn't merely a look of incredulity, it's one of utter betrayal, a look that both says, "Surely you didn't say that," and pleads, "How could you possibly say that? How could you so turn our intimacy against me? Would you really do *this* for the sake of a film? I thought we were just playacting."

Following page

Andy Warhol, *Screen Test No. 2*, 1965. 16mm film, b/w, sound, 66 minutes. Film still courtesy of The Andy Warhol Museum.

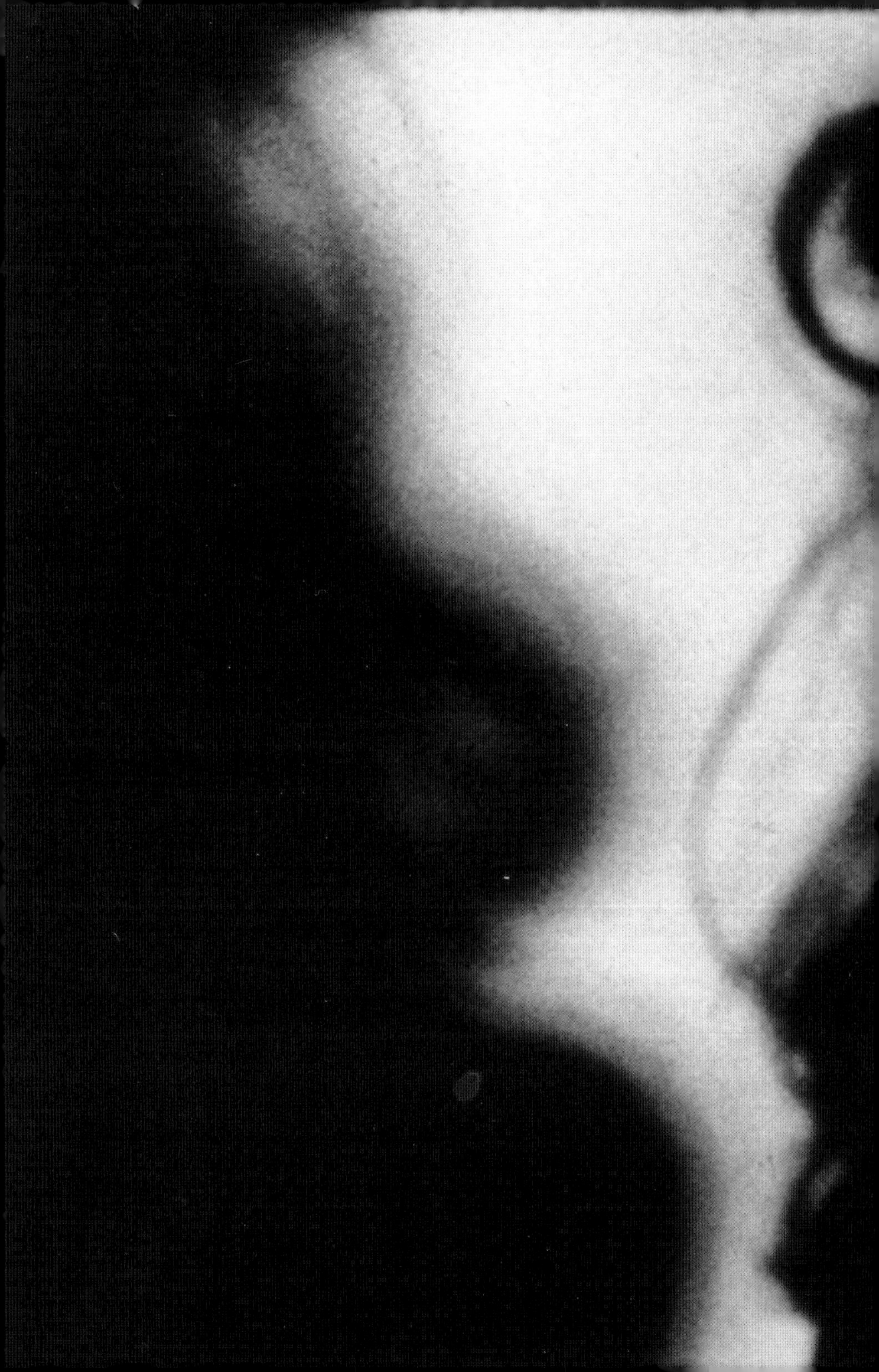

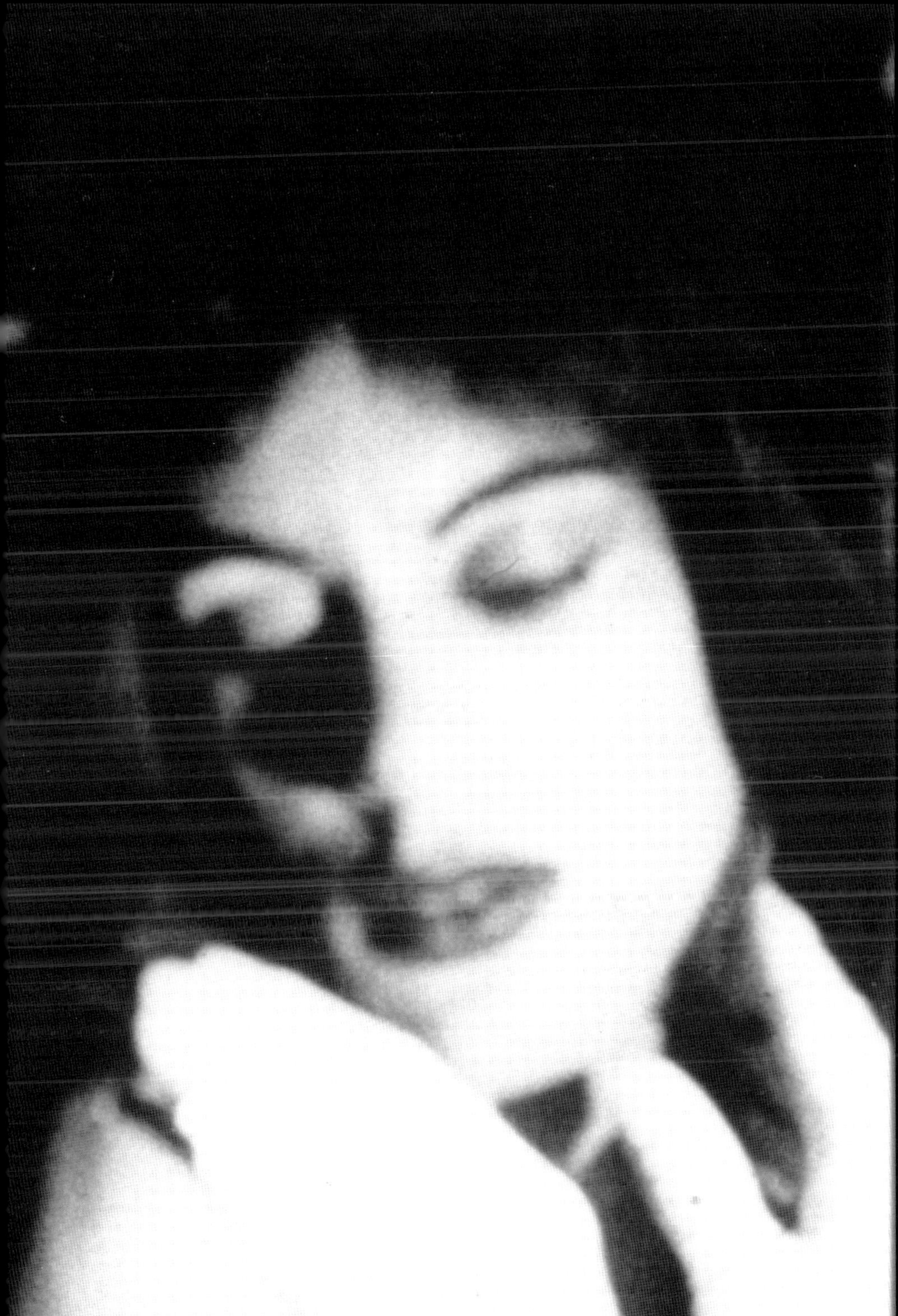

George Plimpton captures the feel of such moments when he describes *Beauty No. 2* in Jean Stein's devastating book *Edie: American Girl*:

> I remember [Chuck Wein's] voice—nagging and supercilious and quite grating.... A lot of the questions, rather searching and personal, were about her family and her father. On the bed Edie was torn between reacting to the advances of the boy next to her and wanting to respond to these questions and comments put to her by the man in the shadows. Sometimes her head would bend and she would nuzzle the boy or taste him in a sort of distracted way. I remember one of the man's commands to her was to taste "the brown sweat," but then her head would come up, like an animal suddenly alert at the edge of a waterhole, and she'd stare across the bed at her inquisitor in the shadows. I remember it as being very dramatic—at least, compared to the other stuff we'd seen—and all the more so because it seemed so real, an actual slice of life, which of course it *was*.[19]

How might we square these scenes of violation and shaming with what I'm describing as an ethical project of giving visibility to a queer world of differences and singularities in the 1960s? What does the viewer's discomfiture at Warhol's techniques of exposure do to the usual processes of spectator identification?

To answer these questions, I need to take a detour through the present, whose sexual politics fuels my interest in this history in the first place.

—

Following New York's annual gay pride celebrations in 1999, the *New York Times* editorialized:

> When police harassed gay patrons of the Stonewall Inn in 1969, the patrons stood their ground and touched off three nights of fierce civil disobedience—prominently featuring men in drag.... The building that once housed the Stonewall Inn on Christopher Street has earned a listing in the National Register of Historic Places, becoming the first site in the country to recognize the contributions that gay and lesbian Americans have made to the national culture. This also marks the gay rights movement's evolution from a fringe activity to a well-organized effort with establishment affiliations and substantial political clout.

Noting that the gay pride parade included Mayor Rudolph Giuliani and Fire Commissioner Thomas Von Essen, the *Times* concluded, "Things have come a long way since those stormy summer nights in 1969."[20]

The *Times*'s view marks the extent to which the various myths about Stonewall and the progress of gay rights have become commonplace and official, even to the point of the newspaper's ritual nod to the prominence of drag queens among the Stonewall rioters. But we might be inclined to skepticism toward this bland narrative of progress through its unremarked report of the mayor's participation in the parade, because not since the days of Stonewall had queer nightlife in New York been so under attack by a city administration. Harassment and padlocking of gay clubs again became commonplace in New York City. This disjunction between the *New York Times*'s sense of our having come a long way and the experience of many of us in New York was the cause for queers to organize, during the time of the gay pride celebrations, a counter-event devoted explicitly to shame. Gay Shame's annual zine was called *Swallow Your Pride*. These may seem like no more than the usual exercises in camp humor aimed at mainstream, normalizing gay and lesbian politics. But given the place of shame in queer theory—and in earlier queer culture, if we can take what I've described in Warhol's *Screen Test No. 2* as in any sense representative of that culture—we would do well to take the idea seriously.

What's queer about shame? And why does it get posed against the supposedly shame-eradicating politics of gay pride?

For an answer I turn to Sedgwick's essay "Queer Performativity: Henry James's *The Art of the Novel*."[21] Schematically, Sedgwick suggests there that shame is what makes us queer, both in the sense of having a queer identity and in the sense that queerness is in a volatile relation to identity, destabilizing it even as it makes it. Sedgwick finds in shame the link between "performativity and—performativity," that is, between the two senses of performativity operative in Judith Butler's enormously generative work *Gender Trouble*, performativity 1: "the notion of performance in the defining instance theatrical," and performativity 2: that of "speech-act theory and deconstruction," in which we find a "necessarily 'aberrant' relation" between a performative utterance and its meaning. In order to demonstrate the latter, Sedgwick departs from J. L. Austin's paradigmatic instance of the performative in *How to Do Things with Words*, that of the "I do," of "I do take thee to be my lawful wedded wife" (how ironic that this has become the very performative that the official gay and lesbian movement in the United States has expended all its recent energies and resources to be able to utter). Sedgwick moves from Austin's "I do" to the more "perverse"—the "deformative," she also calls it—"Shame on you," for which, I want to suggest, "For shame" works just the same, linguistically, performatively, except that, when written, it can also be read the way I'd like it to be read here: as advocating shame. I hope it will become clear as I proceed that favoring shame in the way I intend it is just the opposite of, say, conservative Catholic ideologue Andrew Sullivan's view that contemporary American society lacks sufficient shame. Sullivan's is a conventionally moralistic view of the function of shame; mine is an ethico-political one.[22]

Shame, in Sedgwick's view, is equally and simultaneously identity-defining and identity-erasing; in Sedgwick's words, it "mantles the threshold between introversion and extroversion." Moreover, shame appears to construct the singularity and isolation of one's identity through an affective connection to the shaming of another: "One of the strangest features of shame (but, I would argue, the most theoretically significant) is the way bad treatment of someone else, bad treatment *by* someone else, someone else's embarrassment, stigma, debility, blame or pain, seemingly having nothing to do with me, can so readily flood me—assuming that I'm a shame-prone person—with this sensation whose very suffusiveness seems to delineate my precise, individual outlines in the most isolating way imaginable."

I want to explicate this passage, since it gets, I think, to the crux of the matter. In the act of taking on the shame that is properly someone else's, I simultaneously feel my utter separateness, even from that person whose shame it initially was. I feel alone with my shame, singular in my susceptibility to being shamed for this stigma that has now become mine and mine alone. Thus, my shame is taken on *in lieu* of the other's shame. In taking on the shame, I do not share in the other's identity. I identify only with the other's *vulnerability* to being shamed. In this operation, most importantly, the other's difference is preserved; it is not claimed as my own. In taking on or taking up his or her shame, I am not attempting to vanquish his or her otherness. I put myself in the place of the other only insofar as I recognize that I too am prone to his or her shame.

But who is prone to shame? The answer, for Sedgwick, will necessarily be a bit tautological. A shame-prone person is a person who has been shamed. Sedgwick associates the susceptibility to shame with "the terrifying powerlessness of gender-dissonant or otherwise stigmatized childhood." And therefore, if "queer is a politically potent term... that's because, far from being capable of being detached from the childhood scene of shame, it cleaves to that scene as a near-inexhaustible source of transformational energy."

In this power of transformation, performativity functions both theatrically and ethically. Just as shame is both productive and corrosive of queer identity, the switching point between stage fright and stage presence, between being a wallflower and being a diva, so too is it simultaneously productive and corrosive of queer revaluations of dignity and worth.

In his book about the banishment of sex from contemporary queer politics, *The Trouble with Normal*, Michael Warner argues that we need to "develop an ethical response to the problem of shame." "The difficult question is not: how do we get rid of our sexual shame?" Warner writes. "The question, rather, is this: what will we do with our shame? And the usual response is: pin it on someone else."[23]

How does this work, performatively? Sedgwick explains: "The absence of an explicit verb from 'Shame on you' records the place in which an I, in conferring shame, has effaced itself and its own agency. Of course the desire for self-effacement is the defining trait of—what else?—shame. So the very grammatical truncation of 'Shame on you' marks it as a product of a history out of which an I, now withdrawn, is *projecting* shame—toward another I, an I deferred, that has yet and with difficulty to come into being, if at all, in the place of the shamed second person."

Saying "Shame on you" or "For shame" casts shame onto another that is both felt to be one's own and, at the same time, disavowed as one's own. But in those already shamed, the shame-prone, the shame is not so easily shed or so simply projected: It manages also to persist as one's own. This can lend it the capacity for articulating collectivities of the shamed. Warner explains,

> A relation to others [in queer contexts] begins in an acknowledgment of all that is most abject and least reputable in oneself. Shame is bedrock. Queers can be abusive, insulting, and vile toward one another, but because abjection is understood to be the shared condition they also know how to communicate through such comradery a moving and unexpected form of generosity. No one is beneath its reach, not because it prides itself on generosity but because it prides itself on nothing. The rule is: get over yourself. Put a wig on before you judge. And the corollary is that you stand to learn most from the people you think are beneath you. At its best, this ethic cuts against every form of hierarchy you could bring into the room. Queer scenes are the true *salons des refusés*, where the most heterogeneous people are brought into great intimacy by their common experience of being despised and rejected in a world of norms that they now recognize as false morality.[24]

The sad thing about the contemporary politics of gay and lesbian pride is that it works in precisely the opposite way: It calls for a visibility predicated on homogeneity and on excluding anyone who does not conform to norms that are taken to be the very morality we should be happy to accept as the onus of our so-called maturity. It thus sees shame as conventional indignity rather than the affective substrate necessary to the transformation of one's distinctiveness into a queer kind of dignity. This is why the queer culture of the 1960s, made visible in Warhol's films, is so necessary a reminder of what we need to know now.

—

So I return to the shaming of Mario Montez in *Screen Test No. 2*. As I mentioned before, I wanted in my essay on *Blow Job* to contest the cliché of Warhol's filmic vision as voyeuristic. I argued that formal features in Warhol's films—different formal features in different films, of course—worked to foreclose a knowingness about the people represented in them. Warhol found the means to make the people of his world visible to us without making them objects of our knowledge. The knowledge of a world that his films give us is not a knowledge of the other for the self. Rather, what I see, when, say, I see Mario Montez in *Screen Test No. 2*, is a performer in the moment of being exposed such that he becomes, as Warhol said, "so for real." But unlike Warhol we don't leave the room (nor, for that matter, I'd bet, did Warhol). Rather, we remain there with our disquiet—which is, after all, what? It is our encounter, on the one hand, with the absolute difference of another, his or her "so-for-realness," and, on the other hand, with the other's shame, both the shame that extracts his or her "so-for-realness" from the already "for-real" performativity of Warhol's performers, and the shame that we accept as also ours, but curiously also ours alone. I am thus not "like" Mario, but the distinctiveness that is revealed in Mario invades me—"floods me," to use Sedgwick's words—and my own distinctiveness is revealed simultaneously. I, too, feel exposed.

Tavel, the brilliant, ridiculous scenarist—brilliant, indeed, at ridicule[25]—seemed to provide exactly what Warhol wanted. "I enjoyed working with him," Warhol wrote, "because he understood instantly when I'd say things like, 'I want it simple and plastic and white.' Not everyone can think in an abstract way, but Ronnie could."[26]

Tavel repays Warhol's compliment:

> This operation-theatre he brings us to and in which we at first resentfully feel ourselves to be the patient, suddenly actualizes as the real and traditional theatre: we are audience as always, suddenly alive and watching, horrified after amused, scholarly after ennuied. And alarmed. The "destructive" artist proves again the prophet and makes of his life a stunning cry, withal keeping his mask-distance of laughter and contempt. He emerges gentle from a warehouse of Brillo boxes, having stated his bleak vision, as social an artist as any '30's fiend could ask for.[27]

Tavel continues in the same essay, "The Banana Diary: The Story of Andy Warhol's 'Harlot'":

> The New American Cinema has taken the mask off rather than putting it on. The New American Cinema smacks of Cinema Verité in almost more ways than can be counted. The souls of the beings we view are enlarged before us, even to the point of snapping out of character and blinking into the camera; an instance more and they would be waving at us. That these souls are often wretched, which means our souls are wretched, has brought the accusation of brutality and sadism against the movement. Yet who among us, in his own life, escapes the complex of sado-masochistic chaos or finds his way about in a commodiousness less than brutal?[28]

It should be clear from this, I believe, that Tavel's purpose in *Screen Test No. 2* is to solicit from Mario exactly what we see: Mario's irresistible, resplendent vulnerability.[29] We see his soul enlarged before us most conspicuously at those moments when he is overcome with shame, and when we become aware—painfully—of his shame as what Sedgwick calls a blazon. That blazon, which we share, might well proclaim a new slogan of queer politics: For Shame!

ADDENDUM: MOTHER CAMP

In a "Note to the Reader" in *Mother Camp*, her groundbreaking study of female impersonators, Esther Newton wrote:

> It has been suggested that I explain the significance of the title *Mother Camp*. In the mid-sixties, "camp" was an in-group word which denoted specifically homosexual humor.... The most highly esteemed female impersonators were all "camps," virtuoso verbal clowns.
>
> My use of the word "mother" is slightly more idiosyncratic. I intended it in a double sense. "Mother Camp" as an honorific implies something about the relationship of the female impersonator to his gay audience.... I also meant "mother" as an adjective modifying "camp," the latter word then referring to the whole system of humor. This reflects my belief that camp humor ultimately grows out of the incongruities and absurdities of the patriarchal nuclear family; for example the incongruity between the sacred, idealized Mother, and the profane, obscene Woman. If camp humor takes such problems as its special subject, then the drag queen is its natural exponent. He himself is a magical dream figure: the fusion of mother and son.[1]

At the tender age of twenty-five I succumbed to ridiculousness. It happened on Forty-Second Street, between Ninth and Tenth Avenues, sometime after midnight, at a porn cinema called the Masque Theater. It began with a warning from the devil: "The play you are about to see is a mortal sin. Any person witnessing this play takes part in that sin and thereby risks his immortal soul." The first character to appear, after the devil, is a mother by the name of Turzahnelle. She is about to abandon her child, Orgone, described in the play's text as "the Baby Hunchback, Pinhead, Sex Maniac." Who could love such a creature? Who will save the baby sex maniac from a premature demise on a mountaintop? Who will become adoptive mother to this poor creature? Who else but Mario Montez?—as Carla, the gypsy wildcat. In *Queer Theatre*, Stefan Brecht describes this play, *Turds in Hell*, by Charles Ludlam and Bill Vehr: "In *Turds*, the globular cosmos has become unrolled, it stretches, an undulating expanse, ingrained time, on which events of transfiguration transpire at diverse locations, little flickering flames on a plain, but each a real person living out a whole life (in the forever repeated gestures of his obsession)."[2] Brecht's descriptions, ungrammatical and impossible to follow though they may be, are always wonderfully evocative. I don't remember much about *Turds in Hell*, but I remember Mario. Or at least I think I do: I remember Mario standing on one side of the stage for what seemed like hours, mute, with shimmying body and animated facial expressions, repeatedly, obsessively miming Marilyn Monroe. I was seduced. Though I wasn't a baby sex maniac abandoned on a mountaintop, I think I too wanted to be adopted by such a mother.

It was around this time—things get a bit circuitous here, but that's what happens when you succumb to ridiculousness—it was around this time—1969—that I met, became friends with, and for a while shared my loft with another famous downtown

Puerto Rican drag performer and Warhol superstar. I had just moved to West Twenty-Third Street, across from the Chelsea Hotel, and begun hanging out in the back room at Max's Kansas City. Soon after seeing *Turds in Hell*, I saw another ridiculous theater piece—this one directed by Ludlam's rival theatrical genius John Vaccaro. The play was Jackie Curtis's first, *Heaven Grand in Amber Orbit*. I don't remember much from that play either, except for its atmosphere of sheer chaos. Soon after I saw it, one of *Heaven Grand*'s chorines swooped into the back room at Max's. She had a massive number of stripped coque feathers in her hair, which seemed to electrify her already exceedingly animated head. She was glamorous and zany and loud. No doubt she was on speed. She was Holly Woodlawn. I invited her for tea the next day, and we began to hang out together. When Holly and her sweet young boyfriend Johnny found themselves temporarily homeless, they came and lived with me for a few months, the most madcap few months of my life. Living with Holly, I saw her unglamorous side too, which only enamored me all the more of her glamour, to which I once made a small contribution—which brings me back to the subject of mothers.

My own mother was not always as glamorous as a boy wants his mother to be, but she made attempts when the occasion demanded. For one of these, before I came into the world, she bought a dinner dress by Adrian. Designed in the early 1940s, after Adrian left MGM to open his ready-to-wear business, and hanging throughout my childhood in my mother's cedar closet back in Idaho, it consisted of a straight-to-the-floor black silk-crepe skirt, topped by a bright pink satin bodice covered in black lace. Two heart-shaped pink rhinestone brooches adorned the neckline. It seemed just right for Holly, so I called my mother. "Mom," I said, "Do you still have your Adrian?" "Yes, dear," she said, "it's still down in the cedar closet." "Could you send it to me?" I asked. To this day, I'm amazed that I did that, and even more amazed that my mother didn't ask *why* I wanted her Adrian. She just said okay, and a couple of weeks later the dress arrived in the mail. I gave it to Holly. She put it on. She looked fabulous—which was Holly's favorite word. Holly went out for the evening wearing the Adrian, and that was the end of my mother's glamorous dinner dress.

I never saw my mother wear her Adrian. It was old and out of style by the time I saw her dressed up to go to a fancy dinner party, and my mother's version of glamour didn't include the notion of "vintage" dresses. That would be the invention of a later generation of glamour-pusses, like Mario Montez. For Warhol's post–*Chelsea Girls* film *Ari and Mario*, Mario wrought a strange variation on this scenario of seeing your mother all dressed up to go out while you're left at home with the babysitter. The film's conceit has Mario playing babysitter to Nico's four-year-old son Ari while Nico goes out for the evening. But it's not Nico who's dressed up in the film—she just wears one of her usual pantsuits—but Mario, who is dolled up in a pale aqua pleated crepe gown whose empire waist is emphasized by a large brooch. A matching diaphanous, ruffled jacket is worn over the dress, and the ensemble is accessorized by several strands of beads, bracelets, rings, and dangling earrings, which Nico admires when she returns to the scene at the end. Mario calls them go-go earrings and says that he made them himself. (See plate 1.)

Things get off to a bad start when Ari hides in the closet and Mario is left to coax him out. Unlike me, Ari is unsusceptible to Mario's charms. Mario does his level best. He suggests playing cowboys and Indians. "I'll be the Indian," he says, as he puts a cowboy hat on Ari. Ari doesn't go along, but gets out his jack-in-the-box instead. Mario tries reading from a children's collection of Aesop's Fables—"The Fox and the Grape," "The Tinderbox," "The Shepherd and the Chimney Sweep." Ari seems to pay no attention, but Mario perseveres. "Do you like it so far?" Mario asks, and Ari mutely shakes his head in uncertain assent. "You do?" implores Mario, then looks off camera, clearly perplexed about what to do with this singularly unresponsive little boy. He goes back to cowboys and Indians, this time suggesting that as he sings "Ten Little Indians," Ari could shoot each of the Indians in turn. This goes nowhere, except that we get to hear Mario sing "Ten Little Indians." Mario then proposes to dance like an Indian. "Do you know what they call a female Indian?" Mario asks, momentarily forgetting the answer himself. "A papoose?" he wonders. Ari eventually becomes frighteningly aggressive as he aims his toy rifle at Mario and shoots and shoots. Mario feigns being wounded and pleads, "Don't shoot me again, please," to no avail. Finally he asks, "Isn't there anything else you like to do?" at which point Nico returns to calm her child down (it's obvious, in fact, that Nico had never left the room but simply disappeared behind the camera). The film ends with a tight close-up of Mario's face looking a bit uncertain about his success in the role of substitute mother.

Not surprisingly, Mario is much more accomplished in the role of mother when the little boy is a grown-up, since grown-up boys *are* susceptible to his charms. Such is the case in one of his greatest Warhol vehicles, *More Milk Yvette*, in which he plays Lana Turner, and the part of Lana's daughter, Cheryl Crane, who stabbed Lana's tough-guy lover Johnny Stompanato to death, is played by Richard Schmidt, an attractive young man nearly smaller enough than Mario to be believable as his fourteen-year-old progeny. But obviously Schmidt is neither a teenager nor a girl. And his behavior with his "mother" tends toward the incestuous. He alternates with the eponymous Yvette, who plays Lana's maid, in helping Mario on and off with the many on-camera costume changes that seem to be the film's main subject. He holds a mirror for Mario to put on lipstick. These are perhaps things a child might do for his mother. But sharing a hamburger by eating it together—that is, eating it at the same time from the edges toward the center—seems a bit risqué. And halfway through the film, there's a full-on make-out scene between Mario and Richard. Things get seriously confusing when, not so long after this, the Johnny Stompanato character shows up, swoops Lana off her feet, and plants a

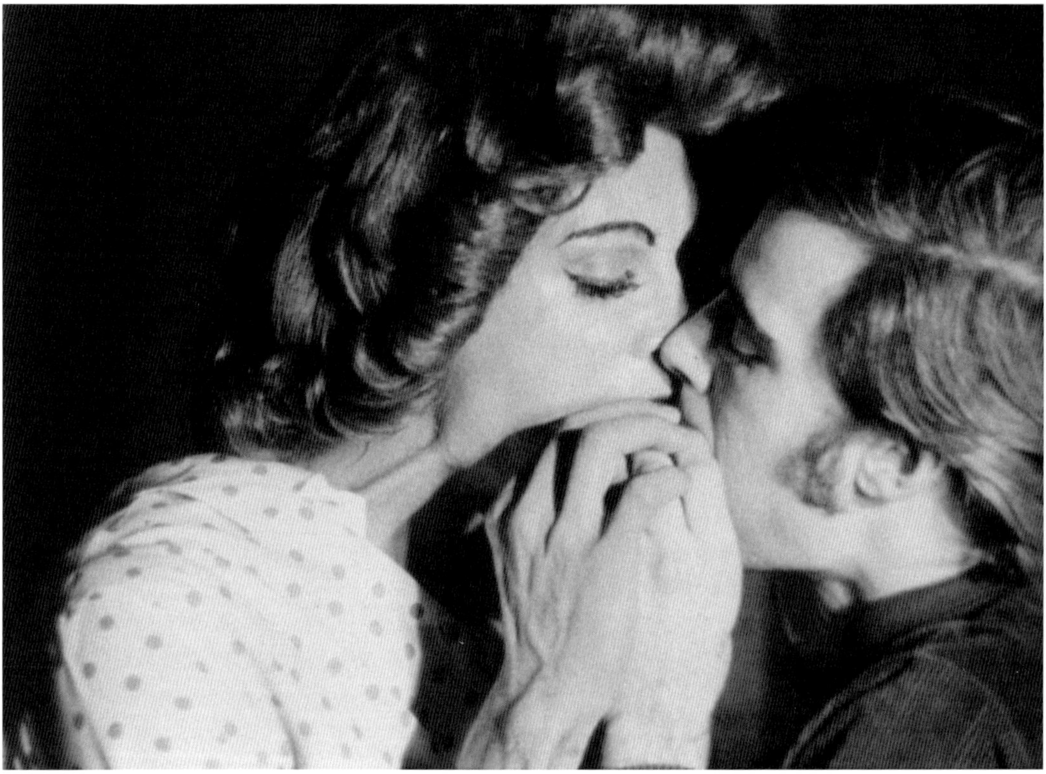

Andy Warhol, *More Milk Yvette*, 1965. 16mm film, b/w, sound, 66 minutes. Film still courtesy of The Andy Warhol Museum.

big wet kiss on her lips. All of these romantic moments—whether between mother and son or mother and gangster-lover—are accompanied by intensified harmonica playing by a Bob Dylan lookalike named Paul Caruso. And most are preceded or followed by love songs sung a cappella by Mario—including "If I Loved You," "Unchained Melody," "Night and Day," and "It's De-Lovely." In fact, the special brilliance of *More Milk Yvette* among Warhol's films is that it succeeds, more or less, in crossing a melodramatic Hollywood biopic (Lana Turner's stormy relationship with her gangster boyfriend, ending in murder), a symbolic representation of a celebrated Hollywood movie-star trait (Lana Turner's sweater-girl moniker), and an impossible-to-sustain Hollywood genre (the musical). Who could have pulled this off but Mario Montez? As Donald Newlove wrote at the time in an essay called "Prothalamion for Wet Harmonica and Johnny Stompanato," it didn't matter that Mario was "light years away from Lana Turner; it is enough that as a star in his own right, he can be any woman he says he is. He could as well be Rita Hayworth, he would do it with exactly the same intonations and gestures."[3] (Newlove is surely right: In Warhol's films alone, Mario played Jean Harlow, Hedy Lamarr, and Lana Turner, in addition to many star turns as, simply, Mario Montez.) Warhol seems to have had the crazy idea that Mario could sing every line in *More Milk Yvette*, as if he were making a film like Jacques Demy's *The Umbrellas of Cherbourg*. And Mario does indeed begin the film singing his lines, to no particular recognizable tune. He enters the frame singing:

> My name is Lana Turner,
> And I'm just coming back from my studio,
> And I've never modeled so many sweaters in my whole life,
> But I had to do it,
> And my boyfriend named Johnny Stomp … [Mario stomps his heels a couple of times, like a flamenco dancer] … Stompanato is waiting for me at home,
> And I do have a son named Cheryl who's waiting for me too.

Needless to say, not even Mario can sustain the task of making up all of his lines and singing them as he goes along. So he continues in what Newlove calls Singspiel:

> Cheryl, oh Cheryl, what have you done to Johnny? Did you shoot him? Oh why? I love him so much. Why did you shoot Johnny? Why? Was he trying to seduce you? Was he? I can't believe that.

Mario sensibly keeps the dialogue to a minimum—in fact, the film is monologic (only Mario speaks—and adds a song now and then). As for Johnny seducing Cheryl—it doesn't happen. The only seducing here is done by Mario, and not of Cheryl alone. When Mario sings, it's not for Cheryl or Johnny, really. It's for the camera. And there's no question but that Mario's charms succeed in their aim to seduce. To describe the film here, I consulted my notes from the first time I saw it. "Very lyrical, extremely beautiful,"

I wrote during the first thirty-three-minute reel. "Extremely lyrical, extremely sexy," I wrote later, after Mario and Richard's make-out scene. Obviously, I was smitten. The movie-star mother played by Mario in *More Milk Yvette*—the magical dream figure, in Esther Newton's characterization—had worked her wiles. Every time I see one of Mario's wonderful performances, I'm taken back to that moment when, thanks to Mario, I succumbed to ridiculousness. If only I'd met Mario earlier—before Holly—my mom's Adrian would have been his.

COMING TOGETHER TO STAY APART

AT ONE POINT, ANDY PROPOSED TO MAKE A FILM CALLED *LUNCH*. HE WANTED TO PUT ME AND EDIE AT A LUNCH TABLE AND HAVE BOTH OF US TALKING, NONSTOP, NOT TO EACH OTHER. BUT WITH DIFFERENT SILVERWARE, DIFFERENT THINGS TO EAT, SO THAT IT WAS A LUNCH ENTIRELY ABOUT NONCOMMUNICATION. IT NEVER HAPPENED, THOUGH. HE DIDN'T DESCRIBE IT LIKE THAT. THAT'S MY SAYING IT. HE JUST SORT OF SAID, IT WOULD BE GREAT TO DO A FILM ABOUT LUNCH. YOU SHOULD TALK, EDIE SHOULD TALK, YOU SHOULDN'T TALK TO EACH OTHER.

GORDON BALDWIN, INTERVIEWED IN *THE VELVET YEARS: WARHOL'S FACTORY*

VARIOUS THINGS WE THINK WE KNOW ABOUT ANDY WARHOL'S FILMS—THAT THEY WERE SILENT OR, WHEN MADE WITH SOUND, THAT THE SUPERSTARS TALKED ON AND ON BUT SAID JUST WHATEVER CAME INTO THEIR MINDS AT THE MOMENT—SUGGEST THAT A SCREENPLAY FOR A WARHOL FILM WOULD MAKE NO SENSE.

But this overlooks the fact that Ronald Tavel *wrote* a number of the acknowledged masterpieces of Warhol's vast film output—*Screen Test No. 2*, *The Life of Juanita Castro*, *Horse*, *Vinyl*, *Kitchen*, *Hedy*, and two sequences of *The Chelsea Girls*—and of the canonical Warhol films, this list makes up a good portion. If we add to this the fact that several of Tavel's Warhol screenplays, staged in the theater, resulted in the invention of the Theater of the Ridiculous both in name and in founding style, then we must admit that this was one of the most productive artistic collaborations in the recent history of the avant-garde.[1] But there are two strikingly odd things about this most fruitful of collaborations: First, the fame and fortune of the two partners is entirely asymmetrical; while everyone knows Warhol, who knows Tavel? And second, the partners worked at loggerheads. Their deliberate failure of cooperation will be my subject here, but before I come to it, let me say something about the regrettable eclipse of Tavel.

The genius of Warhol was not least his uncanny ability always to secure for himself the author-function, and all the more so by protesting that he rarely had all that much to do with making his work, admitting openly that his work was really the yield of others—others' ideas, others' designs, others' images, others' abilities, others' labor. But the more Warhol protested, the more he alone was credited.

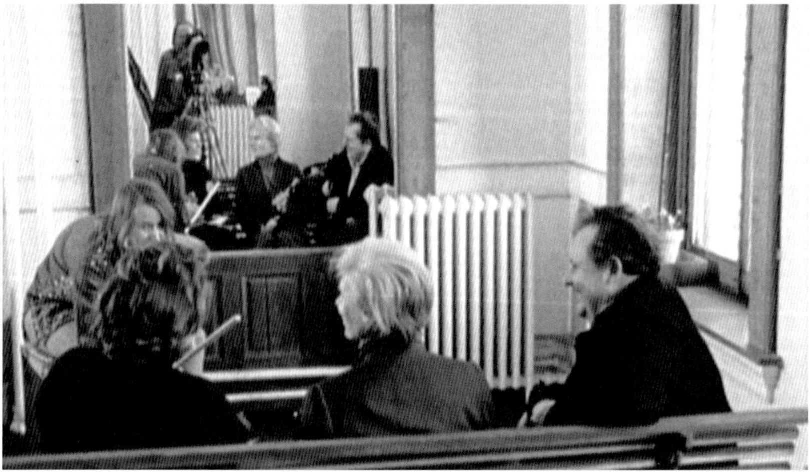

Emile de Antonio, *Painters Painting*, 1972. 16mm film, color, sound, 116 minutes.

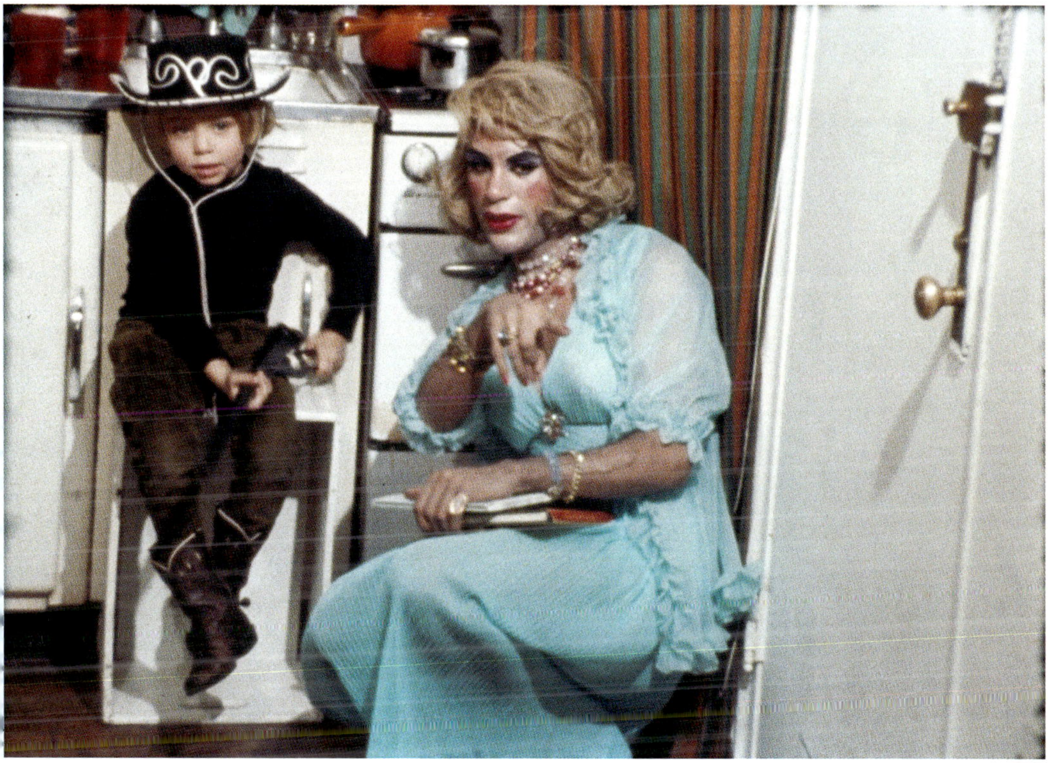

Plate 1

Andy Warhol, *Ari and Mario*, 1966. 16mm film, color, sound, 67 minutes. Film still courtesy of The Andy Warhol Museum.

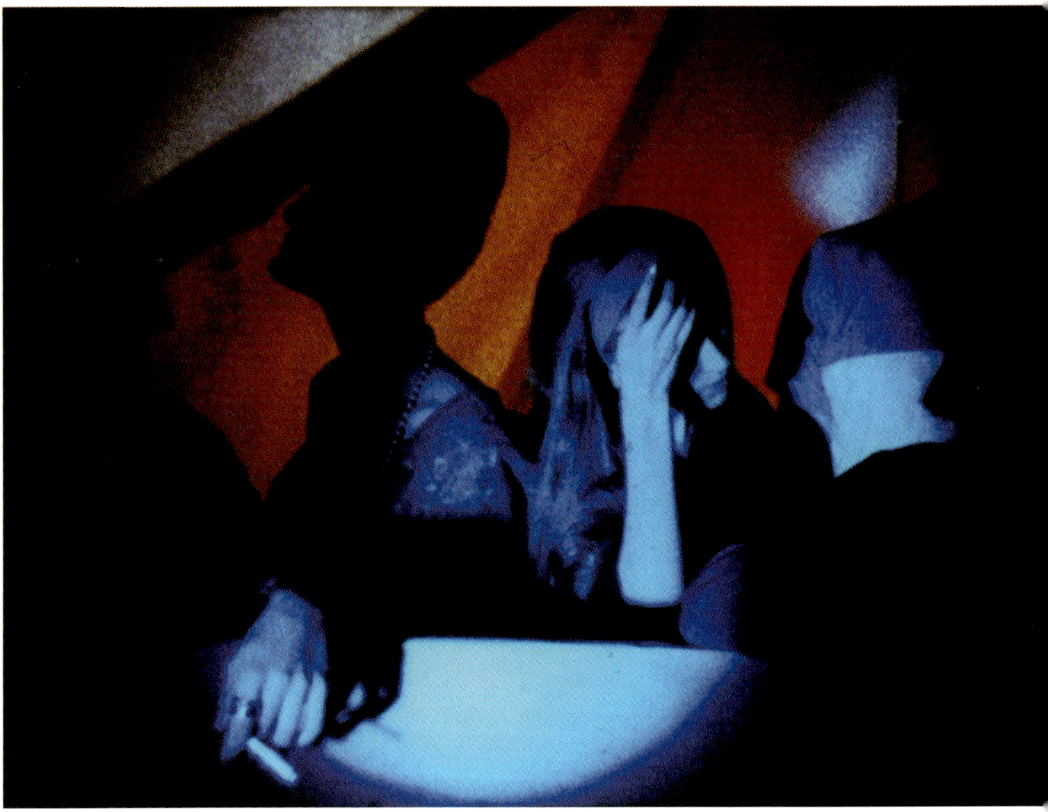

Plate 2

Andy Warhol, *The Chelsea Girls*, 1966. 16mm film, b/w and color, sound, 204 minutes in double screen. Film still courtesy of The Andy Warhol Museum.

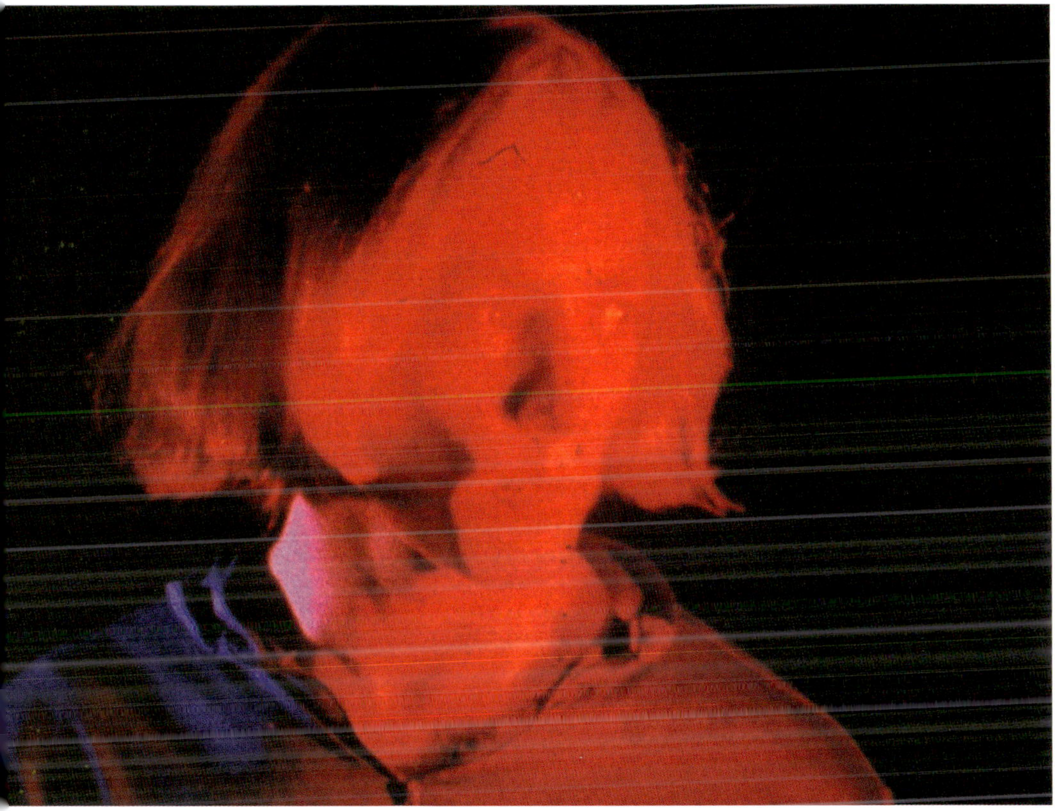

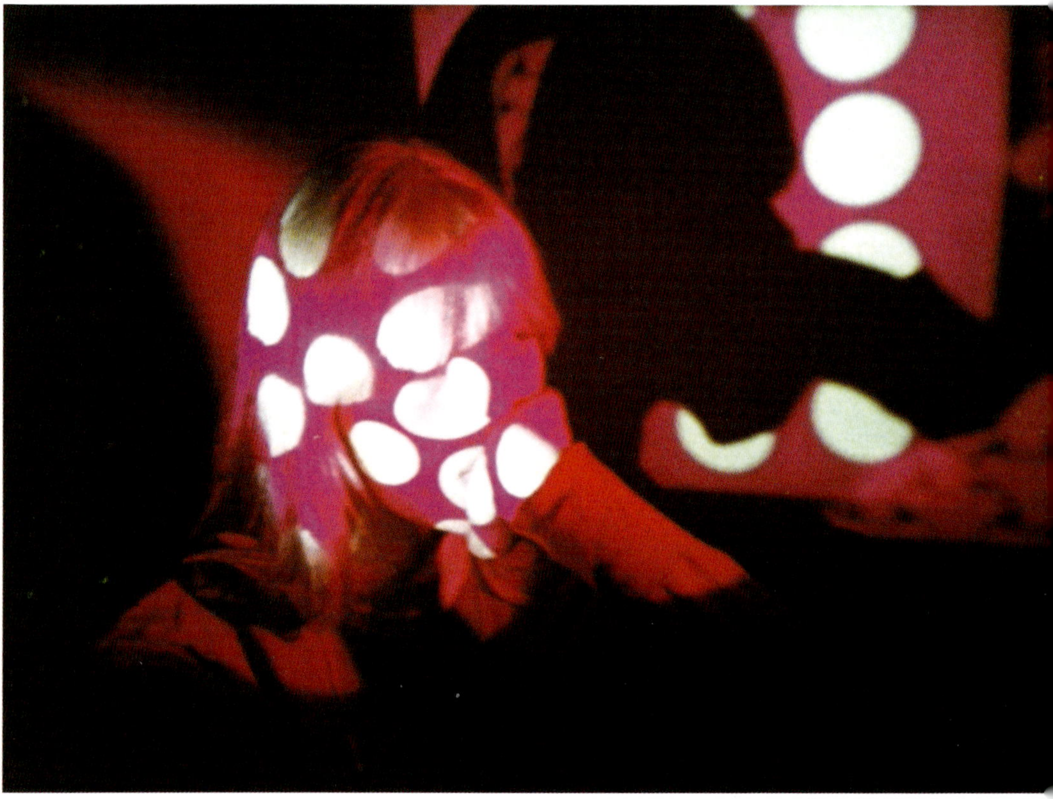

Plate 3

Andy Warhol, *The Chelsea Girls*, 1966. 16mm film, b/w and color, sound, 204 minutes in double screen. Film still courtesy of The Andy Warhol Museum.

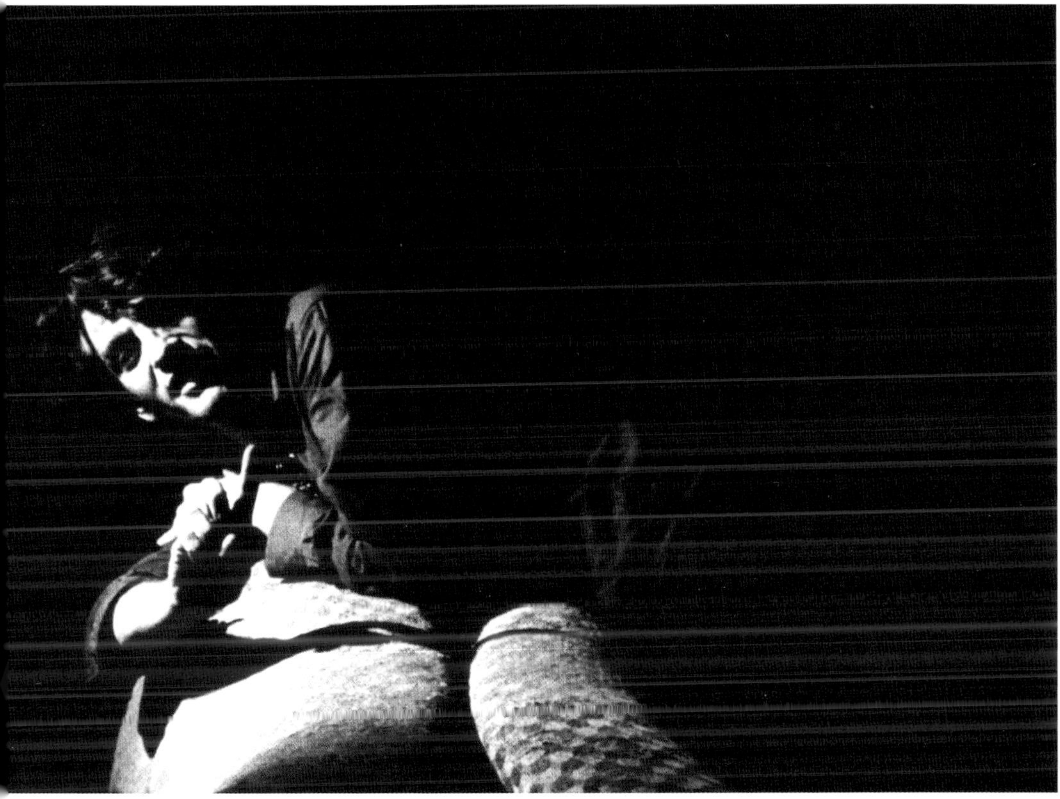

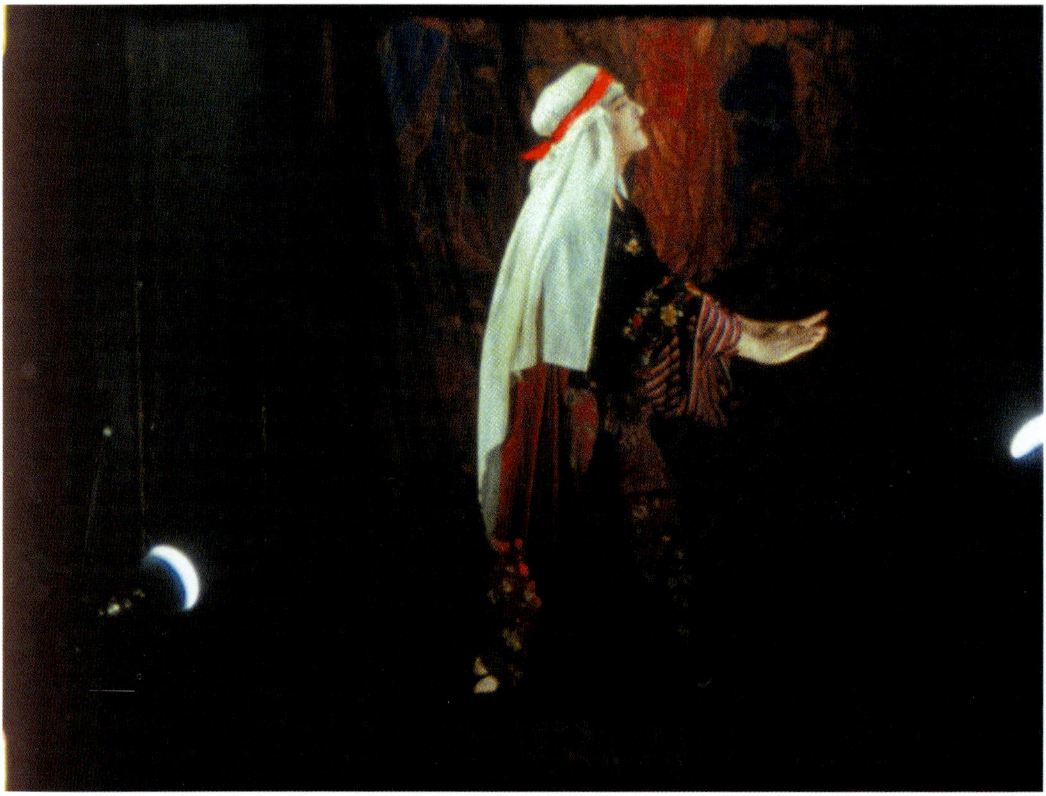

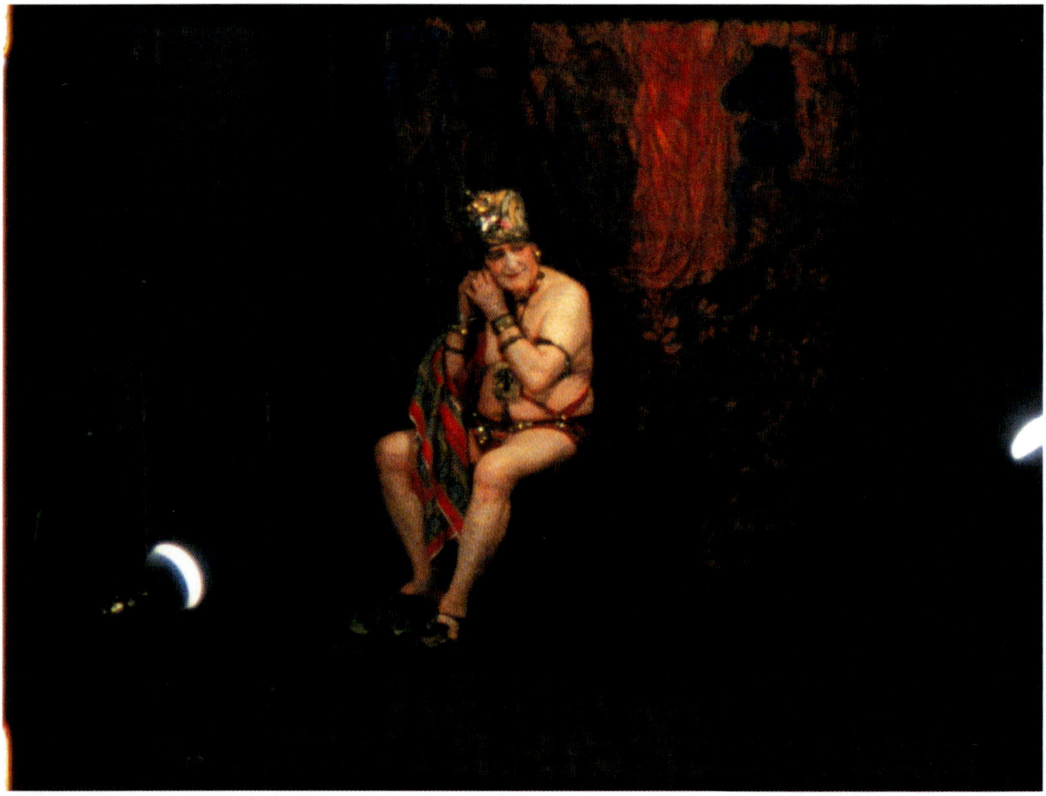

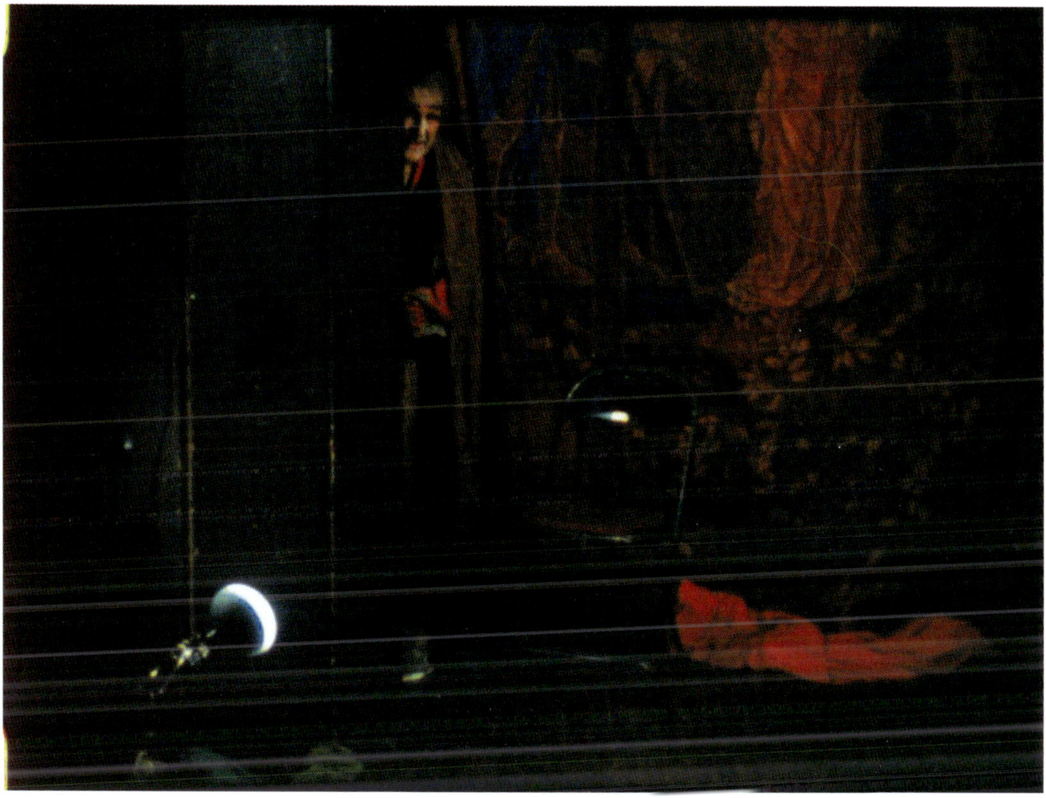

Plates 4–6

Andy Warhol, *Paul Swan*, 1965. 16mm film, color, sound, 66 minutes. Film stills courtesy of The Andy Warhol Museum.

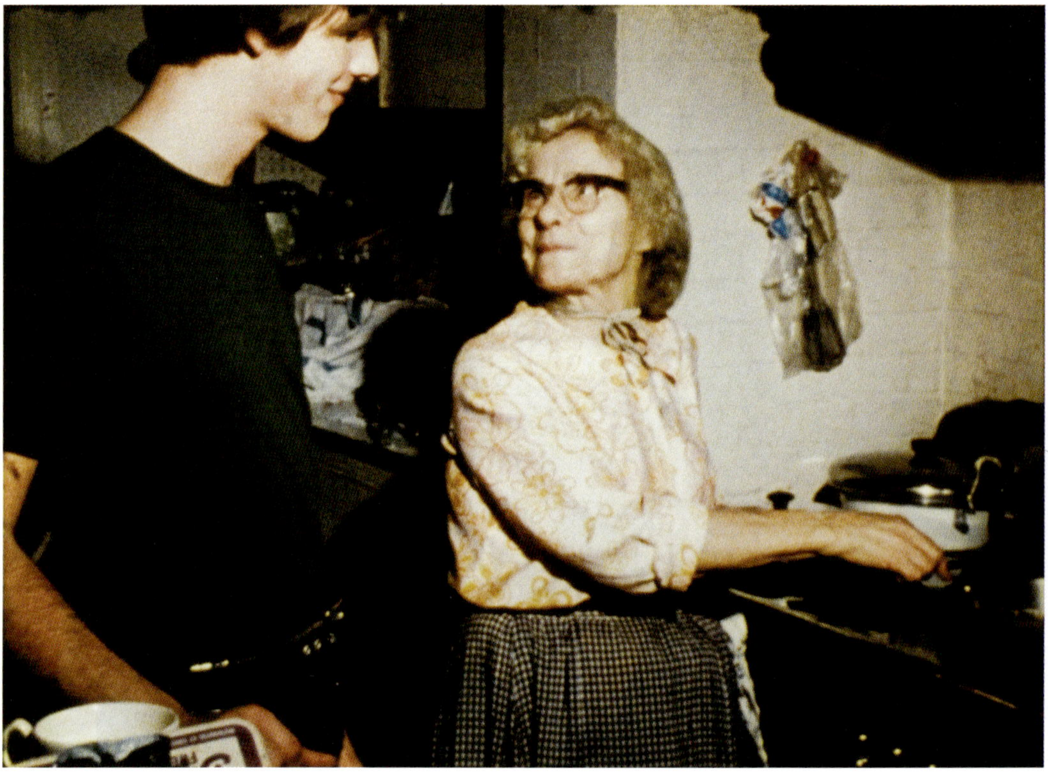

Plate 7

Andy Warhol, *Mrs. Warhol*, 1966. 16mm film, color, sound, 67 minutes. Film still courtesy of The Andy Warhol Museum.

Here's a telling example: In Emile de Antonio's documentary *Painters Painting*—which, notwithstanding its title, is mostly painters *talking*—Warhol sits facing a mirror on a couch between de Antonio and Factory denizen Brigid Berlin. Standing behind them and also visible in the film frame, Ed Emschwiller aims a camera at the mirror. De Antonio says to Warhol, "You said all people are the same and that you wanted to be a machine in your paintings. Is that true?" Warhol demurs: "Uh, is it true, Brigid?" All the other painters in the film—among them Willem de Kooning and Barnett Newman, Robert Rauschenberg and Jasper Johns—answer de Antonio's questions. Off camera, invisible except for his appearance in the Warhol segment, de Antonio gets the artists to pontificate about their work, sometimes—especially in the segments with Helen Frankenthaler, Larry Poons, Kenneth Noland, and Jules Olitsky—by ventriloquizing the powerful critic Clement Greenberg. But not Andy. Warhol puts de Antonio in the picture and gets Brigid to do the talking. If anyone holds forth in this segment, it is Brigid, but even she is canny enough, or maybe just uninterested enough, not to be a Greenberg dummy. Why, though, do I assume (wrongly, it turns out) that it was Warhol who arranged this shot, setting up de Antonio instead of being set up by him? Why do I assign authorship for this one sequence of de Antonio's famous film to Warhol? Simply because it allows Warhol, unlike every other painter in the film, *not* to be figured as claiming authorship of his work, and this is, of course, the standard Warhol gambit. As a result, Warhol's authorship trumps de Antonio's even in the documentary auteur's justly famous film.[2]

Like de Antonio, Tavel is one of the few artists to have been closely associated with Warhol who created a significant independent body of work. But the documentarian's and the playwright's place in our collective memory and histories of 1960s counterculture is also asymmetrical. De Antonio is well known for films about subjects of enduring interest for some of the central political struggles of America's postwar period—*Point of Order* (1964), about the 1954 Army–McCarthy hearings; *Rush to Judgment* (1967), about the Warren Commission investigation of the JFK assassination; *In the Year of the Pig* (1968), about the Vietnam War, and *Millhouse: A White Comedy* (1971), about Richard Nixon—while Tavel is known, by those who do know him, as the playwright of such works of ridiculous theater as *The Life of Lady Godiva*, *Indira Gandhi's Daring Device* (both 1966), *Gorilla Queen* (1967), and *Boy on the Straight-Back Chair* (1969), in addition to the scenarios for Warhol's films that were also done as plays, *Screen Test*, *The Life of Juanita Castro*, *Shower*, *Kitchenette*, and *Vinyl* (initially staged 1965–1967).[3] Like other figures of the 1960s queer underground, Tavel conceived his work within and for an alternative community that did not aspire to and usually didn't get a hearing beyond its own precincts. Tavel's achievement stands in reverse proportion to his acclaim, and no doubt part of his achievement is remaining true to, and therefore restricted to, his alternative milieu.[4] Warhol's films form a central part of this same queer underground, but in Warhol's case, the market value that his paintings eventually accrued has retroactively conferred high cultural value upon all the rest of his work. As Michel Foucault explained in his well-known essay "What Is an Author?" the author-function fundamentally changed at the end of the eighteenth century, when its principle of appropriation shifted from one of surveillance to one of ownership. But ownership is unevenly applied to the various forms of discourse and cultural production.[5] Ephemeral forms, participatory forms, collaborative forms: all present difficulties for the author-function in the era of consumer capitalism. Thus, in a case such as the Warhol–Tavel films, the author-function is easily usurped by Warhol.

Still, I will insist that Tavel is indisputably the author of the Warhol screenplays and that the screenplays resulted in indisputably significant movies.[6] More important, the significance of these works, and their distinctiveness among Warhol's films, is the consequence of the collaboration, a collaboration that must be differentiated from the usual condition of filmmaking, which perforce entails teamwork among writers, directors, producers, technicians, and actors. In the case of the Warhol–Tavel partnership the specific form and quality of the films results from a *confrontation* between Tavel's script and Warhol's manner of filmmaking during the time the two worked together, a manner pithily summarized by superstar Mario Montez. When asked in a 1968 *Film Culture* interview, "Does Warhol rehearse?"—and this question of rehearsal is one that arose again and again in Tavel's working relationship with Warhol—Montez replied, "No—He doesn't believe in editing—Rehearsing and editing are related."[7] For Warhol, indeed, they are.

The Warhol films for which Tavel wrote scenarios are all shot with an Auricon camera, which takes 1,200-foot rolls, or roughly thirty-three minutes, of film. In every case but that of *Horse*, which uses three rolls and is thus about 100 minutes long, and, of course, *The Chelsea Girls*, which is projected two reels at a time, side by side, and runs three and a half hours, the Warhol–Tavel films use two rolls spliced together to make sixty-six-minute films. What makes this duration noteworthy is not its simple calculation but the fact that the actors are required to carry on their activities for over an hour, uninterrupted but for a short break in the middle to reload the camera, and that the technical crew must also sustain its work throughout the length of the film. For the technicians, this sometimes requires little more than maintenance, since the shot is entirely unchanging: The camera never moves, focus is never changed, and lighting and sound levels remain steady. But this is less often the case than the minimalism that has come to be associated with Warhol's cinema might suggest. Indeed, in the Warhol–Tavel film *Hedy*, cast and crew move throughout the vast space of the furniture-storage loft above the Warhol Factory that served as the film's location, and Warhol follows along with his camera, which is even more mobile than the scene it sometimes captures, sometimes wanders away from.

More decisive, though, is the sort of pressure this duration puts on the players. Because Warhol refuses to edit, there is no going back, no fixing mistakes—for that matter, no such thing as a mistake in the sense that it might be rectified by a retake and edited into the finished film. The essential condition of "acting" in a Warhol film is that you are left to your own devices and that whatever you *do* will simply *be* the way you appear in the film. If you make a fool of yourself, a fool you will be, for all to see. In David James's formulation, "The situation is that of psychoanalysis; the camera is the silent analyst who has abandoned the subject to the necessity of his fantastic self-projection."[8]

How does this manner of working use a scenario? Why did Warhol even want a scenario? A possible answer might be: Warhol didn't yet realize that he didn't need one. By that I mean that perhaps Warhol didn't yet realize that to make *sound* films in which his superstars would speak, he didn't need written scenes and dialogue; all he needed was the relentless rolling of his camera. But I don't think we can make such an assumption, simply because Warhol already had reason to know this, since, throughout the period when he was making films with Tavel's screenplays, he was also making films with stories and dialogue—or better, with situations and talk—that had no scenarios. These include the first Warhol sound film, *Harlot*, although *Harlot* is something of an anomaly in its radical disjuncture of sound and image: The scene taking place in the film frame is essentially silent while the soundtrack records three men—one of them Tavel—commenting on the scene taking place at some distance from them. But they also include such well-known nonscripted films as *Poor Little Rich Girl*, *Beauty No. 2*, *My Hustler*, and *Camp*. Throughout the period that Warhol made films from Tavel's scenarios, he made an even greater number of films, in many ways stylistically similar, without scenarios.

So I'll pose the question again: Why did Warhol want a scenario? And I'll answer with a simple paradox: Warhol wanted a scenario precisely because he didn't want one. Tavel gives us a number of clues about Warhol's paradoxical objective. In *The Life of Juanita Castro*, Tavel plays the on-screen director who feeds the actors their lines, one at a time. He says, "Juanita, look at Fidel, and say, 'You never really cared for the poor peasants,'" whereupon Marie Menken, playing Juanita, turns around to face Mercedes Ospina, playing Fidel, and says, "You never really cared for the poor peasants." Asked whether taking on the director's role—in both senses, directing the film and acting the part of the director in the film—had been his intention when writing the script, Tavel replied:

> No, I expected Andy to do it. But he read the script and then asked me to. At that point, Andy certainly didn't want people learning lines. You can see that if you glance at the script. The onscreen director tells everyone what to say and do. I would not have had the balls to suggest that I do that. It could have been one of his ways of destabilizing me. But I had the feeling he made the decision almost instantly. His instincts were

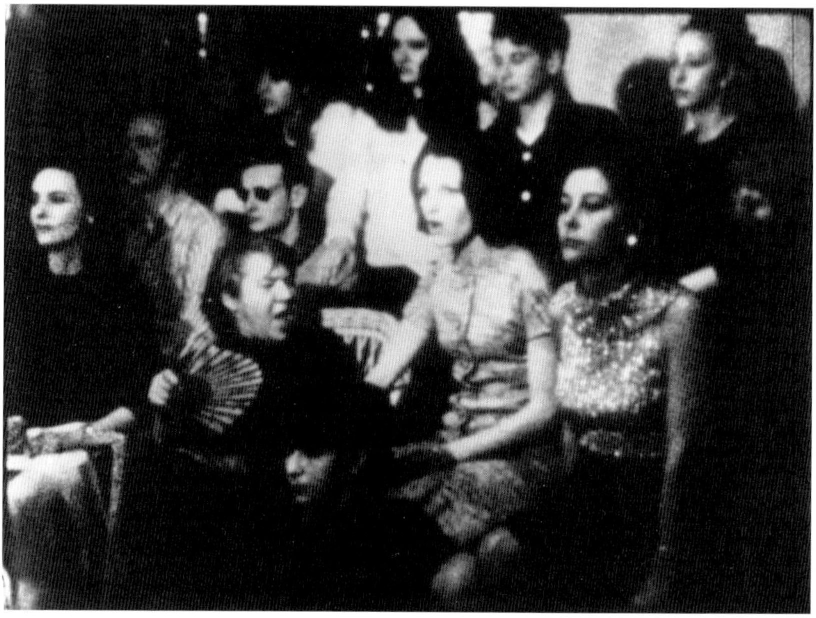

Andy Warhol, *The Life of Juanita Castro*, 1965. 16mm film, b/w, sound, 66 minutes. Film still courtesy of The Andy Warhol Museum.

> so strong. He could depend on them. They seldom failed him.... I handed him the script and he said you do it, Ronny. I was slowly becoming aware that I was one of the people Warhol was studying.... To be incapacitated in that way is part of the tension of *Juanita.*[9]

To be incapacitated, like being subject to the camera's relentless rolling, like being analysand to the silent analyst, aptly characterizes the condition of working with Warhol: to be prevented from learning lines or otherwise preparing, to be kept consistently off-guard. Seeing *The Life of Juanita Castro* now, it is impossible to imagine Warhol himself playing the part of the director. There are too many lines to read, too many complex sentences and unpronounceable words; indeed, the script has entire lines in Spanish, in which Tavel is apparently fluent, while Warhol would certainly have been as much at a loss with the foreign tongue as is Marie Menken, who tries entirely unsuccessfully to repeat the Spanish lines Tavel feeds her (the part was written for Mario Montez, but he declined, insisting that he didn't do politics).[10]

In any case, Tavel caught on to Warhol's game right away, and devised his own way of playing it. About *Horse*, the next film after *Juanita* for which he wrote a scenario, he says, "It was one thing for Andy to remove himself to the extent of having me write and direct the film, but how then did I remove *myself*—as his instructed substitute?"[11] How, in other words, could Tavel destabilize himself, now not *on* camera but *off*, in order to continue as "one of the people Warhol was studying"? Warhol would have us believe that he effected his own self-removal not only by using surrogates—like having Tavel act as director of his films—but also by simply switching the camera on and walking away. But the camera's complex mobility in many films belies this claim; Warhol forced himself, too, to rely on his on-the-spot instincts; he subjected himself, too, to incapacitation.[12] Warhol famously wielded power by abjuring power.

For *Horse*, a hilarious, harrowing, homoerotic spoof of Hollywood westerns, Tavel took his cue about how to keep himself off-guard from his vast storehouse of Hollywood knowledge:

> While watching the odd, unexpected, and sometimes peculiarly slow responses of Charles Boyer and Marlene Dietrich in an art house rerun of *The Garden of Allah* (Selznick International, 1936), it occurred to me that those arresting, but glaze eyed and deliberate reactions may have been achieved via Richard Boleslawski's not letting either of them have any idea of what they were going to, and finally did, say next. I liked this intentional effect of unexpectedness, and imagined it had been achieved by having the filmstars read lines off "idiot sheets" they had never seen before, and over each other's shoulders; while their intriguing "searching" adjustments (as if searching for what to say) were the sincere, stylized results of their not having been certain of where exactly off camera these idiot sheets would next appear.

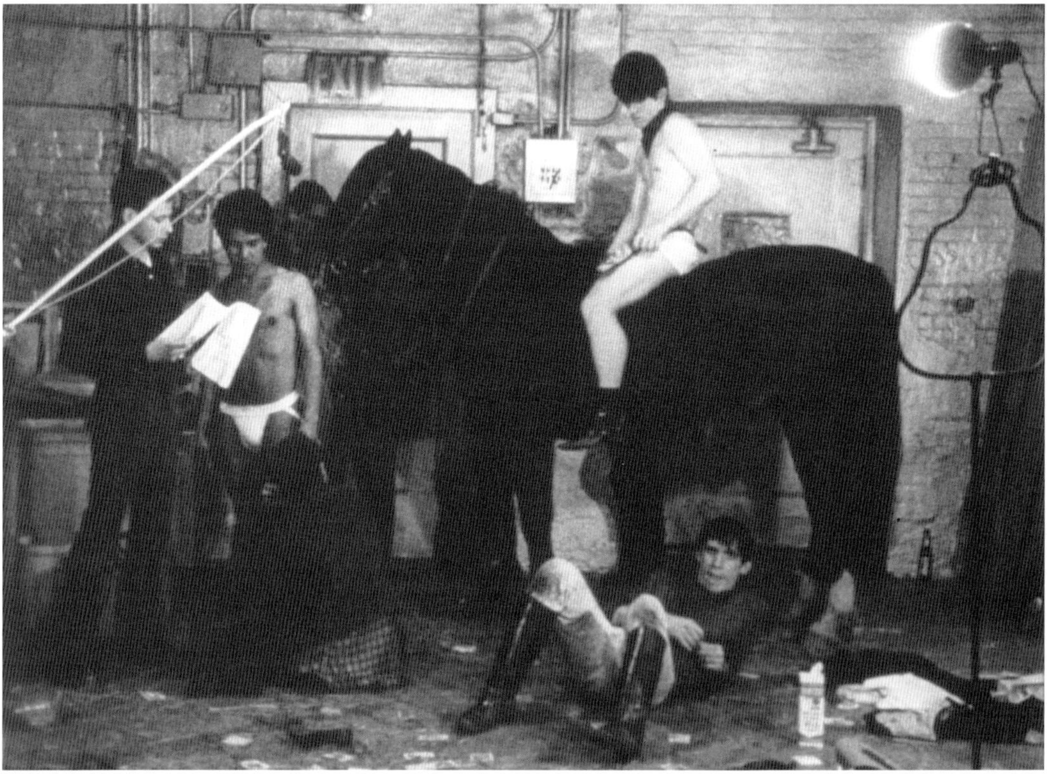

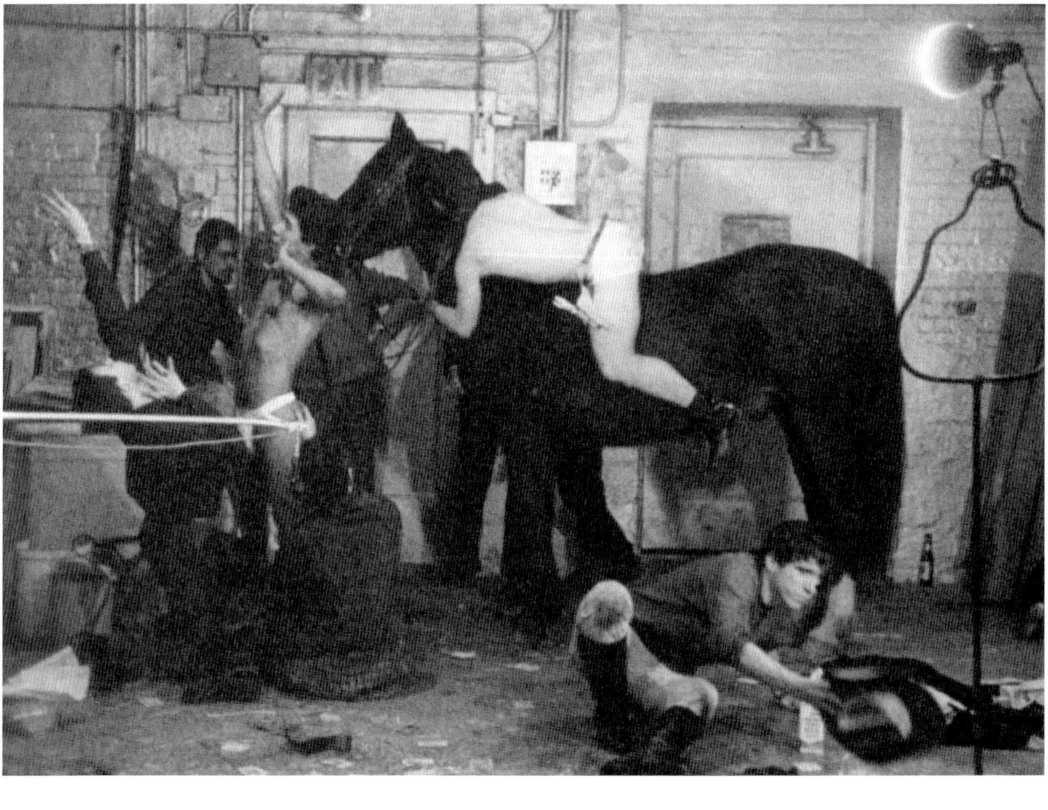

Tavel's task in the case of *Horse* was to get sixty-six minutes of film footage from "four, by fiat, unprepared and thus stage-frightened young men"—Gregory Battcock, Tosh Carrillo, Dan Cassidy, and Larry Latreille—and a horse. To accomplish this, Tavel devised a scheme in which he wrote the names of the actors on four placards and all the action and lines of dialogue on what he called cheat sheets.[13] These latter were ordered in some semblance of a plot and would be held up in sequence by Warhol's assistant Gerard Malanga on cue from Tavel, who moved about the periphery of the set and held up the placard bearing the name of one of the four actors, chosen in accordance with how he saw the story evolving. Seeing his name on Tavel's cue card, the designated actor would turn to Malanga and read his line. "Since Andy's assembly-line format precluded my own memorizing of the dialogue," Tavel recalls, "I would have to hold the script in one hand and select the name cards with the other. This concentration, coordination, and continuous decision on the name calls would stretch my ordinary energy, so I was depending on the anticipated adrenaline under that purposely manufactured stress."

Thus Tavel translated his odd intuition about the wooden acting by the two principals in *The Garden of Allah* into a means of not only prompting his actors to say their unlearned lines but also keeping himself in constant tense motion just off-screen—and sometimes even on-screen: Tavel is occasionally heard giving voice-off instructions in the first reel, but toward the end of the third reel he walks into the frame and, consulting his script, feeds the actors their lines and instructs them in their actions, as he had in *The Life of Juanita Castro*, though with no sense in this case that this was a formal conceit of the film. As the unintentionally comic opera singer Florence Foster Jenkins returns for a second time to the soundtrack to screech the final trio from Gounod's *Faust*, Carillo, by now wearing only a jockstrap, gestures as if he himself were reaching the climax of the operatic ensemble. Tavel seems, though, to find Carillo's poses inadequate and enters the scene to help him out, taking the role of Jenkins's hapless baritone Thomas Burns to Carillo's impersonation of the would-be diva. We might take this for a rehearsal and thus conclude that Warhol wasn't after all opposed to rehearsing so long as a rehearsal is something that takes place on camera, preferably at the end of the scenario being rehearsed.[14]

Andy Warhol, *Horse*, 1965. 16mm film, b/w, sound, 100 minutes. Film stills courtesy of The Andy Warhol Museum.

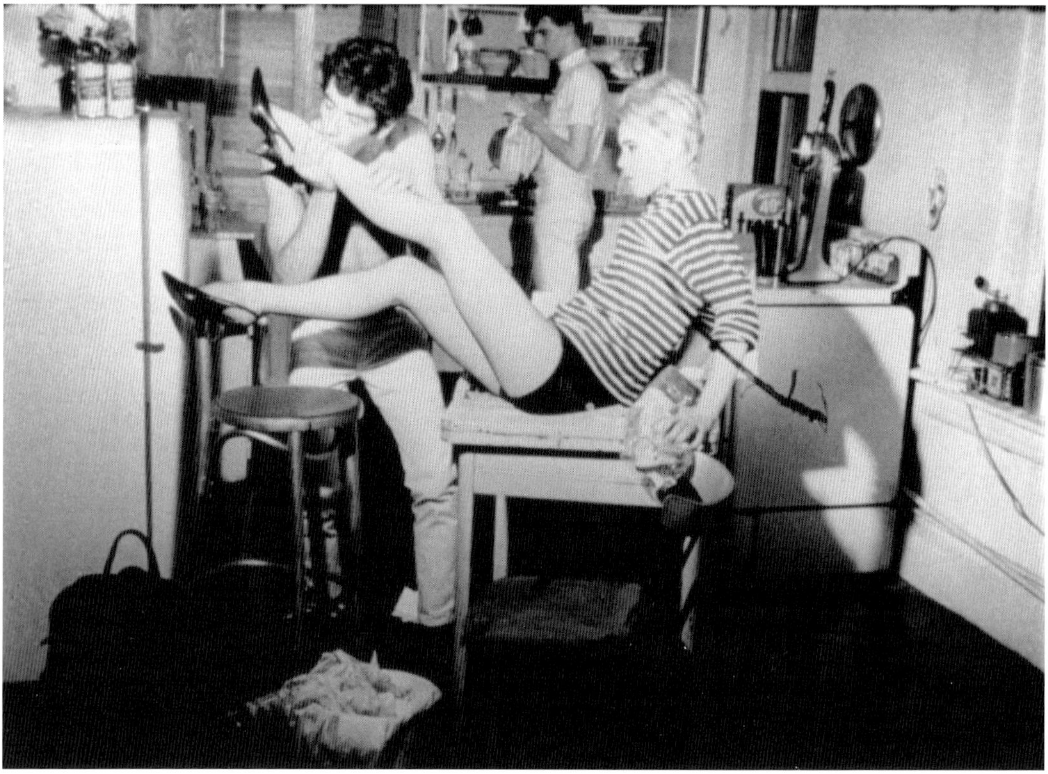

Andy Warhol, *Kitchen*, 1965. 16mm film, b/w, sound, 66 minutes. Film still courtesy of The Andy Warhol Museum.

In any case, it seems Warhol did rehearse one of Tavel's scenarios, but only in an instance in which he no doubt knew it wouldn't yield anything like a scripted performance. Tavel's scenario for *Kitchen* contains the following description:

> The set is a clean white kitchen. A kitchen table and chairs. One wall of the kitchen is in frame and a calendar is on that wall, which is not actually a calendar but a copy of the scenario. Several articles are on the table, and hidden between them is another copy of the scenario. There is also a large book on the table, or two or three books, and copies of the scenario are hidden in the books. When the actors forget their lines, they should pretend to be reading the books, or can get up and go over to the calendar on the wall and read the scenario there, tearing off the pages of the scenario until they reach the place they want as if they were tearing off back dates.

Although *Kitchen* "was rehearsed for a solid week," according to Tavel, Edie Sedgwick, the film's star, was hopeless at memorizing lines, no doubt because she was habitually high on amphetamines during this period of her life. Nevertheless, Warhol had Hollywood ambitions for her, very much liked this particular script, and thus broke with his tradition, although I should add the caveat here that never was a tradition established in Warhol's development as a filmmaker that it wasn't soon enough broken: Silence quickly gave way to sound, black-and-white to color, the absolutely static shot to intricate camerawork, and, in fact, many films are edited. Not only are there edits in some of Warhol's early films—they are indeed many and complex in *Sleep*, and there are crucial ones in *Haircut No. 1*, *Soap Opera*, and *My Hustler*—but also by 1966 Warhol began fairly regularly using so-called strobe cuts, in-camera edits made by turning the camera off and then on again.

In spite of all these facts to the contrary, I return to Mario Montez's insight that Warhol didn't rehearse because he didn't edit, and to my own assertion that Warhol wanted a scenario from Tavel because he didn't want one or, differently put, that he wanted a scenario but didn't want anyone who would take part in its production to see it in advance. These are things that we know not only from what Warhol's associates tell us but also from what we can discern from watching the films. Something that *Horse* and *Kitchen* share, and share with *Vinyl*, too, is that Tavel's scenarios come to an end before the final reel runs out, after which something that resembles a rehearsal begins—or perhaps not precisely a rehearsal, but something like coaching the actors, in the case of *Horse*; wrapping up, in the case of *Kitchen*; or an amyl-nitrate-fueled disintegration, in the case of *Vinyl*. These moments give us an impression of the chaotic activity on Factory movie sets, an impression that is strongest in *The Velvet Underground and Nico*, which captures on film, during the second reel, the police arriving at the Factory to investigate a noise complaint and the attempts by members of the Factory crowd, briefly including even Warhol himself, to mollify the befuddled officers, while the Velvets continue with their rehearsal. It is this almost invisible difference between the actors' playing roles and just playing around—between, that is, in the case of the Tavel films, following the scenario and simply carrying on in front of the camera—to which I want to turn for the remainder of my discussion.

The deliberate discrepancy—or nonrelation—between Tavel's scenario and the film made from that scenario suggests a new condition for relationality itself—a condition, that is, of our confrontations with others and with the world at large. Tavel clearly intuited the tension between the scenario and the film shot from it that Warhol would instigate, and he exacerbated that tension through what he asked the characters in the scenarios to do, by giving their scripted interactions the quality of ridiculousness. But even Tavel's ridiculous versions of human relationships are abrogated by the superstars' narcissism, such that the connections the characters make with one another can hardly be considered relationships at all. Indeed, we might say, with Leo Bersani, that the superstars' narcissism prevents their connections to others "from degenerating into 'a relationship.'"[15] Their narcissism is not, however, what we typically associate with that term—self-centeredness, colloquially, or taking oneself as a sexual object, psychoanalytically.[16] Reading against the grain of Freud's various ideas about narcissism, Bersani has theorized an "impersonal narcissism" or "self-effacing narcissism" in which the ego identifies with "inaccurate replications" of itself, leading to new kinds of connectedness that extend not only to other people but to the world of forms. In such "non-identitarian sameness" lies the possibility, for Bersani, of relationality that depends on neither identification nor disidentification with—on neither merging with nor violence toward—others.[17] Crucially, in this new form of (anti-)relationality, since the self locates itself elsewhere, it cannot at the same time be self-identical. In its narcissistic display, the self also, at least implicitly, recognizes otherness already there *in itself*; it performs its own self-alienation.

It should be clear from what I've said so far that Warhol's approach to filmmaking made it virtually impossible for Tavel's scenarios to "work" in any usual sense of the word, since the actors wouldn't be learning their roles in advance. But in fact Warhol's subversion of Tavel's scenarios developed gradually, while Tavel both played Warhol's own game and perversely wrote scenarios with increasingly elaborate plots and dialogue. At first, though, Tavel wrote screenplays that were not even meant to be seen by the on-screen performers in advance. With the screen-test films (not to be confused with Warhol's four-minute *Screen Test* portrait films), *Screen Test No. 1* as well as the better-known *Screen Test No. 2*, only the off-screen director, played by Tavel, had access to his script; indeed, Tavel wrote the script expressly and only for his own use.[18] Reading from the script, he asked the on-screen performer, shown in close-up throughout, to utter lines, assume poses, and enact situations. The whole point, apparently, was to trip up the performer by suddenly inserting into the interview something that would embarrass or humiliate him (Philip Fagan's shoplifting of ladies underwear in *Screen Text No. 1*; Mario Montez's "real" sex in *Screen Test No. 2*). As the off-screen voice of the tester, Tavel is allowed the confidence and authority that come from having written the lines and remaining beyond the camera lens's range.[19] Following these films, for *The Life of Juanita Castro*, Tavel maintains the authority of writer–director, but must now—as we've seen—perform the role on-screen while unprepared to do so. Warhol thus began to impose what Tavel recognized as destabilizing demands, and no doubt he recognized them immediately for what they were because they were a version of just what he'd been doing to his screen-test subjects.

Things change fairly radically in the next three Warhol–Tavel films, *Horse*, *Vinyl*, and *Kitchen*. One thing remains essentially the same, though: Except for a slight shift in camera angle between rolls and an occasional zoom in and out in *Vinyl*, there is still no camera movement. That too will change with *Space* and *Hedy*. What is new in the Tavel-scripted films immediately following *The Life of Juanita Castro* is the relation of actors to script. This begins with *Horse*. Each of the four actors in *Horse* plays a stock Hollywood western part: the Kid, the Sheriff, Tex, and Mex. Their lines as written in the screenplay, and sometimes as actually delivered in the film, are also Hollywood western clichés: "Why, it's the kid!" "You're a tinhorn," "There's gold in them thar hills," "Someday all this land is gonna be mighty fine cow country," and so forth. Interspersed with these are lines that spoof, or "queer," the genre, lines such as "Take it off," "I'm a celibate," "I'm an onanist," "Beat it, beat it, beat it all day long." Queerer still are the actions, which include an apparent sexual attachment to the horse on the part of all four actors, horseplay as sex play among the actors, and the excuse of the customary Hollywood western's anti-Mexican racism for Mex's sexual humiliation (at one point from off-screen, as the Kid, the Sheriff, and Tex appear to be pummeling Mex, Tavel's voice can be heard saying, "*Feel* him up, don't *beat* him up").[20] Tavel's queer pastiche of the Hollywood western, fully discernible in the scenario, thus has all the characteristics of the Theater of the Ridiculous as Tavel and others would develop them—pop-culture references both obvious and obscure, cornball jokes, perversion, ridicule, persecution.[21] But Warhol doesn't leave it there.

What does he add? Or subtract? Most obviously, there is the set, or the setup. From it we see that *Horse* is a title that we must take quite literally. There is, first of all, a horse, whose name we eventually learn from the credits is "Mighty Bird, courtesy of the Dawn Animal Agency." Mighty Bird stands smack in front of the Factory stairwell and elevator doors. His trainer holds him throughout the film. The middle reel of *Horse*, shown between the two reels that Tavel's scenario scripts, shows *only* this setup. It is a thirty-three-minute shot of Mighty Bird, his trainer beside him, and one of the four actors in the scenario, Larry Latreille, not yet in costume as the Kid, holding a microphone to the horse's mouth. The horse and actors stand in front of the elevator, and nothing happens,

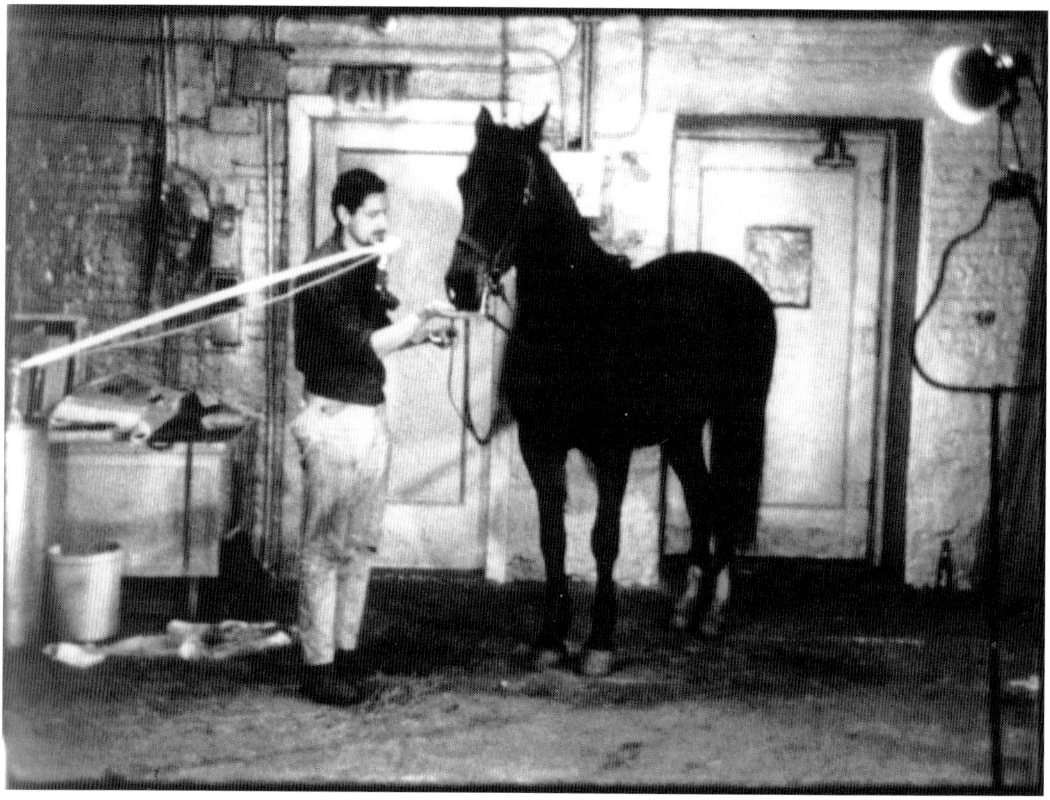

Andy Warhol, *Horse*, 1965. 16mm film, b/w, sound, 100 minutes. Film still courtesy of The Andy Warhol Museum.

or at least nothing "dramatic" happens, nothing requiring Tavel's writing and directing abilities. This reel is, we might say, pure Warhol. Mighty Bird could just as well be Henry Geldzahler in the eighty-eight-minute silent portrait film of him, or the Empire State Building in the eight-hour *Empire*. The ridiculous antics of Tavel's spoof western have been replaced by a Warholian "idea," the idea that all you really need to make a movie a western is a horse. Whatever "incident" makes the film more than just this single idea that generates the film is just the sort of incident that makes the silent, minimal Warhol films the films they are—such incidents as flares of light between edited-together reels, the blinks that interrupt a sitter's stare, or the lights coming on to light up the Empire State Building. Among the incidents, in this case, is the appearance of Edie Sedgwick, discharged from the elevator behind Mighty Bird. A notable horsewoman herself, Edie is both taken with the horse—she walks up to it, nuzzles it, whispers in its ear—and apparently unable to decide whether she belongs in the film at all. This imposition of a recognizably "Warhol" film reel between the two "Tavel" reels serves straightforwardly to mark the "failure" of the Warhol–Tavel collaboration.

In *Horse*'s two scripted reels, the characters' relation to the horse is considerably less natural than Edie's, the trainer's, and Latreille's in the middle reel (although it might be stretching the notion of "natural" to include holding a microphone to a horse's mouth). When the film starts, Latreille as the Kid sits bareback on Mighty Bird. The other three actors sit or stand in front of this queer pair and look directly at the camera. Eventually, they begin to speak lines. They do so awkwardly and with no discernible connection to what they're saying. As we know from what Tavel has told us, they are reading from cue cards. Lines of dialogue have little or no continuity with the lines that precede them, although occasionally there is a relation, albeit a lackluster one. Thus, for example, the Sheriff says, "One of you two is a murderer," and the others say in turn, "It's not me." "It's not me." Whereupon the Sheriff simply repeats his accusation, and the others repeat their denials. From off-screen comes Tavel's voice reading the credits: "Andy Warhol's *Horse*," "The Sheriff is played by Gregory Battcock." This recitation of the credits continues now and again throughout both reels of the film's action. Occasionally the pay phone next to the elevator rings, and Malanga walks into the frame to answer it. At one moment Warhol himself appears for a brief phone conversation. Thus, at no point does the action as written in the scenario take precedence over daily life at the Factory. Or perhaps it would be more accurate to say, daily life at the Factory during this period included, along with all sorts of other activities, making films, in this instance making the film called *Horse*. People come and go, sometimes within the camera's range, while the director directs, the cameraperson films, the sound person holds the boom, and the actors busy themselves playing their roles.

But playing a role in this film is anything but a straightforward matter. The actors read lines, they perform actions, but even when the lines are said by one actor to another or when the actions involve interaction, each actor appears to inhabit his own world. Dialogue and interaction never constitute anything like recognizable intersubjectivity. On the contrary, it is to the camera that each character addresses himself (Battcock frequently turns from addressing the other actors to look in the direction of the camera, as if seeking instruction or approval).

At one point the characters stand side by side facing the camera, directing their silent attention outward. They resemble nothing so much as a group of men standing in a row at a gay bar cruising someone opposite them. They solicit attention, however, by feigning indifference as to whether or not it is paid. It is the cruising style known as stand-and-pose—a decidedly self-contained form of cruising that telegraphs something like: "I am indicating that I want you only to the extent that I am showing you how desirable I am by demonstrating that I am capable of complete indifference to you." From within this narcissistic display, two of the characters, the Kid and the Sheriff, begin to feel each other up. As they do so, they continue to direct their gazes toward the camera, as if to signal that the attention each gives to the other is meant only to further appeal to the look of the camera. Even this literal physical connection with another maintains each in his self-regard.

By the following year, 1966, this relation of actor to camera that we see in *Horse* is also suspended, as the narcissism enacted by the performers begins to be assumed by Warhol's camera itself, which adopts its own self-sufficiency as it moves in and around the actors and set independent of the storyline, of who is speaking, or even of where within the mise-en-scène the actors' activities are taking place. In *Hedy*, as in the nonscripted *Lupe* before it, the camera becomes an autonomous "player," as it zooms in on extraneous details, pans distractedly away from the action, even tilts down to the floor or up to the ceiling. The deep space in which *Hedy* is shot, together with the minimal spotlighting of the action, allows the camera at times to wander off in the direction of total darkness. The lighting, too, takes on this character of self-sufficiency, as it illuminates one character or another, a few together, or none at all. The film's elaborate, melodramatic story of Hedy Lamarr's arrest for shoplifting and subsequent court trial and suicide is both undermined and overwhelmed by the separation of the actors from their roles—what David James calls their constant "falling out" of their roles[22]—together with the camera's and lights' mobile freedom and autonomy and the jarring incursions of soundtrack music by the Velvet Underground. Indeed, it is this constant diversion of our attention from the human drama—however ridiculous the human drama is, however *more* ridiculous it is as written by Tavel, and however *more* ridiculous *still* as played by Warhol's superstars—that constitutes a radical reorientation of relationality in these films.

What we see in these films is that the normative concentration of our interest on the story, on the drama of human relationships, will get us nowhere, will result only in frustration. But as soon as we remove our attention from that story, as soon as we locate our interest in a world in which characters—other *people*—and their stories—of *relationships*—are only one element among countless others, we find unanticipated recompense in new pleasures of looking and new ways to of being in the world. In the Warhol–Tavel films, in addition to the ridiculous scenario, a prop, a space, a shot's composition; its lighting, its framing and persistent reframing; a musical chord, an actor's distraction or extra-diagetic movement: all these aspects of the cinematic image, and more, make claims on our attention and provide sources of pleasure. Whereas typically script, cinematic technique, and performance are concerted to focus our interest on relationships and their storyline development, here they consistently move us beyond them. Indeed, they are the means for the complete dissolution of relationships and stories as we know them. And how else do we know them but as endlessly repeated love stories?

It is, I think, especially moving and significant that this radical break with normative conditions of relationality should be the result of collaboration. Precisely at that moment when Warhol came most to rely on someone else, and moreover on someone else of a highly articulated sensibility, collaboration—coming together, working together—is undone. It is as if Warhol and Tavel each simply went about his imaginative business at odds with the other as the very condition of working together. Moreover, each determined in his own distinctive way, with regard to plot, action, dialogue, setting, lighting, shooting, and especially to the actors, that each and every person or component of the film should maintain an extraordinary level of singularity.

Following page

Andy Warhol, *Hedy*, 1966. 16mm film, b/w, sound, 66 minutes. Film still courtesy of The Andy Warhol Museum.

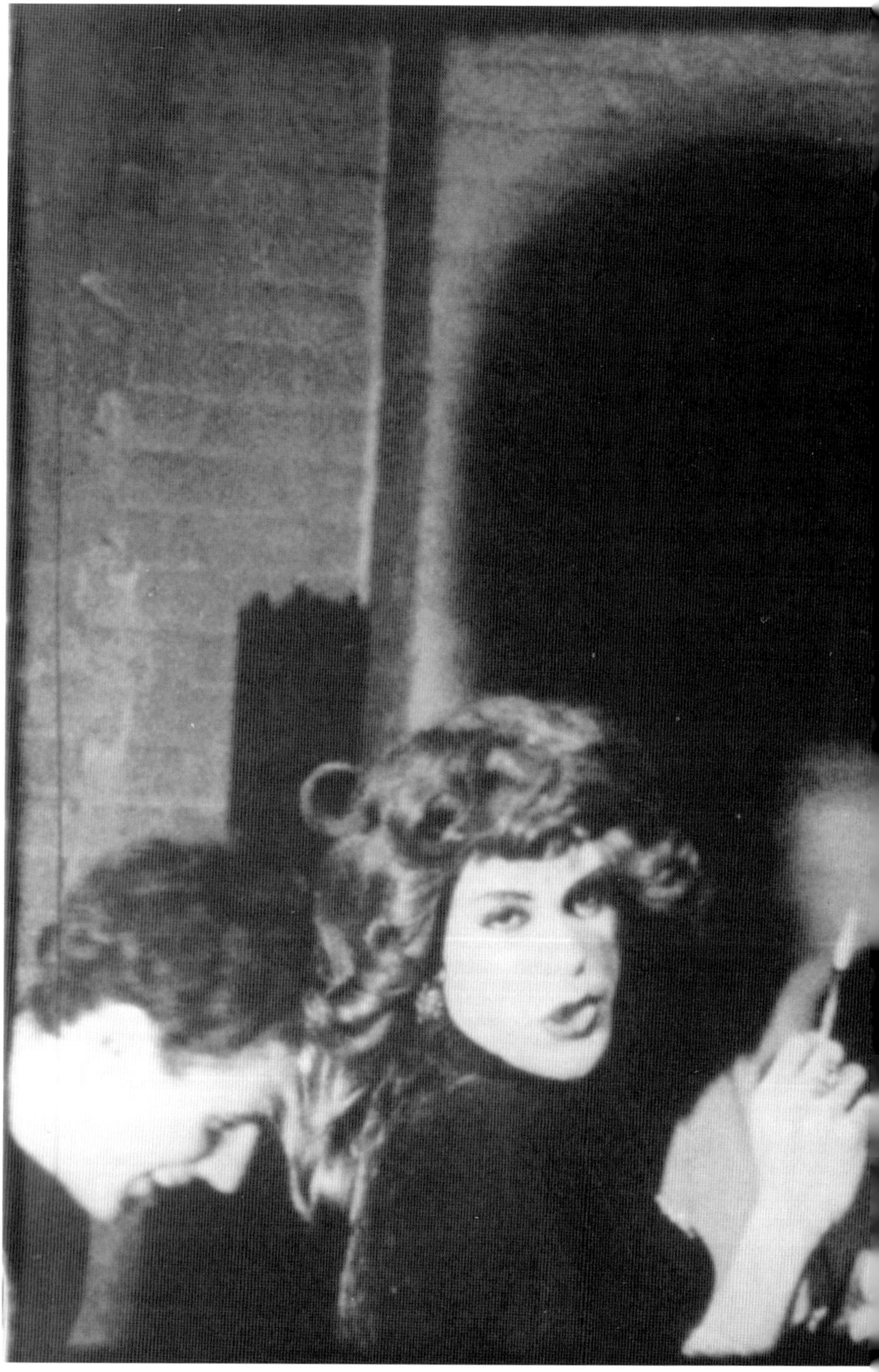

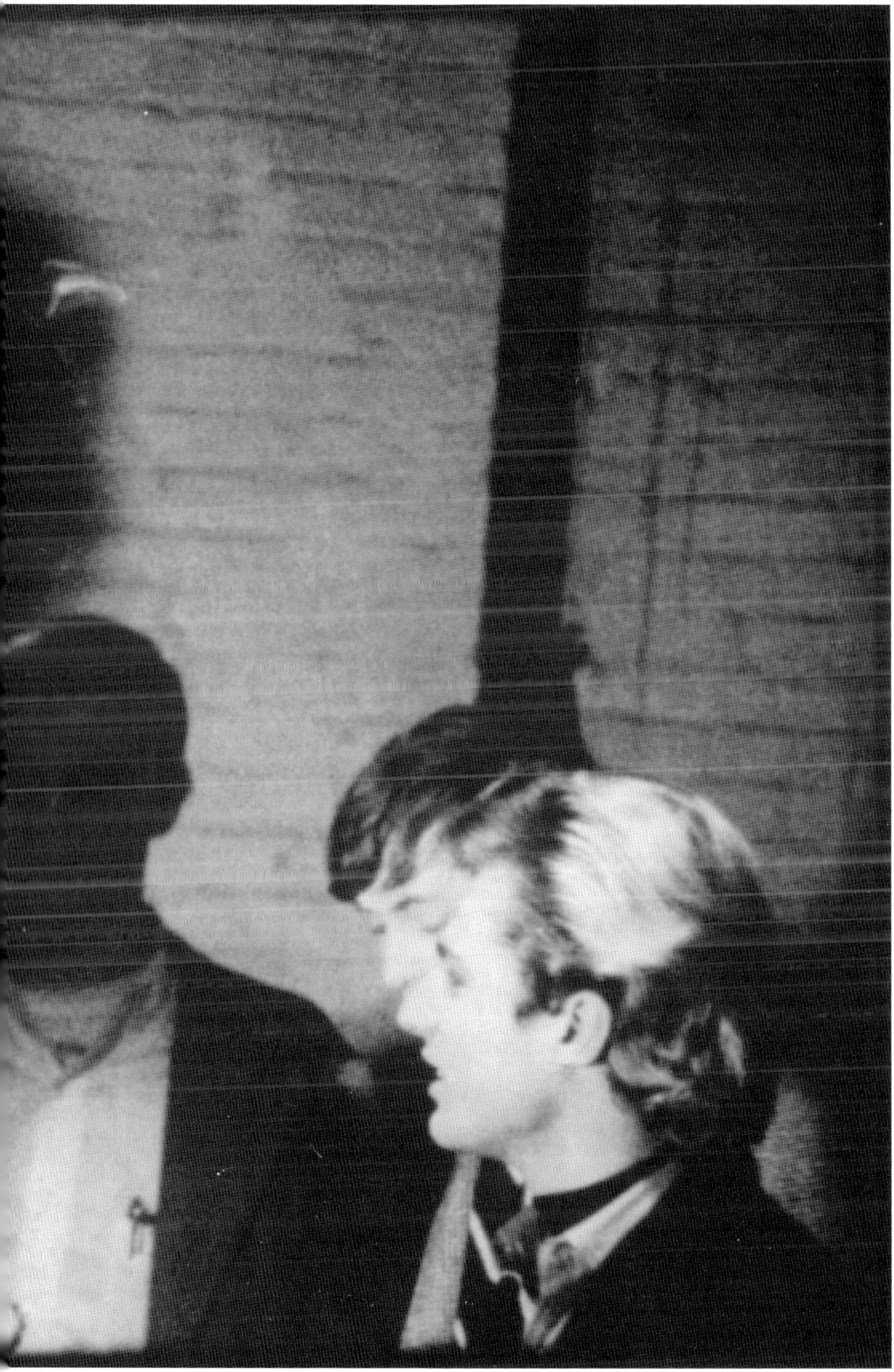

I want to make it clear that this is not the sort of coming together of autonomous elements that we know from the innovative collaborative procedures of Merce Cunningham and John Cage, in which the work of choreographer, composer, and set designer interact by sheer chance; and, interestingly, no artist seemed better to understand this autonomy-by-design than Warhol when he agreed to Cunningham's use of his helium-filled silver Scotchpak pillows—or *Silver Clouds*, as he called them—as the setting for Cunningham's *RainForest* in 1968. Warhol's set would be literally *in the way* of the dancers, and the dancers would set the set in motion entirely by their chance encounters with its elements. But presumably for Warhol and Tavel, Cunningham's procedures are too benign. Individual autonomy is achieved by ignoring the implicit demand placed by one individual on another when the two come together. There is no *impossibility*, no *cruelty*, no *ridicule* acknowledged in Cunningham's dances. Indeed, under the sway of Cage's Zen-derived ideas, there is nothing that we would think of as narcissism in Cunningham's aesthetic.

In Warhol and Tavel's collaboration, the coming together of separate elements is far from a passive chance operation. Rather, it is an active confrontation—working not individually in blithe cooperation but singularly at determined cross-purposes. But neither are these cross-purposes those of the usual competitive relations in which the one attempts to outdo, to master, or to abolish the other, but instead are designed to produce a scene that defies relationality as we know it: a radically new scene in which the self finds itself not through its identification or disidentification with others, but in its singularity among all the singular things of the world. The Warhol–Tavel collaboration is a coming together to stay apart; it maintains both the self and the other in their fundamental distinctiveness, a distinctiveness that is for me the radical meaning of queer.

SPACIOUS

A: I LIKE YOUR APARTMENT.

B: IT'S NICE, BUT IT'S ONLY BIG ENOUGH FOR ONE PERSON—
OR TWO PEOPLE WHO ARE VERY CLOSE.

A: YOU KNOW TWO PEOPLE WHO ARE VERY CLOSE?

THE PHILOSOPHY OF ANDY WARHOL

ANDY WARHOL'S EARLY SOUND FILM *JOHN AND IVY* WAS SHOT IN A SMALL APARTMENT KITCHEN. A FOREGROUND COLUMN OR DOORJAMB—IT'S HARD TO TELL WHAT IT IS SINCE IT APPEARS SIMPLY AS A DARK VERTICAL BAND—DIVIDES THE FILM FRAME INTO A NARROW STRIP OF SPACE AT THE LEFT, WHERE THERE IS A LOW STOOL THAT JOHN OR IVY OCCASIONALLY SITS ON, AND A WIDER AREA ON THE RIGHT, WHERE THERE IS A CLUTTERED STOVETOP WITH A TEA KETTLE SIMMERING ON IT.

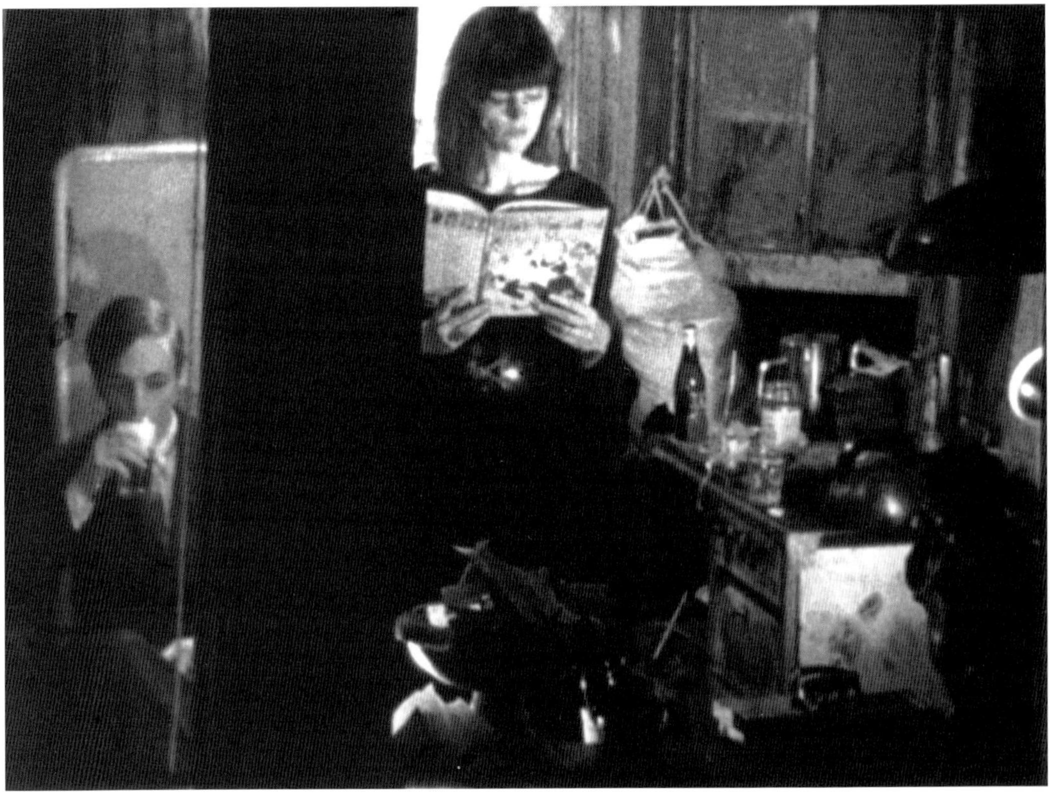

Andy Warhol, *John and Ivy*, 1965. 16mm film, b/w, sound, 33 minutes. Film still courtesy of The Andy Warhol Museum.

Behind the stove is a window, apparently on an airshaft. In striking contrast to the kitchen's squalor, John Palmer and Ivy Nicholson are stylishly turned out. His sports coat has a star-shaped patch at the back on the armhole; her fashion-model coiffure is chic and expensive-looking. Throughout the film's thirty-three minutes, the two of them and Ivy's two young blond children move into and out of the camera's range from screen left.[1] If the rooms in New York City's East Village tenement apartments like Ivy Nicholson's are often very small, this one seems smaller still because the foreground column so insistently obstructs our view of it. You wonder that there was room enough for Warhol's camera. John and Ivy look too large for the space, especially because what they do in this cramped kitchen, aside from constantly coming and going, is dance the frug and fall to the floor below the camera's range for a quick make-out session. Meanwhile the naked little boys run in and out and make the kind of fuss that little boys make. Adding to the sense of confinement, a WABC radio broadcast that comprises the film's most audible soundtrack tells us that the film is shot while the city is in the grip of snow emergency. (We also learn from the radio that it is 5:00 p.m., that the Justice Department has returned indictments in the case of three murdered civil rights workers in Mississippi the previous summer, that "Winston tastes good like a—clap, clap—cigarette should," and that the number one song is the Supremes' "Come See about Me," which means *John and Ivy* was shot in mid-January 1965.)

The foreground column does more than subdivide the screen space: It radically flattens and contracts it—contracts it in the sense that the "action" of the film, especially insofar as that action involves interaction among the film's characters, is confined to the right-hand two-thirds of the screen, the area mostly taken up by the stove. There are some moments when the action occurs across the left- and right-hand spaces, and there is even a brief moment of contained interaction within the narrow band at the left, where John reads a story to one of the boys, sitting in his lap; meanwhile Ivy peels a hard-boiled egg in the more expansive swath of space at the right. Some other things Ivy does: She brushes her teeth with a battery-powered toothbrush, smokes, reads the children's book, pulls up the black tights that she wears beneath her over-the-calf boots, dampens those same tights by rubbing them with a handful of snow taken from the airshaft, picks up one of her boys and holds him, makes instant coffee, dances to songs by the Shangri-Las and the Beatles playing on the radio, blows air into a paper bag and pops it behind John's head while kissing him, and throws a snowball at John. John doesn't do much. He changes stations on the radio. He observes that meeting the camera is like meeting a new person (if this is the way he acts when he meets a new person, he's not very sociable).

But the column paradoxically also expands and opens up the space, and it does so in a way that startles you when it occurs. On a couple of occasions, rather than walk behind the column from screen left to screen right, Ivy moves rightward toward the camera and passes in front of this *repoussoir* element to appear as a looming silhouette in the foreground. At these moments we become aware that the space we've been looking at is not nearly as two-dimensional as it had seemed; in fact, the spatial configuration is one not only of left and right of the column but also of behind and in front of it. Of course, the space on screen has all along appeared to have some depth, but that depth has not until these moments noticeably extended in the direction of the viewer. That this should be so startling is a measure of Warhol's ability to make us see the screen as surface.

Warhol is famously the artist of surface—"If you want to know all about Andy Warhol, just look at the surface: of my paintings and my films and me, and there I am. There's nothing behind it."[2] Certainly, scanning the surface of Warhol's early films is a sensible response to his camera's immobility, but when we look around the screen, what we see is, in fact, space—sometimes shallow, sometimes deep. Scanning the surface and finding space is not only something we do as a result of the static shot; it is also, in the later films, something Warhol's now-mobile camera does for us. In a number of films beginning late in 1965, Warhol tilt-pans all the way up to the ceiling and down to the floor to give us a dizzying sense of *too much* space, a *dis*orienting sense of spaciousness.

The delineation of space is nevertheless comparatively systematic in some of Warhol's films. For *Haircut No. 1*, an early silent film made up of six 100-foot reels spliced together, Warhol shows us the haircut and the room in which it takes place from a different angle or distance in each reel, as if to mark out the mise-en-scène with his camera setups, except that the lighting and framing also make the space difficult to comprehend, so much so in one especially striking shot that the oddly juxtaposed heads of the three actors (there are eventually four) make a frame enlargement look like a collage of cutouts.

Andy Warhol, *Haircut No. 1*, 1963. 16mm film, b/w, silent, 27 minutes at 16 fps. Film stills courtesy of The Andy Warhol Museum.

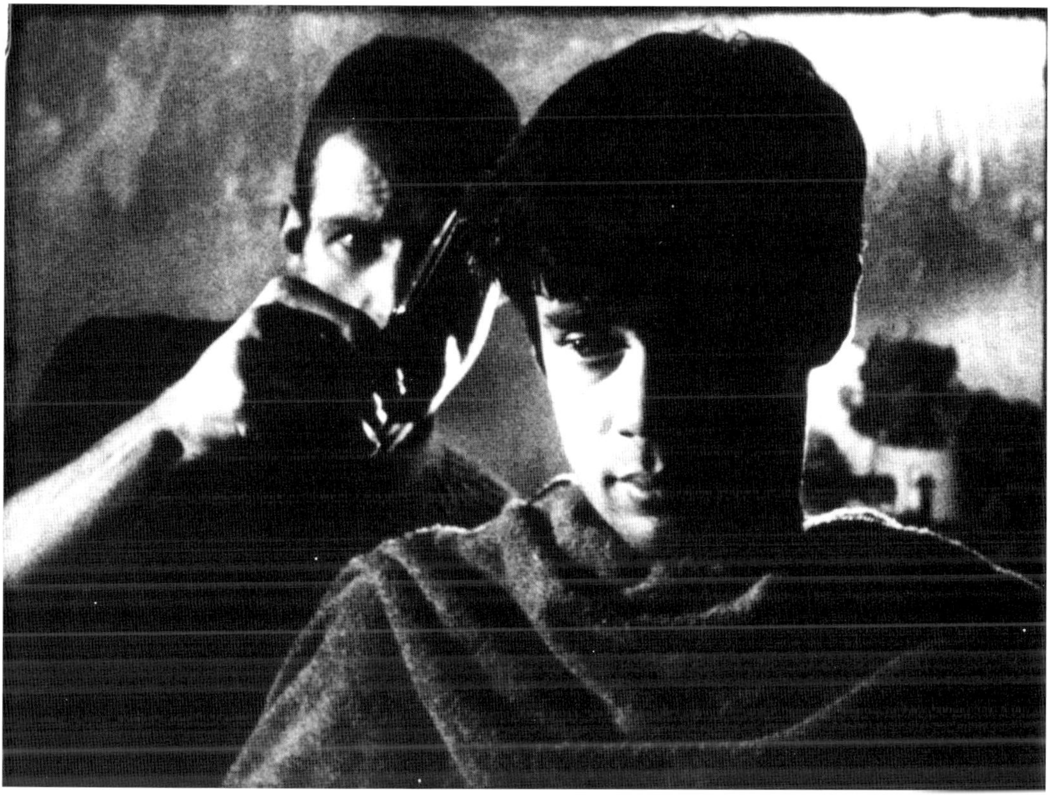

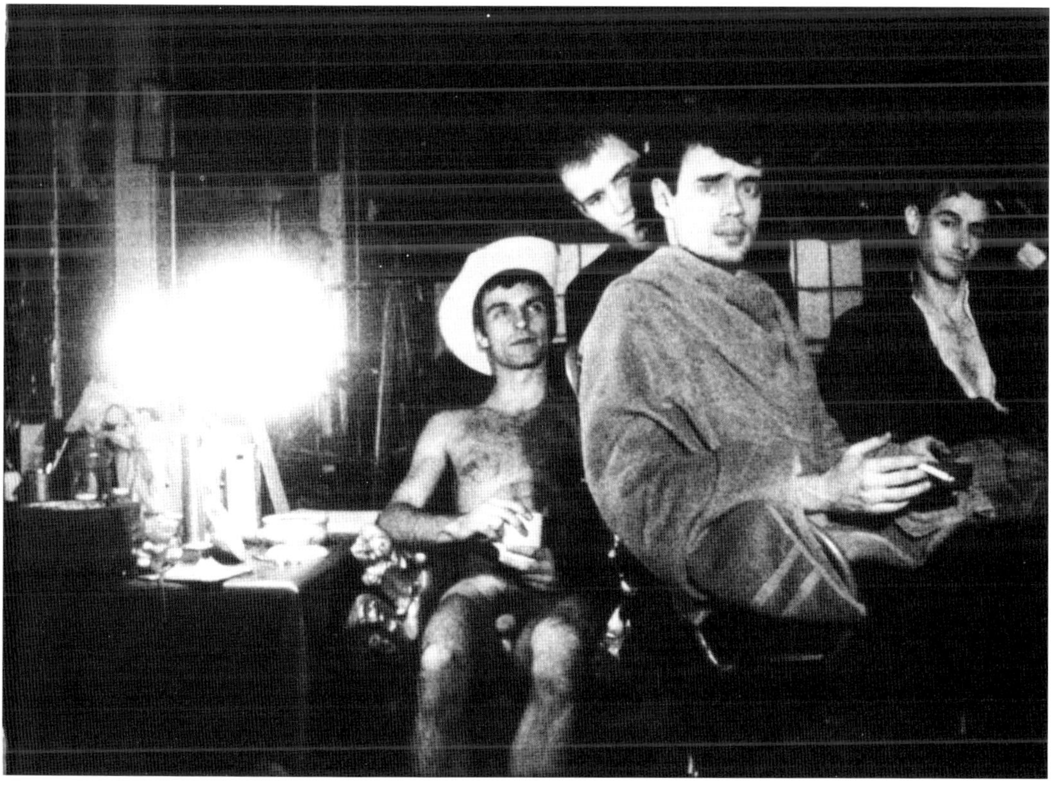

There is also a kind of spatial joke in *Haircut*. Judson dancer Freddy Herko, who isn't getting a haircut but looking on—looking at the camera, posing—appears shirtless at first and then for ensuing camera setups undresses fully except for a cowboy hat. Billy Name's careful, precise, erotic, slightly menacing scissoring of John Daley's hair occurs in the foreground while Freddy sits cross-legged behind them. The joke is that if you are not watching the eponymous event but looking into the background at this sexy guy, you will get a quick payoff as he uncrosses his legs and recrosses them on the opposite side (it's the same maneuver employed by Sharon Stone in *Basic Instinct*).[3] Freddy's crotch-shot is something of a clue to the way to watch Warhol's films. Scanning the surface is how you see, *pace* Warhol, behind it, into spatial depth.

A classic example is *Vinyl*, a film scripted by Ronald Tavel in which Gerard Malanga plays bottom to Tosh Carillo's very professional top in an S&M scene that takes place in the film's left foreground. The right foreground is occupied by Edie Sedgwick, who makes her film debut in *Vinyl*. She wasn't in fact meant to be in the film, but she arrived at the Factory as the shoot was beginning, so Warhol put her up front to the right of the action; she sits there on a steamer trunk, looking insouciant, chain-smoking, occasionally moving her upper body to the beat of Martha and the Vandellas' "Nowhere to Run." The S&M interrogation that is the film's ostensible subject during the second reel is probably exaggerated and in any case not exciting: Malanga's cries of pain sound phony and silly. But if you move your eyes from the left-foreground *Clockwork Orange*–inspired aversion-therapy scenario toward the right background, behind Sedgwick, you see in glimpses a genuine S&M scene in which Larry Latreille as a sexy submissive really is subjected, silently and presumably willingly, to sustained sexual torture, first by Carillo, then by Jacques Potain. Warhol and Tavel seem to want us to recognize sadomasochism as the background condition of whatever normally engages our attention. Certainly the fact that both what underlies a narrative and the narrative itself can play out in a *single shot* is one of the astonishing spatial achievements of Warhol's midperiod films.

What was intended to be the most determinedly programmatic spatial delineation among Warhol's films is a Tavel project called *Space*. Tavel explains that, in order to achieve the degree of abstraction Warhol asked of him, he wrote a script consisting of eight passages of dialogue each for eight readers who would sit in a figure-eight configuration.[4] A roving microphone would be carried from one reader to the next, and the person at the mike would read his or her lines, which were random samplings from radio and TV ads and snatches of conversation Tavel had overheard on the street. A few examples from the script that actually made it into the film:

> Well, when she was alive, all you heard was Marilyn Monroe this and Marilyn Monroe that, and Marilyn Monroe and Joe Dimag [*sic*] and Marilyn Monroe and Arthur Miller and Marilyn Monroe this and Marilyn Monroe that. But now that she's dead you never hear anything about her.

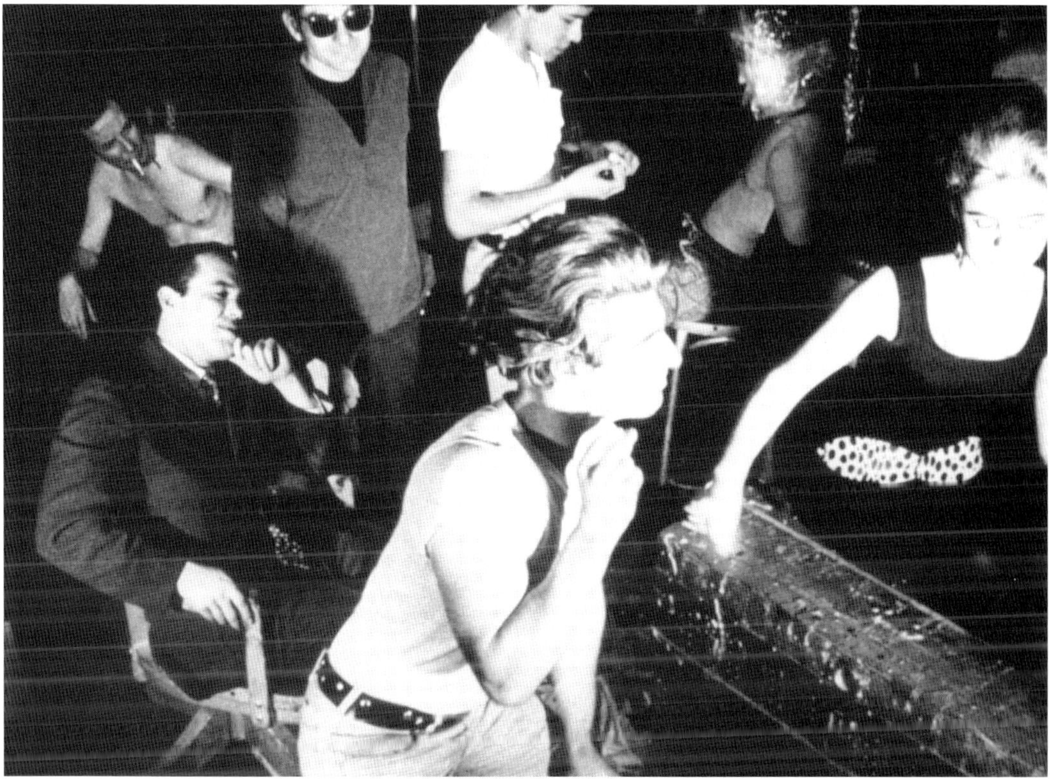

Andy Warhol, *Vinyl*, 1965. 16mm film, b/w, sound, 66 minutes. Film still courtesy of The Andy Warhol Museum.

> I cried throughout the whole movie … dreadful film, dreadful.
>
> Someday, pornography will be accepted, but nudity will never be understood.
>
> I wanted to be a Playboy Bunny. I wanted to be a Bunny that boys play with. A hundred times I filled out applications. But the P.R. man said I didn't fill them out right, and failed to hire me.
>
> I'm a two-time loser. What's your pitch, honey?

Tavel's script was almost completely subverted by the film's cast, especially Sedgwick and her friends Donald Lyons and Ed Hennessey, who show no interest in following the scenario. Instead, Lyons attempts to teach Edie to recite the rosary, while Hennessey eats, drinks, and regurgitates on whoever is unlucky enough to be sitting within close range, "as if this were just the quite most amusing thing one could do in the world during a movie," as Tavel bitterly put it.[5] Those who did follow Tavel's directives, at least initially, are the handsome young folk singer Eric Anderson, who speaks his lines while accompanying himself and others with his guitar, and the extraordinary Dorothy Dean, whom the camera captures far less than the glimmers of her appeal we do manage to see would seem to demand. But for all that this is a film crowded with interesting personalities and pretty faces—Dean, Anderson, Sedgwick, Gino Piserchio (the beauty of *Beauty No. 2*), Roger Trudeau (the beauty of *Kitchen*)—Warhol is in fact more interested in the concept of space, though not necessarily the one plotted by Tavel's script.

Space is among the first of his films in which Warhol experimented with camera movement. Initially the sound person, Kristy Keating, does move the microphone from actor to actor as instructed by Tavel. There are several more than the scripted eight players, all artfully arrayed in a tightly crowded grouping around Anderson. The Factory's half-sphere mirror ball, recognizable from other films such as *Camp* and the Vivian Kurz *Screen Tests*, sits on the floor; it might be taken as a symbol of Warhol's cinematography for *Space* insofar as the mobile camera fragments and confounds our spatial perception of the scene it shows. (The emblematic nature of the mirror ball is underscored by the fact that the second reel of *Space* begins with a slightly out-of-focus close-up of it, after which there is a cut back to the fuller scene; this "establishing shot" followed by a cut duplicates what happens in the film's first reel, which opens with a shot of a sound-check on the set followed by a cut to the beginning of the action.) Whereas the spatial ambiguity of *Haircut* is the result of chiaroscuro lighting, the lighting of *Space* is bright and even. But the combination of camerawork that never shows the scene in its entirety as it insistently pans back and forth and zooms in and out, and the fact that what the camera sees is a jumble of faces, bodies, limbs, furniture, objects, and mirrors, makes it impossible either to fathom from moment to moment or to reconstruct in memory the space of *Space*. Moreover, Warhol only rarely moves his camera in sync with the microphone, so the sound we hear doesn't accord with the characters we see talking. There are especially disorienting moments in the film's second reel in which we see a hodgepodge of pretty faces both in front of the mirror and in it—Edie-in-the-mirror, Eric, Edie, Norman Levine, for example, or Edie-in-the-mirror, Ed-in-the-mirror, Edie, Gino. The space does indeed collapse into surface at these moments, and that surface is exquisite. We might thus read Warhol's suggestion to "just look at the surface" here as an admonition: If we look beyond the surface to the "substance" of *Space*, all we see is the childish nonsense of the hootenanny that the scenario has deteriorated into. And while Edie Sedgwick is no more capable of singing along to "Michael, Row the Boat Ashore" or "Puff, the Magic Dragon" than she is of learning the rosary or reading Tavel's lines, her physical presence and her face never cease to dazzle.

The dazzle of her face is the surface *and* substance of *Outer and Inner Space*, Warhol's first experiment both with video and with double-screen projection and at the same time another complex spatial diagram. Callie Angell interpreted the "outer" and "inner" of the title of this extraordinary fourfold portrait as signaling "the dichotomy between Sedgwick's outer beauty and inner turmoil" and also as describing the "two very different spaces of representation occupied by the video-television medium and by film."[6] Indeed, not only is the electronic image of Sedgwick's face flattened by its even lighting as compared with the shadows that sculpt depth into her filmed face—shadows that in fact result from the face's being illuminated by the slightly larger picture on the TV monitor that sits beside and slightly behind it—but that image is also manipulated electronically at times to make it disintegrate into a moiré pattern that makes it even more surface-like. The film's title might also describe the camera's view of the space of the set and of its two subjects—Edie's video image and Edie herself, twice—as it describes a backward U shape from outer to inner and back to outer, or, to employ the language of cinematography, from medium shot right juxtaposed with close-up left, to close-ups left and right, and finally to close-up right, medium shot left. Of course, this spatial demarcation from outer to inner and back to outer is really a function of the double-screen projection: Warhol began with a close-up in reel one, moved out to a medium shot, began reel two with a medium shot, and then finished by pulling in to the close-up with which he'd begun. We don't see this outer and inner space *as space*, however, even when the two reels are projected side by side; rather we follow the spatial demarcation *in time*: We map the U shape of the space mnemonically.

Warhol also plays a different kind of spatial game with *Outer and Inner Space*: He shows us the actual space in which Sedgwick sits, facing the camera, in front of the TV monitor showing her profile, thus making clear how the highly abstract tight close-up on the left-hand screen is constructed. He then dissolves that space by pulling the right-hand shot in to close-up to fill both screens with juxtaposed profile and three-

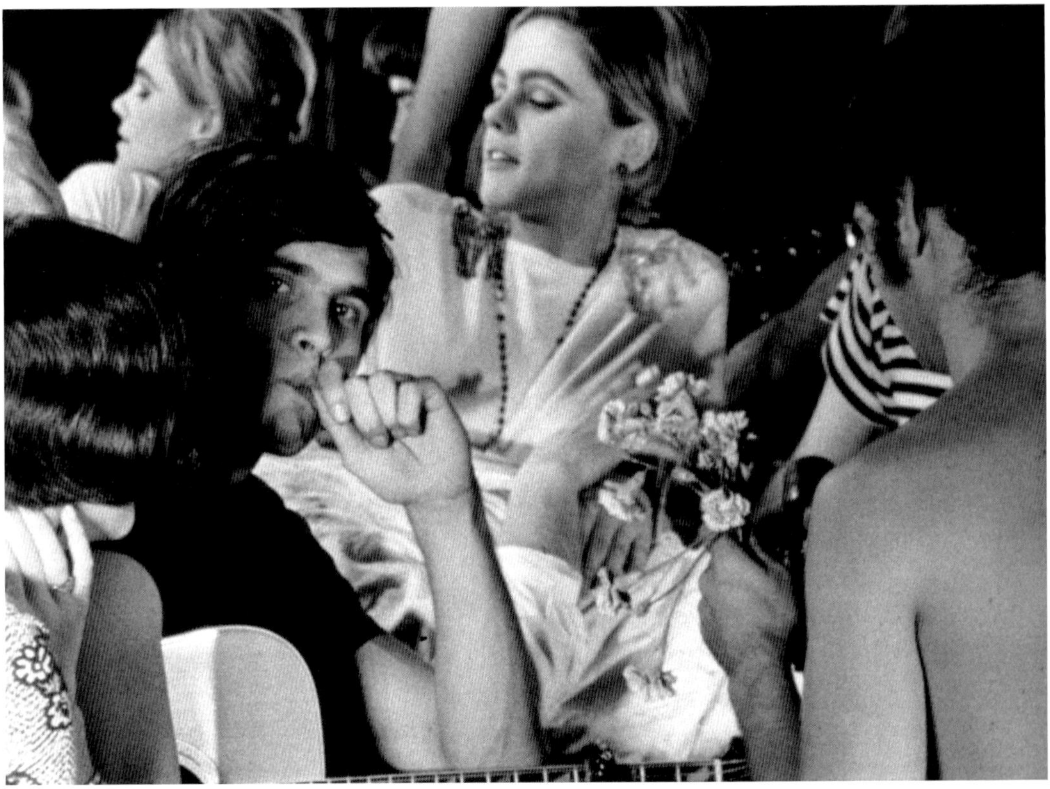

Andy Warhol, *Space*, 1965. 16mm film, b/w, sound, 66 minutes. Film still courtesy of The Andy Warhol Museum.

quarter views, quadrupling Sedgwick's visage. We now experience the film purely as a surface lineup of video profile/filmic three-quarter/video profile/filmic three-quarter images. Sedgwick chatters to someone off camera in all four versions of herself, though she moves her head much more often in the film register than in the video one. We hear only snippets of what she says—a word here, a phrase there, hardly ever a complete sentence. From time to time she seems to react to her own voice emanating from the monitor beside her, but we infer this more from her movements than from hearing what she says. At first, we strain to listen, but very quickly we give up and simply watch the shimmering mobility of her facial expressions and her enormous dangling earrings. The film's sound is thus a sort of ruse, making us think that perhaps there's a story, a conversation, gossip—something that we should be in on. A transcript made by a lip-reader teaches us otherwise: Sedgwick reprises "Puff, the Magic Dragon" from *Space*, and that's about as interesting as it gets.[7] What she says doesn't matter. What matters is that a constant patter of her vocal sounds accompanies her changing facial expressions and bobbing head. *Outer and Inner Space* is a work of vividly animated portraiture, a unique experiment in complicating and extending—spatially, temporally, sonically—the early silkscreen paintings of Marilyn, Liz, Elvis, and Jackie and the nearly 500 *Screen Test* film portraits that Warhol made between 1964 and 1966.

Of course, a great many, if not indeed most, of Warhol's films can be thought of as portraits: the early, silent ones obviously—*Sleep* (John Giorno), *Fat* (Robert Indiana), *Blow Job* (DeVerne Bookwalter), *Empire* (the Empire State Building), *Henry Geldzahler*, *Taylor Mead's Ass*, *Shoulder* (Lucinda Childs), *Mario Banana* (Mario Montez)—but the later, sound ones too—*Face*, *Poor Little Rich Girl*, *Beauty No. 2*, *Afternoon*, and *Lupe* (more portraits of Sedgwick), *Paul Swan*, the Ronald Tavel scripted *Screen Test No. 1* (Philip Fagan), *Screen Test No. 2* (Mario Montez), and *Suicide* (Rock Bradett), *Mrs. Warhol*, *Eating Too Fast* (Gregory Battcock), *Bufferin* (Gerard Malanga).[8] Various reels of *The Chelsea Girls* are essentially portraits of Ondine, Brigid Berlin, Eric Emerson, and Nico. A number of films—*Kiss*, *Haircut*, *Couch*, *Camp*, *Restaurant*, *The Velvet Underground and Nico*—are group portraits; *John and Ivy* is a double portrait, a portrait of a couple; *Blue Movie* is a double portrait of Viva and Louis Waldron, a portrait not of a couple but of a fuck (the film's alternate title).

The Closet is a double portrait of Nico and Randy Bourscheidt. Although they are pictured alone together in a closet, a closet big enough for only two people, they are not a couple, and there certainly isn't going to be a fuck. *The Closet* is a space of *not* coupling, of not even getting close. In her desultory way, Nico tries to get Randy to show some interest in her. Feigning incomprehension, Randy demurs. The following dialogue takes place three-quarters of the way into the film, after Randy has confessed to being perfectly happy to stay in the closet:

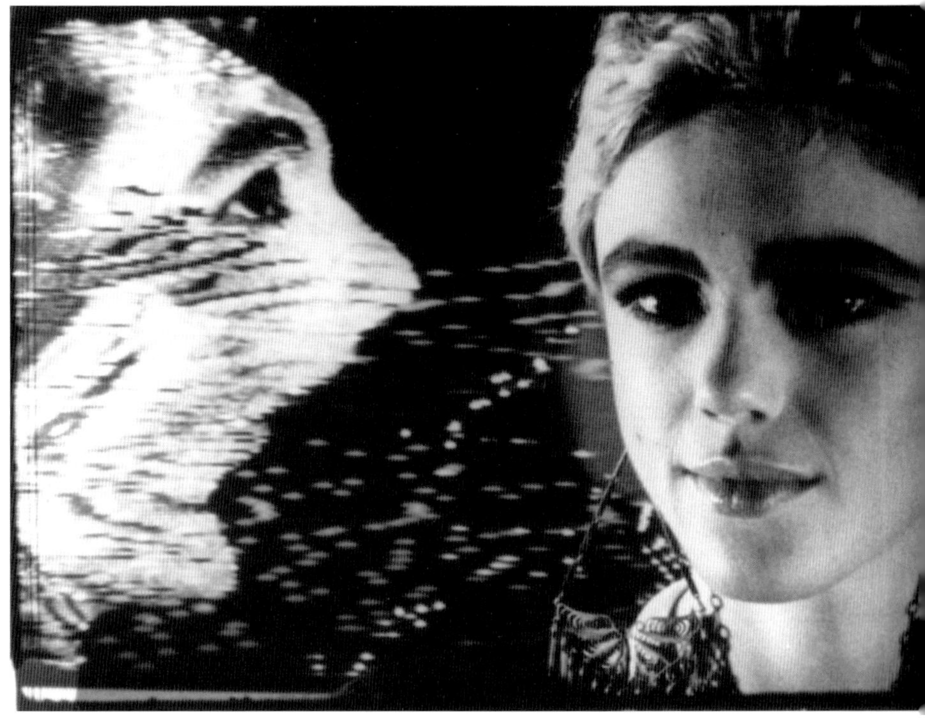

Andy Warhol, *Outer and Inner Space*, 1965. 16mm film, b/w, sound, 66 minutes, 33 minutes in double screen. Film still courtesy of The Andy Warhol Museum.

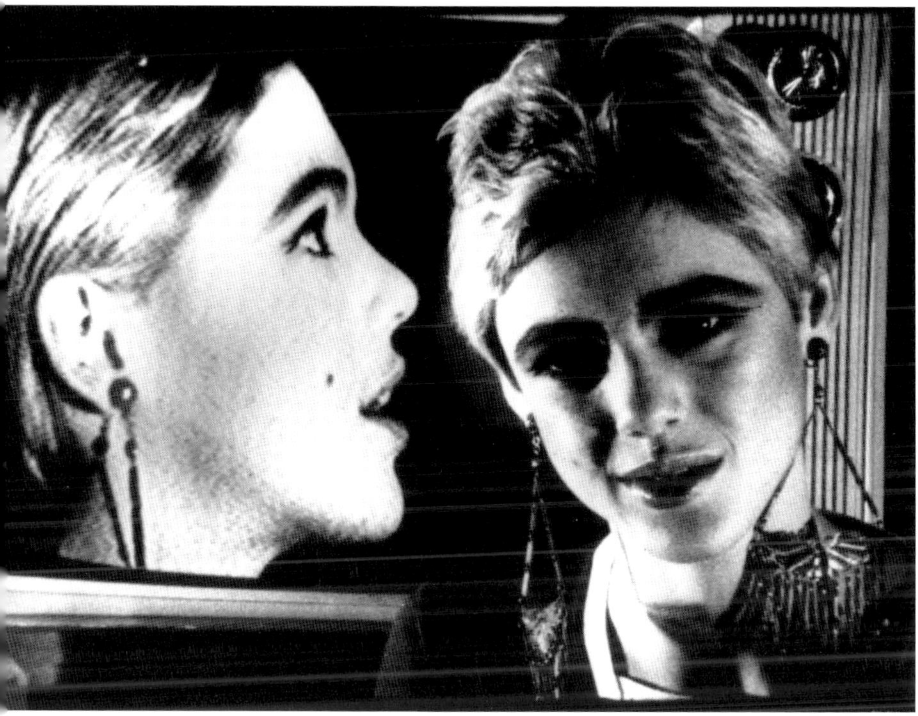

Nico: "Do you think anything seems interesting?"

Randy: "Uhm, yeah."

Nico (waits, then exasperated): "*What*?"

Randy: "Sometimes you."

Nico: "Do you have to get used to something that seems interesting, or the other way around? Do you *want* to get used to something that seems interesting."

Randy: "No."

Nico: "Definitely?"

Randy: "No, because things are usually interesting because you don't know anything about them."

Nico: "Don't you think you can be interested in something you get used to?"

Randy: "Yes, but it doesn't make any difference, because ..."

Nico: "Therefore you have to go looking for new things. Therefore you have to go out of here."

Randy: "Well, things change in here. You know, you change, and I change."

Nico: "We should all be interested in things we don't want to be interested in."

Randy: "Uh, right."

The Closet begins with a slightly askew shot of a closet door, an old-fashioned door with moldings and a brass doorknob (we think: "Oh no, this is going to be a film of a closet door like *Empire* is a film of the Empire State Building, and a closet door is not at all interesting to look at"). Nico's and Randy's voices can soon be heard behind the door. They discuss snakes molting. After about eight minutes, Randy pushes the door open. The angle of the original framing remains, and we see that the camera has been positioned low enough that with the closet door open the two actors, evidently sitting on low stools, are captured in three-quarter view. The back of the open door is partially visible at the right. Neckties and silk scarves hang down from above. Nico wears a white Foale and Tuffin pantsuit; Randy wears an Aran sweater over a white button-down shirt. Nico's hair is, of course, very blond, Randy's, light brown. The closet's interior, like its outside door, is painted stark white. Bright, even lighting bleaches out the scene, making the whole film appear as blond as Nico herself. After a moment of adjusting to the light, the two continue their timid, diffident, not always audible conversation:

Nico: "Do you actually know where we are, now?"

Randy: "No, I can't remember."

Nico: "Is Central Park, New York, a part of New York?"

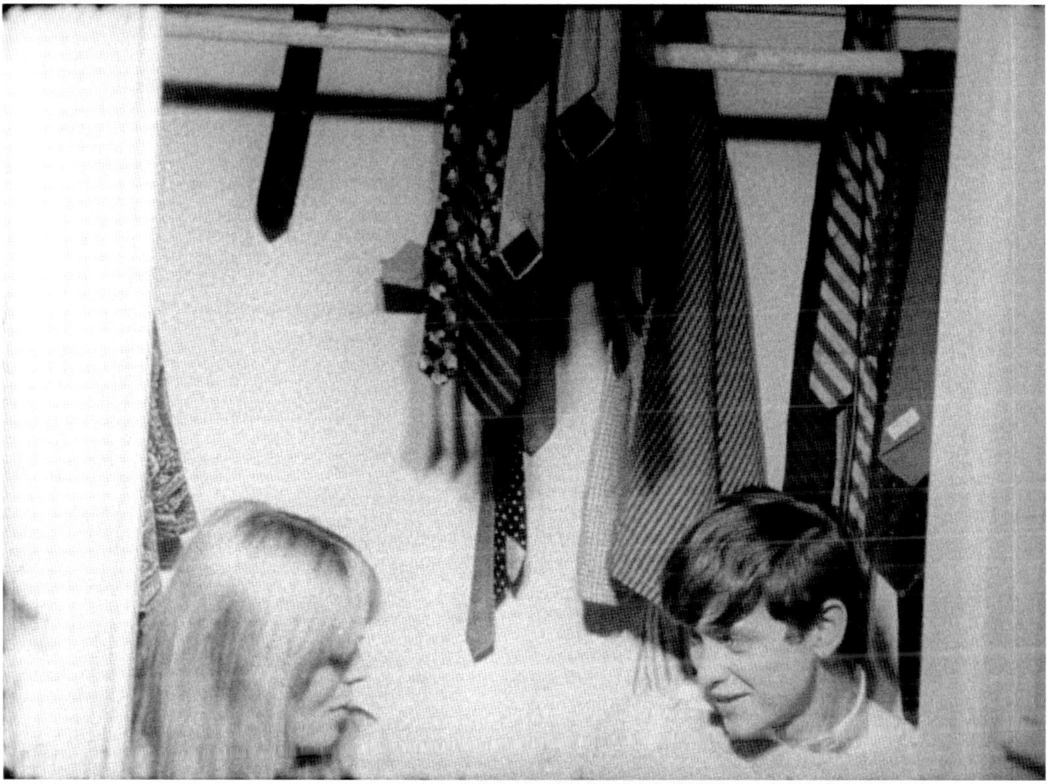

Andy Warhol, *The Closet*, 1966. 16mm film, b/w, sound, 66 minutes. Film still courtesy of The Andy Warhol Museum.

Randy: "Yeah, Central Park is right there" (points to his left).

Nico: "I thought it was that way" (points to her right).

Randy: "Oh, that's right, I think it is."

We realize that this will not be a scintillating conversation, so we stop straining to understand the poor-quality optical-sound recording. As if in response to our dissatisfaction, the camera moves. It zooms in to a close-up tight enough that Nico has to lean into the frame to be seen. Nico disappears left, so we look at Randy. His restless body language, darting eyes, nervous smile, and quizzical tone all suggest that he's camera-shy, not to mention Nico-shy. Nico is a goddess, and Randy is just a sweet kid, star struck, bashful, and undoubtedly sexually intimidated.[9] At various moments, Nico plays with Randy's hair, his sweater, offers to feed him a sandwich. There are long, awkward silences. Midway through the film, Nico asks, "Are you afraid of me?" Randy hesitates, smiles.

Nico: "I'm not trying to embarrass you."

Randy (inching slightly toward Nico): "Uh, no (long pause), why?"

Nico: "Do you find there's a similarity between us?"

Randy: "Uh, not really, no."

Nico: "No?"

Randy: "No, your hair is much longer than mine."

Nico: "Not really."

(Randy laughs, reaches across, gingerly touches Nico's hair, nervously laughs again.)

Nico: "That's not an essential thing."

Randy: "Not really ... our faces?"

Nico: "Hmm?"

Randy: "Our faces?"

This dialogue begins with a close-up of Nico's face. After she asks, "Are you afraid of me?" the camera zooms out to a medium shot to capture Randy's reaction. It holds there until Nico asks whether Randy finds a similarity between them, then begins a slow pan to the left that leaves him out of the picture by the time he answers her. By the time he reaches for her hair, Nico is squeezed into the right-hand side of the picture, and by the time he asks, "Our faces?" we can see only a narrow sliver of her at the edge of the frame. The camera is trained on the doorjamb and a blank wall.

Warhol's camerawork has a pleasingly perverse relation to the cramped space and languorous pace of *The Closet*'s seduction and refusal. The camera holds steady for long stretches, as if to accentuate the going-nowhere quality and uncomfortable silences of the conversation, but it sometimes becomes very active, even if its repertory of moves is kept to a minimum. It's as if Warhol has just discovered some things his camera can do and is trying them out. He zooms in from medium shot to close-up, tilt-pans down to the floor and up to the shelf above the actors' heads, pans and swish pans left and right. For example, here is what Warhol does with his camera in the sequence immediately following the conversation I've just recounted. We start with the medium shot showing the wall, the closet doorjamb, and a narrow fragment of Nico at the far right. The camera slowly pans right, zooms in to a close-up of Nico, tilt-pans down to Nico's pants leg, tilt-pans back up, zooms out to a medium shot, zooms back to the close-up of Nico, pans left beyond Nico, then all the way right to Randy, back left past Nico, then swish-pans right to Randy. After two more slow pans to the left followed by swish pans to the right, there is a zoom out to a medium shot of Randy and a pan left to the narrow fragment of Nico at the far right with which we began. There is a tilt-pan down to the closet floor, right, and up so that Nico's and Randy's heads appear respectively at the bottom left- and right-hand corners of the screen.

This framing of the two's heads at opposite sides of the screen doesn't exactly isolate the two from each other: they are, after all, sitting next to each other in a coat closet. Sometimes the camera zooms in on their tight proximity, showing only adjacent body parts—Nico's knee next to Randy's elbow, Nico's left hand beside Randy's right. But in *The Closet* proximate isn't close. On the contrary, sixty-six minutes of togetherness seem not to have brought Nico and Randy one bit closer to each other. Nico gets nowhere with Randy; she never so much as learns his name. Near the end of the film, Nico takes off her jacket and Randy hangs it up between them, then says, "It's like two closets." Nico plays peekaboo, hiding behind the jacket, pushing it aside, then hiding behind it again.

Randy: "Do you think you could forget I was here?"

Nico: "Oh no, never. I don't forget faces."

Randy: "You don't know my name though."

Nico: "No. What is it? Romeo?"

Randy: "No."

Nico: "Why not?"

Randy: "Uh."

Nico: "Why don't we play Romeo and Juliet?"

Randy: "Shall I get down on my knees?"

Nico: "Oh no. You could be Juliet, and I'm Romeo."

Randy laughs, throws Nico's jacket sleeve at her, and the film runs out.

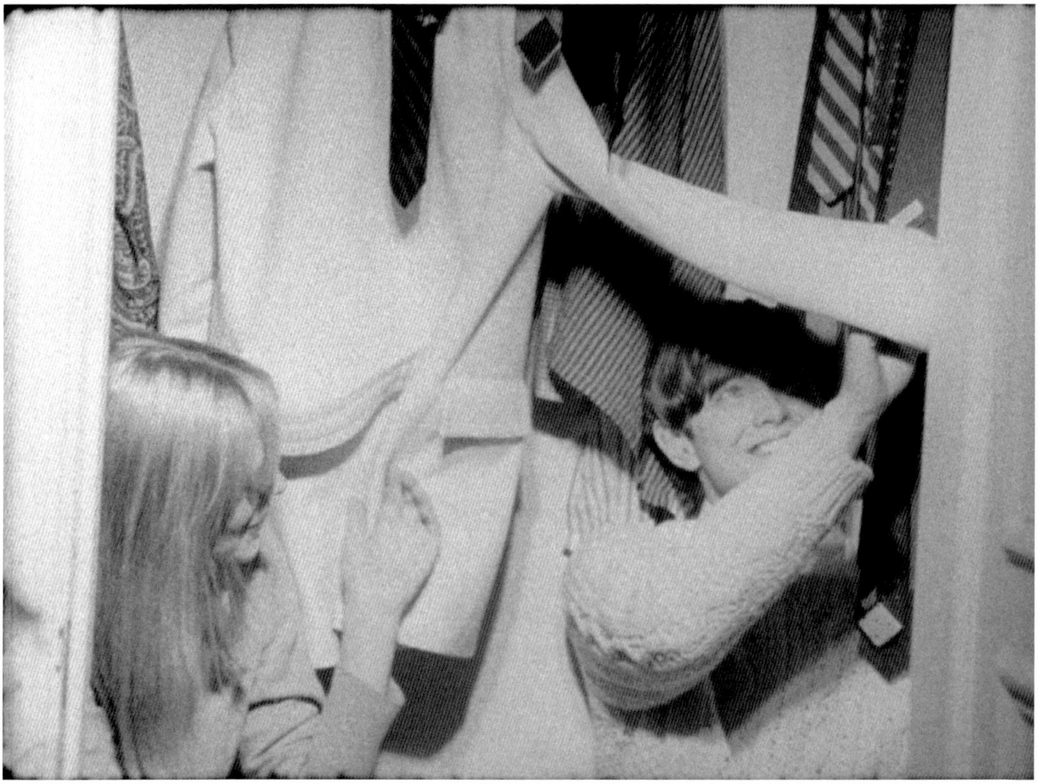

Andy Warhol, *The Closet*, 1966. 16mm film, b/w, sound, 66 minutes. Film still courtesy of The Andy Warhol Museum.

Nico doesn't make the most convincing Romeo; you could hardly describe the feeling she gives off as ardor (Randy in fact likens her at one point to an icicle). *The Closet*'s seduction is so subtle that the participants are able to behave more or less as if it's not taking place at all. And we think: "Maybe it's just a stunted conversation between two actors with no chemistry; maybe it's just a pretext for Warhol to move his camera; maybe it is, after all, just a film of a closet, like *Empire* is a film of the Empire State Building." In the meantime, the closet has become a strangely fascinating place.

> Nico: "It's very sad to be in a closet all your life, don't you think? Don't you feel sorry for me?"
>
> Randy: "No. I don't know what we'd do if we got out."
>
> Nico: "There would be more variation, I'm sure—variations of color."
>
> Randy: "I know, but that doesn't make any difference … you just get used to them. There are some variations in here."

Confinement in *The Closet* is rendered less claustrophobic, so much more *variable*, by Warhol's mobile camera, which, while always keeping the closet in frame, constantly reconfigures and opens out its space. Confining enclosure is, by contrast, especially palpable in the second reel of *My Hustler* (which predates *The Closet* by a year) because the unmoving shot of a small beach-house bathroom shared by Paul America and Joseph Campbell—called the Sugar Plum Fairy in the film—follows upon a reel shot outdoors on Fire Island, with, for Warhol in mid-1965, all sorts of camera movements—pans, swish pans, tilt pans, zooms in and out—and even two cuts. Close-ups of Paul lying on the beach zoom out to long shots, and toward the end of the reel the camera follows Paul from a great distance as he plays in the waves with Genevieve Charbin. Even close-ups of the group on the beach-house deck (Ed Hood, who plays the john to Paul's hustler, and variously John McDermott as the houseboy, Genevieve, and Joe) give an illusion of spatial depth because of a large beachscape painting hanging inside the house that is sharply visible behind the assembled characters. In one especially spacious shot, the camera pans away from a close-up of the group on the deck along the facade of the house, zooms out to a long shot of the sand dunes and other beach houses in the distance, and continues to pan while zooming back in as it reaches its destination in a close-up of Paul lying on the beach. During this complex shot, we hear Ed make a proposition about his Dial-a-Hustler callboy to Joe and Genevieve: "The bet is this: that neither one of you can make him, and you can both try—of course, you can't try too hard, you can't try everything. I don't want your clothes coming off, Genevieve…."

Apart from the early and essentially unique *Tarzan and Jane Regained … Sort Of*, shot at various sites in Los Angeles in 1963; the lost "documentary" *Andy Warhol*

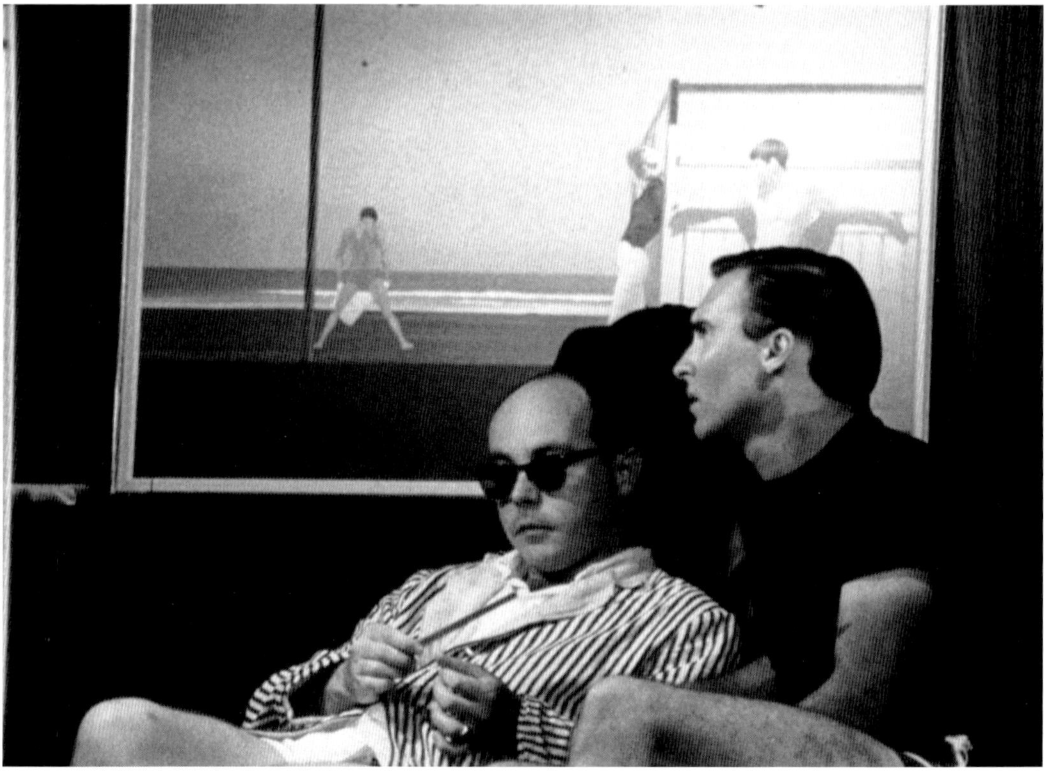

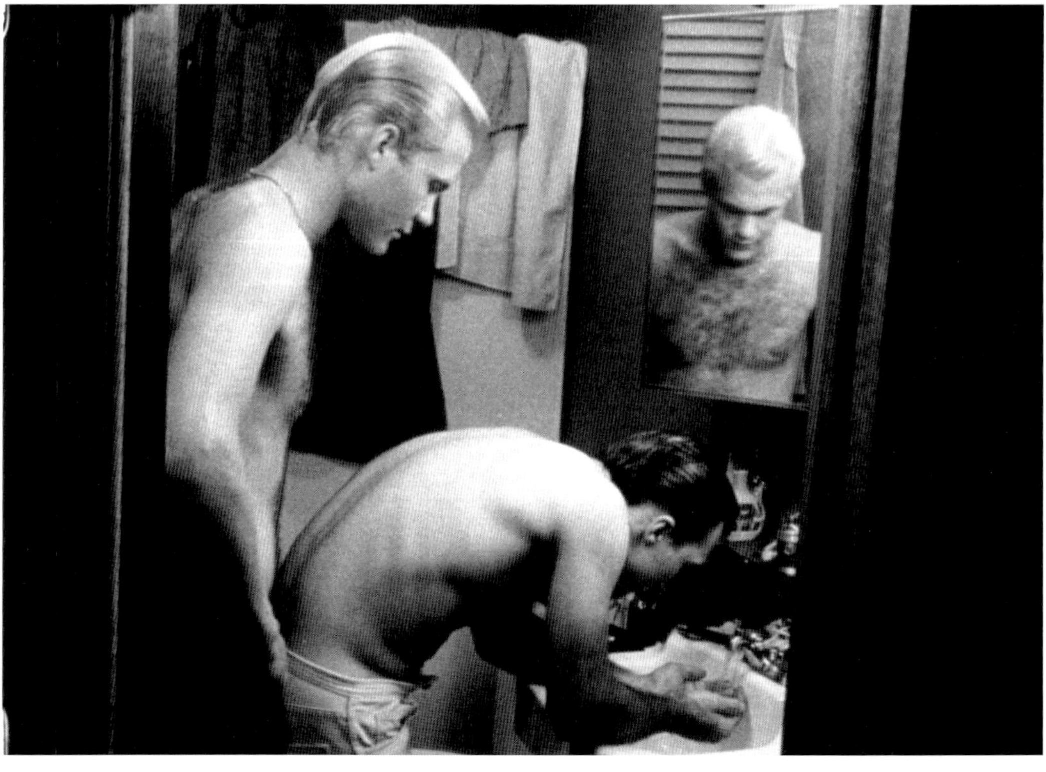

Andy Warhol, *My Hustler*, 1965. 16mm film, b/w, sound, 67 minutes. Film stills courtesy of The Andy Warhol Museum.

Films Jack Smith Filming Normal Love; and one sequence of *Soap Opera* set in an urban backyard, Warhol made no films on outdoor location before *My Hustler*. And it was only around this time that he began to move his camera and include edits in a thirty-three-minute reel (as we've seen in *Space*). So when Warhol reverts to a stationary, unedited shot of a bathroom interior in *My Hustler*'s second reel, we're all the more struck by how cramped the space is—and more so too because of the physical intimacy coupled with the emotional distance of the two guys.

Parker Tyler describes the scene well:

> Cozily flank by flank in the cottage's tiny bathroom, the pair engage in some beautifully deft verbal sparring. The hush that can sound like an interminable desert of silence in Warhol's films is here as precisioned into tense pauses as the most carefully crafted dramaturgy. One has a notion the directorial genius that makes everything in this true-life put-on look utterly right is a real objective hazard; I suspect it was due simply to the perfect understanding between the two performers as to just what was involved. Adagio, sotto voce, it leads into a veiled proposition from the old-pro—tactically prolonged through an endless shave and wash-up—that the blond, in return for the other's invaluable list of tried customers, must first render his body up to the old-pro himself.[10]

We see them from the side, while seeing their faces in a medicine-cabinet mirror. They jockey for position in front of it, changing places again and again throughout the reel. They see each other in the mirror too. They check each other out surreptitiously while paying closest attention to themselves. Their narcissism is stunning, even for a Warhol film; to say that they primp is an understatement, if only because they do so for thirty-three minutes straight. They shower, dry off, shave, brush their teeth, comb their hair, clean their ears with Q-tips, clean their nails, apply talcum powder, dry themselves again, comb their hair again, and again, and again. Paul takes a piss. Joe watches out of the corner of his eye. Joe sprays deodorant on his underarms and mists cologne on his shoulders and in his hair. He dries Paul's back, rubs it, moves his hands around to Paul's chest and massages it. He does all these things while pretending disinterest in Paul's body, even as he says, while grasping Paul's chest, "It just depends on how cooperative you're going to be … I mean, you've got a beautiful body, you know." The cooperativeness and physical beauty he's discussing ostensibly concern Paul's potential as a hustler, not as a score of his own. And since Joe admits to being an experienced hustler himself, his interest is not—again ostensibly—in Paul, even though he does say, in his most overt verbal come-on, that after hustling for a while, "you get accustomed to it, not that you don't like girls or anything, but you actually sort of … ah … sort of enjoy making it with a younger guy once in a while." Paul plays dumb: "Whaddaya mean a younger guy? What are you talking about?" … "Why, how old are you?" Joe doesn't answer that. The question of older men brings him back to johns and what they'll expect from Paul. "A john is a guy that, you know, appreciates you for being … ah … what you are, or what he thinks you might be." Joe knows one john, for instance, who doesn't demand much.

> He doesn't want your ass. He doesn't want to get sucked off. He just wants to play with you.… But he doesn't just lie there. He talks to you. He says things like, you know, "Make it ooze, make it ooze," and you say, "Make it ooze, make it ooze." And then you say, "I got a hot load coming. I got a hot load, hot load, hot load." You know, you break up in laughter but it's real. That's the way he gets his jollies, and you figure, well, that's the way he's getting his jollies and I'll get my jollies when I get my thirty-five bucks twice a week for fifteen minutes.

Joe's ploy is, as Tyler notes, to get Paul to make it with him as a commission for introducing Paul to some of his johns, but Paul steadfastly fails to comprehend what Joe is offering—or pretends to fail to comprehend. Joe's exasperation finally leads him to impugn Paul's masculinity.

> Joe: "So what is your game, anyway? I mean, you're not exactly the ordinary guy on the street."
>
> Paul: "Whaddaya mean?"
>
> Joe: "Well, I mean your hair's pretty long. You've gone with a couple of johns. You're not out here with a girl. You were an athlete in school. Whaddaya, you got out of school, you were in the army, right?"
>
> Paul: "No."
>
> Joe: "You weren't in the army?'
>
> Paul: "No."
>
> Joe: "Navy?"
>
> Paul: "No."
>
> Joe: "Marines?"
>
> Paul: "Nothing."
>
> Joe: "Why not?"
>
> Paul: "4F."
>
> Joe: "4F? An athlete?"
>
> Paul: "I have a bad knee."
>
> (Joe turns away in feigned disgust.)
>
> Paul (protesting): "I do."
>
> Joe: "Yeah, sure."

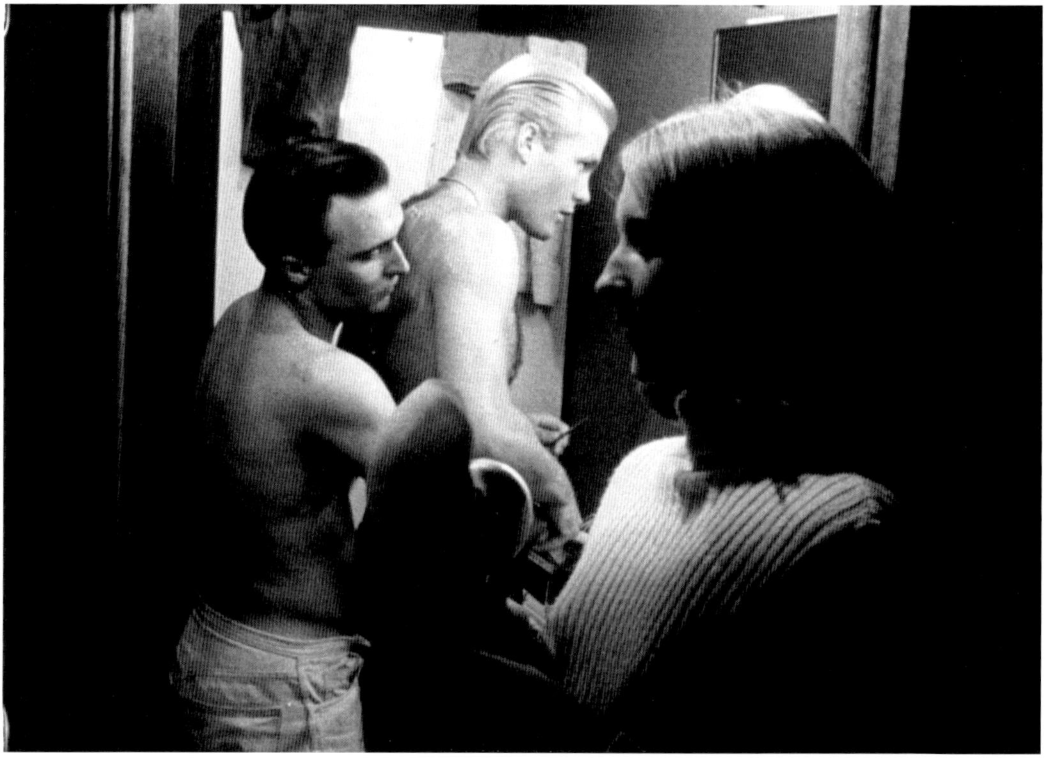

Andy Warhol, *My Hustler*, 1965. 16mm film, b/w, sound, 67 minutes. Film still courtesy of The Andy Warhol Museum.

Right after this insinuation, Joe rubs Noxzema on Paul's back and moves his hands around to caress his chest again. Twice while doing so he eyes the camera. His furtive glance startles: All of a sudden we are made aware that there is an outside of this bathroom space we've been confined to. Joe returns his hands to Paul's back, then reaches around to his abdomen and down to his belt. . . .

At just this moment, Genevieve appears in the doorway in extreme close-up, her head in shadow, her profile outlined by the bathroom light. "Oh, for Christ's sake," Joe says, and he backs away out of the frame. "Hey, Paul," says Genevieve, "you could go away with me, you know. I'm going away next week, for about a year. I've got some money, and I'm going away to France. It's very beautiful there . . . It's better than staying here and being like Sugar Plum." Genevieve gets no response, so she moves on. Ed takes her place in the doorway: "Hello, Paul. Paul, have you ever seen that much cash in one wallet? Do you know how much more there is where that comes from? Do you know the places I could take you? . . . I could get you girls, Paul, beautiful, rich girls . . . I could teach you things, Paul. I'm extremely well educated. I have a large library." Ed departs, and Dorothy Dean takes his place. Dean hasn't appeared in the film thus far. We have no idea what she represents in the story, apart from what she says now: "Well, sweetie, you may be lovely, but can you stay lovely? I mean how long can this go on? Not forever. I think it's more to your advantage to decide what you want to do . . . You are very pretty, but you're not exactly literate . . . Sweetie, I will get you educated, which won't harm you, and after that, do what you want. I mean, why be tied down to these old faggots?" Dorothy pauses and begins to apply her lipstick, and the film runs out.[11]

Throughout this succession of offers to escape, Paul silently cleans and buffs his nails while Joe stays in the background, out of the camera's range except for a few glimpses of him in the mirror. Paul never so much as glancingly acknowledges his propositioners. He looks up from his fingernails only to stare at himself in the mirror. Although the subject of his half hour of banter with Joe was whether to continue hustling, he now shows no interest in offers of money, travel, and education in payment for his companionship. Indeed, he shows no interest in moving beyond the bathroom mirror and the game he and Joe have been playing in front of it.

Joe Campbell and Paul America's performance in this second reel of *My Hustler* must count as one of the great improvisational tours-de-force in Warhol's cinema. Not only do the two men sustain the illusion of an actual conversation between experienced and inexperienced hustlers while at the same time constantly grooming themselves, but they also strike a perfect balance between tough-guy talk and the game of seduction. Joe is kind of a letch, but he's also kind of a stud. Paul is a faux-naïf tease, but he's also intimidated. Each wants the other but can't quite admit it—to himself, to the other, to us. Or is this just the impression they're creating?

The claustrophobia that I suggested resulted from the contrast of *My Hustler*'s second reel with the mobile camerawork and outdoor expansiveness of its first reel is compounded by the game these two play. We feel it, but evidently Paul doesn't, or in any case he doesn't mind. Like Nico's offer to get Randy out of the closet, Genevieve's, Ed's, and Dorothy's offers to get Paul out of the beach-house bathroom are rebuffed. Why leave, when there's so much variation right here? You would have to run off together—as a couple—with one of these three characters toward a predictable end, if not the proverbial happily-ever-after ending. In here, you can continue to play around in the space of *not coupling*, a space that hasn't been much explored in the movies—or anywhere else, for that matter. It is one of the signal achievements of Warhol's cinema that it resists denouements.[12] Warhol's films don't have happy endings. They don't have endings at all. They just end.

MISFITTING TOGETHER

REEL ONE, RIGHT-HAND SCREEN, "NICO IN KITCHEN": *THE CHELSEA GIRLS* BEGINS WITH A TIGHT CLOSE-UP ON NICO'S BLOND BANGS, SO TIGHT THAT WHEN NICO MOVES HER HEAD RIGHT OR LEFT SHE DISAPPEARS FROM THE FRAME.

Using a small scissors and a double-sided makeup mirror, which occasionally reflects light into the camera, she trims her bangs, and she speaks with Eric Emerson and Ari, her little boy. When Nico asks Eric to make some coffee, he turns the water on, which drowns out the already-hard-to-make-out dialogue. The camera zooms out to a medium close-up that shows Eric standing next to Nico and washing the coffee pot. Nico sits down, below the frame, and the camera eventually pans down and left to find her. Ari walks into the frame to embrace his mother, who speaks to him in French. Five minutes have gone by, so the sound is turned down to just below audible as reel two, "Father Ondine and Ingrid," begins, sound on, on the left-hand screen. The camera pulls out to a medium shot. Eric stands next to Nico, then moves in front of her. What seems to be an almost invisible cut returns him to his position on the right side of the screen. Nico stands up, the camera zooms in to a tight close-up at her waist, in deep shadow, then pans up to her head, above it, and back down to frame her bangs, which she resumes trimming. Lighting and focus are adjusted. The film continues as it began: Nico, in tight close-up, trims her bangs.

Throughout reel one, the camera zooms in and out, pans back and forth, up and down and around, but it inevitably returns to Nico's bangs and holds on them. And Nico continues to trim them, brush them, comb them with the edge of the scissors, toss them, blow on them, flick bits of hair out of them, look at them in her makeup mirror. She smokes, drinks, smiles, but no matter what might momentarily divert her—talking to Eric, playing with Ari—she always returns to her bangs, and so does Warhol's camera. At some point we might realize that Eric and Ari, with their nearly identical pageboys, also have bangs; maybe it's when Eric combs Ari's with his fingers just before Nico fiddles at cutting Ari's hair for a few seconds. But only Nico's bangs matter. We see how artfully they're shaped, following as they do the curve of her eyebrows, slightly pointing toward the bridge of her nose at the center. We see both what a job it is to keep them so perfect and how effortlessly Nico seems to manage it. Right up to the moment when the film runs out, Nico concentrates—can one say concentrates *distractedly*?—on her bangs. But the film runs out not as we might expect during one of those precisely framed tight close-ups to which the sequence has returned again and again as if drawn by magnetic force, but during a medium shot that indifferently frames the scene through the door to the kitchen; Nico is partially cut off at the extreme left as Ari reaches toward her from below, Eric is silhouetted at bottom center next to the doorjamb, and a blank wall in dark shadow occupies fully a third of the screen on the right.

If, in spite of silhouettes and shadows, reel one is basically white—Nico the Nordic blonde, Eric the strawberry blond, Ari the towhead, all in a uniformly lit kitchen with white enamel cupboards and appliances—reel two, on the left, is black. It opens with a medium close-up of Ondine in which everything is pitch darkness but his face, his hands, and a hint of white turtleneck worn under a dark, hooded robe. Ondine is midsentence.

He shades his eyes with his hand as he looks directly into the light that shines on him from off-screen left and dramatically highlights his jagged features. “Get in here,” he demands, and soon enough we hear the New Jersey–accented whine of Ingrid Superstar. Catholic confession is the conceit of the sequence, with Ondine playing father confessor, although he taunts more than he listens. Ingrid chats idly about her boyfriend; Ondine asks a few easy questions like “Where did you meet him?” Ingrid, bored, clams up for a while, then asks, “Now, what was the question again?” Ondine: “The question was, Why are you a lesbian?” She insists she’s not, he insists she is, and the camera zooms out to a medium shot to reveal Ingrid for the first time and the odd setup of the “confessional”: two couches positioned back to back. Ondine kneels on one, resting his elbows on its back; Ingrid sits facing forward, away from Ondine, toward the light. She wears sunglasses. Ondine soon changes the game from confession to psychoanalysis. “Now start to recall,” he tells her, “I want to hear everything.” Ondine hovers over her, bobbles around. The camera bobbles too; indeed its movement is dizzying as it pans and zooms and finds bits of nothing to see. Ondine changes the game once again: Now it’s a job interview, and since Ingrid doesn’t meet the qualifications, he asks her to leave. She does, and he too gets up and walks out of camera range. “That’s all,” he says as he departs. But of course it’s not all; the camera is still rolling, so they have no choice but to return to their positions and their banter. Ingrid insults Ondine, then asks his forgiveness. He feigns hurt feelings: “You’re speaking to a very sensitive priestess, the high priestess, and I’m not Maria Montez either.” “Who’s Maria Montez?” Ingrid asks. “*Who* is Maria Mon*tez*?” Ondine says, incredulous, then adds, as if it weren’t a non sequitur, “I don’t know.” Ondine is always quick. When he insists he’s not a Roman Catholic priest, Ingrid wonders, “Well, what are you doing as a priest?” “Posing,” he replies, without missing a beat. The two of them bicker, yell at each other, tussle physically, and the camera gets right into the action, as if it were one of the troublemakers. It careens, streaks by its objects, abstracts the scene, but eventually it finds its way back to Ondine’s craggy features, the equivalent here of Nico’s bangs in reel one.

—

The Chelsea Girls changed my life. Very soon after I saw it, in 1967, I quit school, moved to New York City, and got a job working as an assistant to the legendary fashion designer Charles James, who lived in a suite of run-down rooms at the Chelsea Hotel. James laced my morning coffee with amphetamines. His tantrums rivaled Ondine’s infamous speed-fueled outburst at the end of *The Chelsea Girls*. He had an attractive young guy there one day, tied by his wrists, naked, to the bed, the sort of bed that features as the setting for a number of *The Chelsea Girls* episodes. I survived just two weeks in James’s employ, but a few years later I moved to a loft across the street from the Chelsea Hotel and began spending late nights hanging out in the back room of Max’s Kansas City, where I met some of the Factory crowd, including the mercurial Ondine.

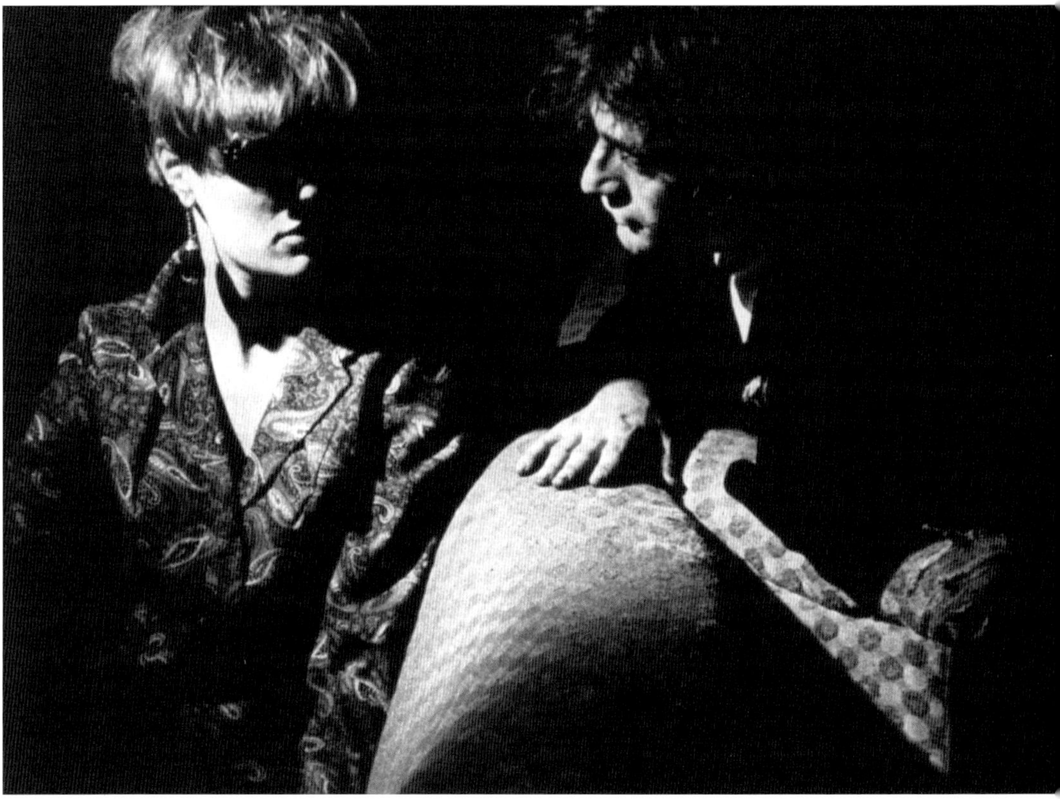

Andy Warhol, *The Chelsea Girls*, 1966. 16mm film, b/w and color, sound, 204 minutes in double screen. Film still courtesy of The Andy Warhol Museum.

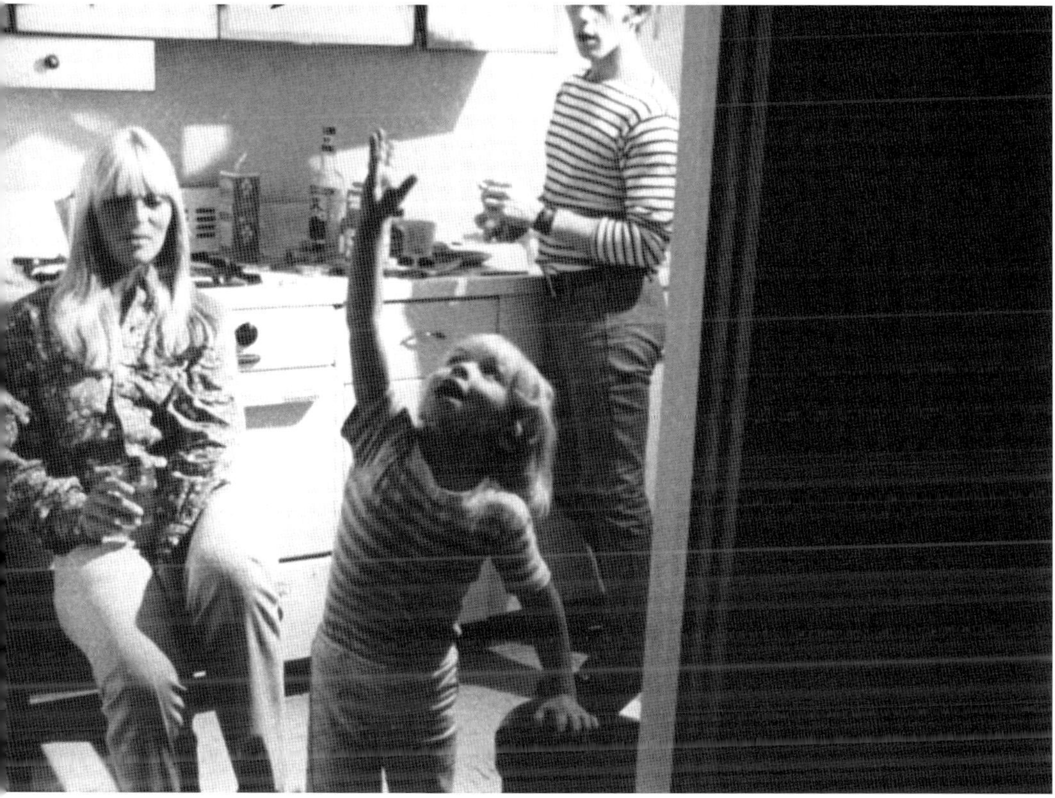

The Chelsea Girls was my first encounter with underground film. I was a college student in New Orleans at the time, and *The Chelsea Girls* was playing at the local art cinema during the film's national theatrical release. That it was shown commercially and widely reviewed throughout the United States, Canada, and Europe says much about 1960s film culture: After all, *The Chelsea Girls* is a three-and-a-half-hour, split-screen, nonnarrative movie about a bunch of queers and junkies at a seedy residential hotel in what was then *not* an upscale New York neighborhood (Chelsea *boys* were far in the future). The Chelsea Hotel's manager was so insulted by the film that he threatened to sue Warhol for designating the film's episodes by hotel room number (many sequences were in fact shot at the Chelsea Hotel; others clearly were not). But in spite of its vaunted depravity—or because of it—Jack Kroll of *Newsweek* called *The Chelsea Girls* "a fascinating and significant movie event," "the *Iliad* of the underground," and found its characters "as meaningful as Jack Gelber's garrulous junkies, Edward Albee's spiteful comedians, John Updike's poetic suburbanites."[1] Writing for *Art and Artists*, Brian O'Doherty compared Warhol's achievement in film to Joyce's and Burroughs's in the novel and wrote that *The Chelsea Girls* was "quite possibly the first masterpiece from a generation that has learned to handle the medium of film as casually as an artist used to handle paint long ago before painting was threatened with obsolescence."[2] Toby Mussman called *The Chelsea Girls* "Warhol's masterpiece to date" and likened it, for its violence, to Buñuel's *L'age d'or*, Hawks's *Scarface*, and Fuller's *The Naked Kiss*.[3] Other superlatives and comparisons abounded, most of them preposterous. *The Chelsea Girls* was called "*The Sound of Music* of the underground cinema"; Warhol was likened to Bosch, Caravaggio, Dante, Dickens, Victor Hugo, and D. W. Griffith; and Vincent Canby suggested in the *New York Times* that Jonas Mekas, who had arranged national distribution for *The Chelsea Girls*, was "beginning to sound like Darryl F. Zanuck."[4]

Perhaps the oddest tribute paid to *The Chelsea Girls* was Nam June Paik's suggestion, in his manifesto "Expanded Education for the Paper-less Society," that it offered the best format for capturing on film still-living notables of the twentieth century, mostly in Paik's proposal philosophers and theologians:

> Nothing is more urgent and success-proof than to film the images and voices of aging great thinkers of today, and yesterday, in sufficient and surplus quantity, who might pass away any day, such as Marcel Duchamp, Jaspars [Jaspers], Heideggar [Heidegger], Gabriel Marcel, Ortega Y Gasset, Lucasc [Lukács], Toynbee, Radaklishnan [Radhakrishnan], Ernst Bloch, Niebuhr, Puller [Fuller?], Sartre and Russell. The interviewer should be a qualified philosopher himself and the camera crew as minimal as possible, so that Jaspars [*sic*] or Heideggar [*sic*] can talk as naturally as the "Chelsea Girls." An NBC or NET-style expensive film technique is not only unnecessary, but may be harmful for this subject.[5]

Warhol did claim to have had the idea to make a twenty-four-hour film of Duchamp but couldn't get funding for it;[6] so far as I know, he never considered putting Jaspers or Heidegger on film.

The Chelsea Girls was not, of course, unanimously acclaimed. Bosley Crowther denounced it as a "peep show put on" in the *New York Times*, and the vice squad busted it in Boston.[7] Rex Reed called it "a 3½ hour cesspool of vulgarity and talentless confusion which is about as interesting as the inside of a toilet bowl."[8] Reviewers seemed to be both impressed and outraged that *The Chelsea Girls* had moved from the Film-Makers' Cinematheque, where it "belonged," to a "real" movie theater uptown. Crowther's fulmination was occasioned by just this fact: "It was all right so long as these adventures in the realm of independent cinema stayed in Greenwich Village or on the south side of 42nd Street.... But now that their underground has surfaced on West 57th Street, and taken over a theater with real carpets ... it is time for permissive adults to stop winking at their too-precocious pranks."[9] Andrew Sarris began his grudgingly positive review in *Cahiers du Cinema in English* on the same note:

> *The Chelsea Girls* has made the move uptown from the Film-Makers' Cinematheque to the Cinema Rendezvous, where, ironically enough, many family-type flicks have premiered or returned for the kiddies over the years. Needless to say *The Chelsea Girls* is not for the kiddies, nor for adults of kiddycar coyness. Functional voyeurs will be bored to distraction. Warhol doesn't exploit depravity as much as he certifies it. Most pornography is anti-erotic because of the crudity of its certification, but *The Chelsea Girls* isn't even pornographic. The flashes of male Caucasian nudity depress the viewer with intimations of a pitiful passivity. Warhol has refined the old Hollywood tease into a kind of tepid torture in which organisms talk away their orgasms.[10]

Sarris's annoyance that *The Chelsea Girls* didn't turn him on recalls the famous remark made by an anonymous United States senator to a *Newsweek* correspondent about Jack Smith's underground classic *Flaming Creatures*. In 1968, Smith's film was exploited by the Right to impugn Lyndon Johnson's chief justice nominee, Abe Fortas, who had voted to overturn the New York State Court's obscenity ruling against *Flaming Creatures*. After seeing the film in a viewing arranged by Senator Strom Thurmond at the Senate office building, the senator in question famously commented, "That movie was so sick I couldn't even get aroused."[11]

Limp dicks on-screen and off- are not all that Warhol shared with his movie mentor Jack Smith. Smith turned every screening of his *Normal Love* into a one-of-a-kind performance by playing selections from his vast record collection to accompany the silent footage and by resplicing the film's sequences in the projection booth while showing it. During its opening run at the Film-Makers' Cinematheque, *The Chelsea Girls*, too, differed from screening to screening. Some of the film's original episodes are no longer part of the film at all; one reel of what we know as *The Closet*, for example, was initially shown as part of *The Chelsea Girls*.[12] The form the film now takes, decided on by Warhol when it moved to a commercial theater, consists of twelve reels with nine different "episodes," most of which are just one reel long, three of which are two reels, one of these shown side by side, the others not.[13] Some reels are played with sound on, others with sound off or turned down very low. The image of the final reel is turned off during the last few minutes while the sound continues to play. Because of the double-screen format, with the first reel on the right begun five minutes before the one on the left and indeterminate time lapses for reel changes, every screening of *The Chelsea Girls* is effectively unique.[14] This live-performance characteristic makes it impracticable to see the film except at regular theatrical screenings, which might partially account for the fact that, though creating a sensation when it first appeared and widely considered Warhol's greatest cinematic achievement, *The Chelsea Girls* has garnered scant serious critical attention.

Warhol himself remembered *The Chelsea Girls* as both "the movie that made everyone sit up and notice" and the quintessential Factory home movie: "If anybody wants to know what those summer days of '66 were like in New York with us, all I can say is go see *Chelsea Girls*. I've never seen it without feeling in the pit of my stomach that I was right back there all over again. It may have looked like a horror show—'cubicles in hell'—to some outside people, but to us it was more like a comfort—after all, we were a group of people who understood each other's problems."[15] What were Warhol's and his friends' problems? Speed? Bitchiness? Narcissism? Warhol doesn't say, perhaps because he thinks they're self-evident when you watch *The Chelsea Girls*. In any case, for him, *The Chelsea Girls* is less a depiction of problems—"a horror show," "cubicles in hell"—than solace for them, a "comfort." What does he see that so comforts him?

He sees—we see—two reels projected in tandem. Two together as one: the ideal, the very definition of the couple. But *The Chelsea Girls* *un*couples. Although the film's cardinal number is two—two reels, two events at a time (though slightly staggered)—the two come together serendipitously, indiscriminately—one might even say promiscuously. And doubling readily becomes multiple: three characters, four, five, and more; now this story, now that one, now another, now that one again. Or it can be single: the "Hanoi Hannah" sequence playing on both screens simultaneously, or the left-hand screen's "Colored Lights on Cast" group,[16] prominently including Eric Emerson, seeming to be the spectators of Eric's narcissistic self-exploration and monologue on the right-hand screen. (See plate 2.) Still, the significant relationships in *The Chelsea Girls* are mostly those that are created as chance encounters between the two screens: coincidences, resonances, dissonances, alignments, syncopations, rhymes, and contrasts: black-and-white juxtaposed with color, a predominantly dark reel juxtaposed with a predominantly light one, a pair or a group on one reel, a lone man or woman on the other.

There are also relationships among the reels not juxtaposed. These too may be formal or technical: lighting, framing, zooms in and out, the famous "typewriter pans" (show pan right, rapid pan left), moving in and out of focus; or they might be emotional: Hannah (Mary Woronov) berates Scum (Ingrid Superstar); Ed Hood berates Mario Montez; Marie Menkin berates her son (Gerard Malanga); Ondine berates Ronna Paige. Various superstars appear from one reel to another. Mary Woronov is Hanoi Hannah in reels five and six and Gerard Malanga's girlfriend in the "Marie Menkin" sequence (reel eight), and she climbs onto the bed in "Boys in Bed" (reel four). Lots of people get on the bed initially and continuously occupied by Ed Hood and Patrick Fleming (reels four and seven): Mary, Ingrid, International Velvet, Angelina "Pepper" Davis, Gerard, René Ricard. Mario doesn't climb onto the bed, but he comes into the room, sings a couple of songs, and steals the show before being dismissed by the petulant Ed Hood. Ingrid is all over the place. She appears in "Father Ondine and Ingrid" (reel two), "Brigid Holds Court" (reel three), "Hanoi Hannah" (reels five and six), and "Colored Lights on Cast" (reel ten). Eric appears in "Nico in Kitchen" (reel one), "Eric Says All" (reel nine), and "Colored Lights on Cast" (reel ten). Gerard appears in "Boys on Bed" (reel four) and "Marie Menkin" (reel eight). Ondine stars in the two sequences as Pope Ondine (reels two and eleven). He, like Nico, appears in the film's first and final double-screen projection, but his role is a continuation of the same episode whereas Nico's isn't. (See plate 3.) Because of the five-minute time lag between beginning the first and second reels, *The Chelsea Girls* begins and ends with a close-up of Nico, but there is otherwise extreme contrast in the opening and closing pair: Nico in black-and-white, Nico in color; Nico happy, Nico sad; Nico talking, Nico silently crying to the strains of the Velvet Underground.

It's not always easy to achieve the detachment that makes it possible to see and remember these between-and-among-the-reels interactions, because there is a constant pull toward the reel whose sound we hear as we watch, as if by paying attention to that one and ignoring the other we could follow the story. But as is the case with Warhol's films generally, a different kind of attention produces greater rewards. Yvonne Rainer, whose own early films date from just this time, was one of the first to recognize this, in her 1967 *Arts Magazine* piece "Don't Give the Game Away":

> I began to watch on second viewing the inside edge rather than one screen or the other. Nico's child's head next to the looming Ondine; the moody purplish nervous detail of the Malanga scene next to a corner of the static loaded bed. The inside edge delineates another story, another interaction of characters, and more than any other part of the frame contains the condensed imagery, emphasizing how the image mashes up against the edge and is restrained from spilling out. This is a familiar concept in painting, if somewhat unfashionable in that area at the moment. To see it visualized to such an extreme in the cinema is a new experience.[17]

Rainer then extrapolates how what we might call *The Chelsea Girls*' edginess comes about from this pressure on the frame's edge and the breach resulting from seeing past it, seeing through or over it:

> One very soon begins to see that there is a strict protocol governing most of the interactions, which when defied produces jarring results, as when Hannah tells Superstar, "You aren't *supposed* to like it," or when Ondine gets upset when told he's a phony. The rules of the game narrow down to "maintain your character" and "don't give the game away." … This particular set of limitations—working within them and treading dangerously at their outer edge—evokes an extravagant logic and provides much of the dark humor of the film.[18]

One way of understanding *The Chelsea Girls*' "extravagant logic" was elaborated—incredible as this may seem—in the *New York Times* Sunday Arts and Leisure section a few months after Rainer's article appeared: "These dreamy swingers, playing their little games, clearly question the most basic assumption of our culture—namely that heterosexual coupling, happy or unhappy, moral or immoral, is a socially significant enterprise worthy of the closest possible scrutiny. Hollywood's tinsel titillation and the art house film's hard bedrock fornication are replaced by a new sexual mythology, a cool, low-keyed playful polymorphism."[19] This was written by Rosalyn Regelson, who clearly approved of the playful polymorphism: "Move over and make room for me on the bed," she writes. Who, I wondered, was Rosalyn Regelson, and what was she doing in the *New York Times*? It turns out she was the freelance journalist who wrote an article, also published in the Arts and Leisure section, that I remember reading right around the time I began hanging out in the back room at Max's, an article called "'Not a Boy, Not a Girl, Just Me.'" The title is a truncated version of a famous utterance by the article's subject, Jackie Curtis—"Not a boy, not a girl, not a faggot, not a transsexual—just me, Jackie"—whose first play, *Heaven Grand in Amber Orbit*, was being performed at the Play-House of the Ridiculous. Regelson wrote of John Vaccaro's production that "though the stage is crude and ugly with actors in madhouse rags and painted grotesque faces, it is oddly un-grim, rather as though Grotowski were wedded to Groucho Marx."[20] (I had recently seen *Heaven Grand* and met Jackie and Holly Woodlawn, who was in the play, at Max's, and I was amazed at such a sympathetic article appearing in my staid Sunday newspaper.) Regelson also wrote a *Times* piece on the New Feminist Repertory theater, a group that, she asserted, "challenges the myth we have lived under for the past few decades—that the basic order of the universe rests on the suburban family which consists of Strong Male, dependent consumer Female, and 3.5 growing dittos"—not children, not kiddies, *dittos*.[21] In still another Arts and Leisure piece, Regelson skewered Susan Sontag's revered essay on camp as "like that of a Holiday reporter giving the tourists the word on the In places in some exclusive resort."

> Miss Sontag's *schlock* version of camp is that of a suburban housewife, all Tiffany lamps and antique shop velvet gowns and Bogey movies.
>
> Real homosexual Camp is in fact the opposite of this "style" without content. Like authentic Jewish humor (before the fall into suburbia) it is an ironical response to a hopeless situation in which the world is structured against one's existence. Courage for survival is gained through humorous criticism via irony and parody of the unjust and phony aspects of the structure.[22]

Regelson certainly had it in for the suburbs, but she knew a thing or two about camp: When I entered her name in the World Cat database I came up with a reference to her 1951 master's essay at Columbia University entitled "Gay Saint: The Life and Work of Ronald Firbank." No doubt she really belonged on that bed-full of playful polymorphs at the Chelsea Hotel.[23]

So, was it camp that sustained Warhol? Perhaps during the 1950s, but in 1966, when he made *The Chelsea Girls*, or 1980, when he wrote in *Popism* about being comforted by the film, camp doesn't seem sufficient explanation. In her various *Times* stories, Regelson is surely right to see Warhol's film, feminist and ridiculous theater, and Jackie Curtis's guttersnipe, gender-fuck glamour as "moving into uncharted territory," but she tends to be a bit hung up, as we said in those days, on assaulting the values she attributes to suburbia—prescribed gender roles, heterosexuality, and child rearing—and she is singularly inattentive to anything about *The Chelsea Girls* but its "story." Apart from a passing mention of the film's "two schizoid screens," Regelson has nothing to say about what Rainer called the film's "other story," the one that results from watching the two screens together. Warhol himself is typically disingenuous about this other story. In a 1971 interview with Gerard Malanga, he says,

> The idea of the split/image in *Chelsea Girls* only came about because we had so much footage to edit, and I wasn't into editing at the time, and the film would have been too long to project in its original form time-wise. By projecting two reels simultaneously, we were able to cut down the running-projecting time in half, avoiding the tedious job of having to edit such a long film. After seeing the film projected in the split/screen format, I realized that people could take in more than one story or situation at a time.[24]

Earlier, Warhol told Joseph Gelmis, "I put two things on the screen in *Chelsea Girls* so you could look at one picture if you were bored with the other."[25] Now, we know, of course, that Warhol had essentially stopped editing three years earlier, after *Sleep*; and that film, together with *Empire*, *Henry Geldzahler*, and many others both before and after *The Chelsea Girls*, makes it obvious that Warhol didn't worry about his movies being overly long or boring. More important, *The Chelsea Girls* was not Warhol's first experiment with double-screen projection. The earlier *Outer and Inner Space* and

Lupe (the latter shown also as three reels projected alongside one another) both testify to Warhol's grasp of the complex effects that might result from side-by-side projection. Of the two, *Outer and Inner Space* seems the more designed, with its virtually mathematical video/film, medium-shot/close-up structure, whereas *Lupe* is a study in mostly happenstance contrasts from screen to screen between stasis and movement, sound and silence, vertical and horizontal panning, camaraderie and loneliness, little-girl pink and blue peignoirs. The abrupt, unmotivated cut to Edie Sedgwick's head in the toilet bowl—shot from different angles—at the end of each of *Lupe*'s reels shows just how calculated Warhol's side-by-side juxtapositions could be (hardly surprising from the master of serial composition in painting).

Calculations are mostly abandoned in *The Chelsea Girls* in favor of an interplay between the real time of performance (which for Warhol is also *reel* time—the thirty-three minutes of the 1,200-foot film magazine of the Auricon camera) and sheer contingency—the fractional differences of timing in the side-by-side reels as they are shown by the projectionist at each screening.[26] Still, within this chance structure Warhol asserted control—or perhaps I should say *re*asserted control, since his stipulations were fixed only when *The Chelsea Girls* went uptown. The opening juxtaposition of the low-contrast, "white" "Nico in Kitchen" reel with the high-contrast, "black" "Father Ondine and Ingrid" one, together with the fact that the closing juxtaposition returns us to the central characters of these opening episodes while varying the contrast to one of color next to black-and-white, suggests that randomness has its limits in Warhol's aesthetic.[27] Warhol's controlling hand is most obvious where it *seems* most exceptional, in the event-driven (and old-fashioned-sounding) instruction for reel seven: "Sound until female impersonator exits." All other projection/sound instructions accompanying the reels for *The Chelsea Girls* are strictly time-based—for example, for reel nine, "Eric Says All": "All sound after end of sound on reel #8." That, by the way, is surely an event-driven (or performance-driven) decision too: Eric Emerson's monologue is one of *The Chelsea Girls*' tour-de-force performances. Ondine's performance as the Pope of Greenwich Village in reel eleven is, famously, another, and Warhol instructed, "All sound." So, too, Mary Waranov's dominatrix Hanoi Hannah ("All sound"), Brigid Berlin "holding court" ("Begin with sound as soon as threaded"), and Marie Menkin's shrewish mother ("Sound"). And so, too, Mario Montez's renditions of "'S Wonderful" and "I Got Sun in the Morning" and Ed Hood's competitive fit in response both to Mario's captivating performance and to Patrick Fleming's apparent captivation by it. Ed appears to be reprising his role in *My Hustler* in the two sequences of the boys—and girls—on the bed, frantically fending off everyone's attempts to get their hands on Patrick. Not that Mario has any such designs: "I'm just a housewife, that's all," he insists. It's one of the campiest moments of *The Chelsea Girls*. You can see both why Regelson would interpret it as a jab at suburban mores and why Warhol kept it audible.

But I repeat: Sound in *The Chelsea Girls* is a lure. Our attention is drawn to it; our eyes tend inexorably to follow our ears. And it does, certainly, have its rewards, for example Eric's seductive, narcissistic, "I'm the top," conquest-queen soliloquy. But don't get hooked on Eric. If you do, you're in for trouble. Listen to his chilling, vivid image of coupling as the total dissolution of two into one: "I wish I was a piece of sweat or a drop of sweat being licked by someone. Dripping down their neck and having a tongue sweep along and sweep me up and taken into the body—completely in. To go that far in someone's body, that'd mean you were all them, or they were all you, whoever was the controller. I guess they'd be me because I'm usually the controller. I'm on the top. Nice place to be."[28]

Cocky guy, Eric. Some people think he's a little funny, like "funny funny," as he says. But, as he tells it, he just grooves on having sex with a gentleman. He likes being a top. He likes playing with you like a top (like a toy he can spin).

> You'll enjoy me and I'll enjoy you. We'll play. We'll sing songs together. We'll dance. I'll dance for you. I'll sing for you, and then one day you'll come too close. You'll want me but you won't be able to have me. I say *you* but I mean whoever's next. I've enjoyed many, and many have enjoyed me. I know how to make people enjoy me. I know how to make people happy. I just do what they want me to do.... I can be happy with them for a while but then it gets to be too much and I just have to up and leave completely. For a while they feel bad, usually for a long while they feel *real* bad. They shake their heads and try to forget about me, but I'm not that easy to forget about. I'm the kind of person that lingers in someone's mind. Once they've had me it's hard to do without.

Brian O'Doherty called Eric's soliloquy "probably the closest Warhol will ever come to a testament—his attitudes to pleasure, the world, his handling of the world's attitudes to him." What an odd notion! Warhol grooving on his own body? Warhol a top? No. I think Warhol would more likely see Eric's soliloquy as a cautionary tale and Eric himself as a dangerous lure, a lure leading to the kind of problems for which *The Chelsea Girls* might provide comfort. Better to enjoy Eric the way he would enjoy you: as one of many. Look at the other screen—Eric is there too, among the others. Ingrid, Pepper, International Velvet, Ronnie Cutrone, Silver George. Look at both screens—the play of colored lights, blue on this side, red on that, spotlit here, backlit there; close-ups of Eric on both, a small one on the left mashed up against the edge, a large one on the right, too large for the frame; a close-up of Ingrid beside the one of Eric, both about the same size, for the moment. A moment later and there will be another story, then another. "Another story ... a new experience," as Yvonne Rainer recognized. Two screens side by side, but not *fitting* together. Rather, as Warhol said in a different context, "somehow misfitting together."[29] Misfitting together—that sounds comforting.

MOST BEAUTIFUL

ANDY WARHOL LIKED DANCE.

He made a painting in 1948 with that as a title: *I Like Dance.* I don't know whether or not his liking dance extended to liking *to* dance, although he did belong to the modern-dance club during his college days at the Carnegie Institute of Technology, and his dance-diagram paintings suggest that maybe he tried at one time to learn ballroom technique. He was famous for hanging out in discos—from Arthur and Studio 54 to Area and the Palladium—and for a while he had his own club at the Dom in the East Village; and he referred to his suite of shadow paintings from 1978 as disco décor. Still, I don't recall ever seeing a photograph of him dancing. He was a balletomane in his "swish" days in the 1950s, and this interest in theatrical dance extended well into the pop era. Not only was Warhol a fan of Yvonne Rainer and other Judson dancers, but he also continued to frequent New York City Ballet. He and Edie Sedgwick made a spectacular appearance at the gala opening of George Balanchine's *Don Quixote* at City Ballet in 1965. According to the society pages of *Time* magazine, Edie climbed to the fourth-ring gallery of the New York State Theater promenade during intermission to dance the twist while Andy and his entourage offered a champagne toast from the main floor below.[1] I imagine Warhol was canny enough to know that this little stunt could have been seen as a send-up of Balanchine—who took the role of the Don himself—offering the tribute of his new ballet to his Dulcinea, Suzanne Farrell.

Dance also plays a significant role in Warhol's work. Warhol agreed to have Merce Cunningham use the *Silver Clouds* as the set for *RainForest* in 1968. Five years earlier, using photographs from Cunningham's 1958 *Antic Meet*, Warhol had made several silk-screen portraits of Cunningham, and in 1979 he reused one of the *Antic Meet* photographs for a screen-print poster for Cunningham's company. The 1963 Cunningham silkscreen painting is one of many portraits by Warhol of dancers, starting with a blotted line drawing of Doris Humphrey made for the cover of *Dance Magazine* in 1953 and including the line drawings of John Butler that comprised his one-man show in 1954 at the Loft Gallery. He also made photobooth photos of New York City Ballet principal Edward Villella in 1963 and a number of 1970s silkscreen portraits of Martha Graham and Rudolf Nureyev. But Warhol's preferred medium for depicting dancers was film. There are *Screen Tests* of Judson choreographers Lucinda Childs (including one focused on her shoulder), Kenneth King, and Freddy Herko. *Haircut No. 1* features Herko along with fellow choreographer and dancer James Waring and Judson lighting designer Billy Linich (later Billy Name). There are films of Herko doing his roller-skate dance and Jill Johnston dancing at the Factory. In *Lonesome Cowboys*, Eric Emerson demonstrates his ballet moves to Joe Dallasandro; John Palmer and Ivy Nicholson frug for a few moments in their tiny kitchen in *John and Ivy*; and *Vinyl* ends with a frugging party among many of the performers, including Gerard Malanga and Edie Sedgwick. Edie dancing the frug at the Factory is, in fact, one of the iconic images of her. Gerard is famous not only for his popper-fueled frugging in *Vinyl* but even more for his whip dance, often done with Mary Woronov, including in the short portrait film *Salvador Dalí*. Mario Montez sings and dances his way from one part of the furniture loft to another for the first "scene change" in *Hedy*, and he does a wicked Latin dance in *Camp* as Warhol's camera zooms in and out.[2] The dance number comes after Mario has sung a one-verse version of "I Wish I Could Shimmy like My Sister Kate" (for some reason Gerard introduces Mario in *Camp* as Inez Martinez). *Camp* has another, remarkably touching dance number in which Baby Jane Holzer dances a duet with Paul Swan. Swan's is the first in *Camp*'s series of performed routines. He dances his most famous dance, his 1915 tribute to World War I soldiers, *To Heroes Slain*, reprises it, and then Jane helps him up to his feet (Swan is eighty-two years old at the time, and his dance ends with him feigning death). Jane apparently gives Paul a kiss, off camera. He responds by suggesting that they do an impromptu version together. "You do whatever I do," he proposes, and she, clearly used to being partnered on the dance floor, gamely follows right along.

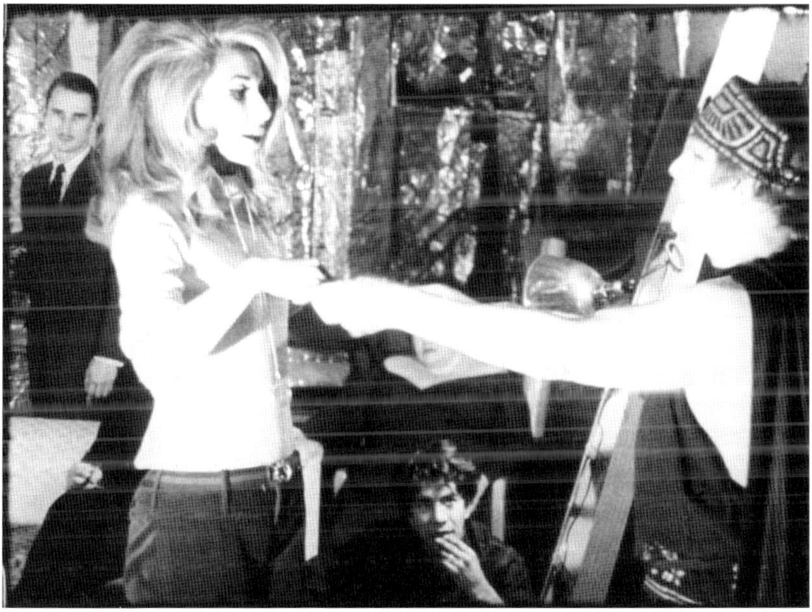

Andy Warhol, *Camp*, 1965. 16mm film, b/w, sound, 66 minutes. Film still courtesy of The Andy Warhol Museum.

Jack Smith shares the stage with Swan in *Camp*. They seem an unlikely pair—but maybe not. After a series of performances of varying degrees of fun (the fun of Donyale Luna's cat walk wearing a fur coat and matching fur-trimmed dress is halted too soon by the film running out, whereas Mar-Mar Donyle's shenanigans early on are so tedious that you think they might never end, and indeed after a while Jack and Tally Brown begin to demonstrate their annoyance by lying next to each other on the couch and mooning for the camera, thus assuring us that we're not the only ones who are put off). Tally's act is to play temporary MC in order to introduce Jack. But first she weighs in on the question of camp, the ostensible subject of the film: "I don't happen to believe in the existence of camp," she says. "So, I'm going to do things for you that are absolutely serious, as I believe indeed everyone before me has done. I don't think anybody's camping. I think we're all doing ourselves." (This is clearly nonsense, since she's just made perfectly clear that she didn't find Mar-Mar's routine serious; then again, it isn't really camp either.) "Here," she goes on, "are a few aspects of myself." She proceeds to do an imitation of Yma Sumac, which would seem to qualify as camp if anything in the film does. Then comes her introduction: "It's my pleasure to introduce a very talented man that I've had the pleasure of working with very often. He always does something absolutely sensational. I never know what it'll be ... Do you want to do that tune, baby? Ladies and gentlemen, the one and only, the inimitable ... Jack Smith!" Jack doesn't move from where he's been standing at the back of the room. Tally has to go get him and drag him to the mike. She then begins to sing: "A cigarette that bears a lipstick's traces / A shrunken head in unexpected places." Smith does nothing at all for a moment, but eventually reaches into his pocket and pulls out a shrunken head, puts it noisily on the microphone, and begins to dance as the Ramsey Lewis trio recording of "The 'In' Crowd" kicks in again—it's been played off and on throughout the film's second reel, which began with Gerard reading his poem "Camp." The poem begins:

> Blown the truck drivers
> Under the west side elevated highway
> After 2:00 am in the rain
> Behind staircases in tenement buildings
>
> Chased out of Tompkins Square Park
> Out from the enclosed courtyard
> Beside the men's room
> By a plainclothesman

And the grass hillside
Where I was buggered in Riverdale by a Cornell student
While the last commuter train of the New York Central passed by[3]

Camp, for Gerard, seems to be just another excuse for braggadocio.

After his shrunken-head gag, Jack stands silent at the microphone. Finally he asks, tentatively, "Should I open the closet now, Andy? Should I open the closet? Should I open the closet?" A very long silence, and finally someone yells, "Cut." "Why cut?" Jack asks. "Shall we open the closet?" He puts on his dark glasses. "Let's open the closet." Silence. "Let's open the closet. Can we?" Finally it seems to be agreed that they'll open the closet, and the entire crew moves to where the closet stands—dances over, really, to the strains of "The 'In' Crowd," which kicks in again. The closet turns out to be a big art deco cabinet with Lucite dowels on the doors. You can clearly see a Batman comic inside.[4] Jack stands next to it and plays at the mystery of opening it for nearly ten minutes. He looks alternately pained, confused, worried, exasperated, sardonic, mischievous. He puts on and takes off his sunglasses. He reaches through the dowels and grabs a key. He holds it up, displays it in close-up, aims it like a tiny gun. He moves the mike, directs the lighting. Feeling the dowels on the door, he intones, "Translucite plastic." He opens the closet, throws the key inside—demented laughter comes from off camera. He directs the camera to be brought forward. He reaches in, maybe touches the Batman comic, but we don't know: The close-up is on his face. He shuts the door, and "The 'In' Crowd" starts up again—appropriately enough, since this whole drama of Batman in the closet is a Factory in-joke. In 1964 Warhol shot what seemed destined to be *the* great epic underground film, *Batman Dracula*, whose eponymous character was played by Smith. It might also have been Smith's greatest film performance, but sadly we may never know, because Warhol left the film in the can, unassembled and unedited. So Smith's scene at the closet in *Camp* is a manifestation of his seething fury at Warhol for not finishing the film.[5] Big drama follows Smith's reaching into the closet. Because the crew seems not to want to move the camera in toward the cabinet, Jack and Tosh Carillo decide to do things the hard way and move the cabinet toward the camera, but it's a heavy and unstable thing and nearly collapses on them. Straining to hold it in place and simultaneously caressing it, Jack stammers, "Art moderne … breakfront."

The improvised apodictic declaration is sheer genius. "Art moderne … breakfront": It's nothing more than what this heavy object he's struggling with—and what he's got the camera, the crew, the cast, and the spectators to focus all our attention on—it's nothing more than what, in fact, it is: an art moderne breakfront. We are at the opposite end of the performance spectrum, it seems, from Swan's *To Heroes Slain*, a mimed dance elegy performed by a man at the nadir of his powers.

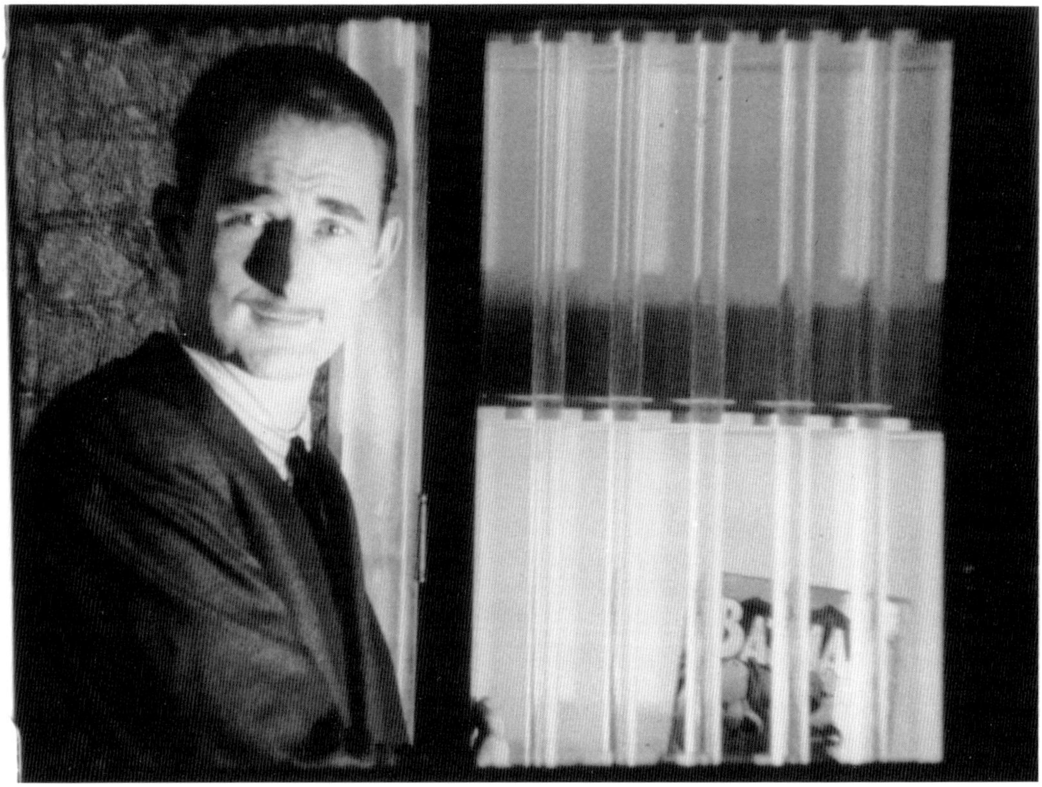

Andy Warhol, *Camp*, 1965. 16mm film, b/w, sound, 66 minutes. Film still courtesy of The Andy Warhol Museum.

In 1914, just before he made *To Heroes Slain*, Paul Swan was billed on theater marquees as "The Most Beautiful Man in the World" and proclaimed in the *New York Evening Journal* "The Prettiest Male in Captivity."[6] His beauty was so renowned that it provided the laugh line of a Fred and Adele Astaire routine, when Adele would scold Fred, "Don't think *you* look like Paul Swan," a line Ira Gershwin would later use in a song for the musical *Funny Face*. We have a good idea what Swan looked like and how he danced, since there is an extant film of him from 1916 called *Diana the Huntress*.[7] Swan was in his early thirties at the time. He was what is known as an aesthetic dancer, like Isadora Duncan, Ruth St. Denis, and Ted Shawn. Largely untrained but for some lessons from ballet dancers Mikhail Mordkin and Andreas Pavley, he seems to have made it up as he went along.[8] A farm boy from a strict Presbyterian family in Crab Orchard, Nebraska, Swan escaped and became worldly. He met Nazimova in New York in 1909 and painted her portrait (Swan was a painter, sculptor, and poet as well as a dancer), and he saw Nijinsky and Karsavina dance *Le Spectre de la Rose* in 1911; he worked in Hollywood, appearing in *The Ten Commandments* and *Ben Hur*. Reviews of Swan's dancing were ecstatic. *Theater Magazine*, 1913: "Swan: An American Who Revives the Greek Ideal": "He is the first of our countrymen brave and bold enough to champion the dance.... Although he is ... an artist, he dares to be dancer; and though he is a dancer, he dares to be a man. Such is his temerity, and when you consider that the world still suspects artists of being only half-men (the other half may be goblin, woman, divinity or devil), it is indeed temerity."[9] In Paris in the early 1920s Swan began giving nude, or almost-nude, dance recitals. One reviewer wrote: "Even if there were no music, no costumes, and no dances, and he should stand alone upon the stage, no doubt Paris audiences would gather to admire him, for a figure like his has not been seen in Europe since Apollo Belvedere's model went home to sit near the Gods."[10] A decade later, when Swan was well into middle age, the reviewers remained convinced: "He dances nude," one wrote, "a Greek bas relief animated by the immortal spirit. One would like to understand what is the chemistry which could create such perfection."[11] A final performance before fleeing Paris in the wake of war was met with the following by the critic of *Le Matin*: "His harmonious body is ever enhanced by the art of his ideal attitudes. Always searching new rhythmic figures, poetic and original expressions, this astounding artist was warmly applauded."[12]

Swan returned to New York in 1939, where he settled into the former Carnegie Hall studio of Charles Dana Gibson, of Gibson Girl and an-onion-instead-of-an-olive fame; for a while, Swan's roommate in Studio 90 was Anita Loos, author of *Gentlemen Prefer Blondes*. One of their fellow tenants was Agnes de Mille, who was in the process of making the dances for what would become the Broadway musical *Oklahoma!* The success of de Mille's *Rodeo* at American Ballet Theater in 1942—not to mention Martha Graham's *Appalachian Spring* in 1944 and George Balanchine's *The Four Temperaments*

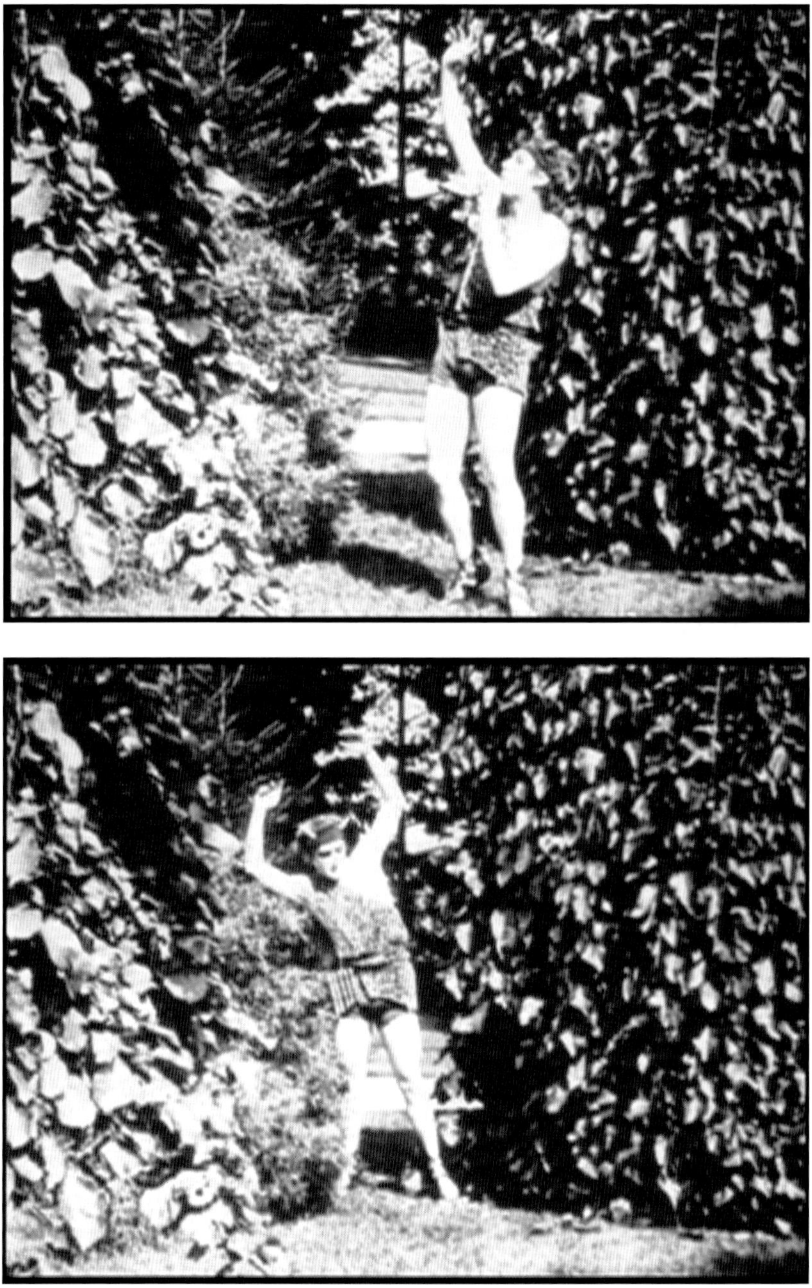

Charles Allen and Francis Trevelyan Miller,
Diana the Huntress, 1916.

in 1946—makes clear just how much the American taste in concert dance had changed since Swan's early successes in the 1910s. Nevertheless, in the mid-1940s Swan began giving the weekly dance recitals that would, two decades years later, become the subject of Warhol's 1965 film *Paul Swan*. In the 1950s, these recitals were frequented by Marcel Duchamp, Robert Matta, and Alexander Calder. The younger artist Robert Barnes, who often went with them, wrote of Swan's recitals: "God, if there was a Duchampian theater, it was Paul Swan.... Matta found Paul Swan, made Marcel go, and then he became a fan. And the best thing that he did was the Bacchanal of the Sahara Desert in which he danced naked, virtually; he had veils, very gay. All by himself, he would do the bacchanal ... loving his veils and ending up totally naked."[13]

Swan doesn't do *The Bacchanal of the Sahara Desert* in Warhol's film; he doesn't dance naked—or even virtually naked. But he *does* appear virtually naked a number of times during costume changes. In *Paul Swan*, Warhol's camera, stationary in the first of the film's two reels, is trained on a set that consists of a tapestry backdrop, a folding chair, and several spotlights. At the left side of this "stage" is a black folding screen, behind which Swan occasionally disappears to search out a new costume. When changing costumes, he moves back and forth between this off-stage space and the makeshift dancing area. His costumes are themselves sometimes skimpy, consisting of flimsy briefs and tunics, pinned on with safety pins. Often as not, he removes one costume and gets into the next on camera, thus appearing stark naked but for a g-string. "Change there?" he asks at one point. "Well, I've got a little something on, anyway." In the second reel, when Swan spends an inordinate amount of time behind the screen, an off-camera voice tells Swan, "They want you to fix yourself out in front of them, because they still have the movie camera going." Swan replies, "Oh, I don't care," then thrusts his naked butt out beyond the screen. This seems to me the most telling sequence of Warhol's film—not the butt thrust, although that's telling in its own way too, but the fact that in a sixty-six-minute film, Swan spends over half of it *not performing* his dances or poetry but changing costumes, and in this particular sequence in the second reel he spends over fifteen minutes off camera looking for the pair of sandals that he insists must be worn with the French peasant costume he's in the very drawn-out process of putting on. As Callie Angell was quick to notice, Swan's performance "recall[s] the equally disorganized, equally uncompromising performances of Jack Smith."[14]

Smith's performances were notoriously slow to get going, if indeed they ever did. It was hard to tell, because he spent endless time futzing with his costume, getting his slides in order, complaining that nothing was going right. A passage from Stefan Brecht's description in *Queer Theatre* of Smith's *Secret of Rented Island* captures the feel of his work:

> Smith kept getting the pages mixed up, losing his place, he was fighting the paper, asking the assistants for page 12 (was provided with it), showing the queen in the cart the right place,—in one sequence this latter gave various lines previously given, you were suddenly in the wrong place in the play, Smith pretending to be lost ("What's going on?!"). The performance, especially in the dramatic third act, under Smith's despairing, exasperated direction,—nobody is doing anything right!—keeps lapsing into work on the presentation.... Something wrong or missing: Smith disappears with nervously energetic steps to see to or fetch it.[15]

When I first saw *Paul Swan*, it was that fifteen minutes behind the screen that struck me as a truly Smith-like failure to get on with the show as the very substance of the performance. Although Swan constantly complains that the costume changes take too long, he goes right on dilly-dallying. Between the first two numbers, a recitation from Omar Khayyam's *Rubáiyát* (see plate 4) and a mime-dance that he announces as *The Elements: Earth, Water, Fire, and Air—the Movements Seen and Unseen in Nature*, Swan protests, "Oh, goddamn, I can't do this, this way. It takes too long." He finishes putting on his sandals. "It takes too long," he moans again. "It spoils it. I can't do it." But then he consoles himself: "I suppose you can cut all that out, can't you?" He seems, on the contrary, perfectly well aware that nothing is going to be cut out, so he keeps right on performing his costume changes, increasing their duration as he goes. After a rendition of *To Heroes Slain*, he takes a full ten minutes to get into his outfit for what he finally announces as "two Oriental numbers: *The Nightingale and the Rose* and *The Temple Bells Are Ringing*." "This takes too long," he complains again. "The audience has all gone home, waiting. I'm sure of that. You're a paid claque." He follows these disingenuous laments by methodically putting on his cheap jewelry. (See plate 5.) First, he tries putting his breastplate necklace over his headdress. It won't fit over it, so he has to take the headdress off and start over, necklace first, followed by the headdress. He puts on a sandal, then another necklace; this one presents no problem because it has a clasp. Next come upper-arm bracelets, then wrist bracelets, earrings, another necklace (which makes it over the headdress), more bracelets, five or six rings, the other sandal. He fiddles with his scarf, goes halfway behind the screen, and adjusts his briefs. "There," he declares.

The "Oriental" dance numbers, which together take just over four minutes, are followed by a fifteen-minute costume change, during which Swan spends most of the time behind the screen while the camera shows nothing but an empty set. Swan ignores the off-stage voice that cajoles, "Paul, come do it out here." He's determined to find his black sandals. Paul's piano accompanist, Richard, goes behind the screen to help. "They have to be black," Swan insists. "Where *are* they? I had them on this morning ... The pants are too tight. I have to ... Where would those slippers be?" Paul pokes his head out: "Doing the best I can, gentlemen," disappears again. (See plate 6.) "Where in the hell?

Goddamn it! They ought to be around again because I was wearing them all morning." "Turn the camera off," he mutters. "Where *would* they be? The slippers have to be right here."

The off-stage voice becomes more insistent: "Paul, don't wear the slippers."

"See if you can pin that. That's what I didn't want to do out there. No, no, you know those black slippers. I wear them all the time." Swan emerges for a split second to fetch the red cape from the stage floor. "Excuse me, won't you," he says and ducks back behind the curtain. "I think that's the queerest damn thing there ever was. Couldn't be up there." Finally he appears, dressed. "There," he says, but that's not the end of it: "I wonder where those black damn things could be."

"Paul, why don't you just wear what you have ..."

"These shoes won't do—got bells on them ... Where the hell is that ... ?"

"Richard, tell him those shoes are okay."

"They were right here this morning."

"Paul, maybe you can just improvise with the shoes that you have there for the time being, or the black socks."

"They have to be here. Isn't that very odd?"

Swan seems to be only partially reconciled to performing in the wrong footwear. "If any of you boys put those shoes in your pocket, I'll have you arrested. They aren't here. So there: end up in a great fight." He smiles impishly and announces, "*Musical Lines on the Canvas of Space*. This is the first one."

Swan's protracted preparing-to-perform-as-performance is something that Swan shares not only with Smith but also with Mario Montez in his work with Warhol. Think, for example, of the beginning of *Screen Test No. 2*, where Mario fiddles for the longest time tying a scarf into his wig, trying to get the knot to fall in a becoming way. Or *Hedy*, where Mario (as Hedy Lamarr) postpones going to trial with the delaying tactic of a long, drawn-out costume change (meant also to be a seduction and distraction of the store detective played by Mary Woronov). Or *More Milk Yvette*, where much of the film time is taken up with Mario (as Lana Turner) changing from ensemble to ensemble. Dressing (and undressing) on camera, the on-camera toilette, is a constant feature of Warhol's films: Edie Sedgwick doing her makeup in *Poor Little Rich Girl* and *Lupe*; Paul America and Joe Campbell primping before the bathroom mirror for the entire second reel of *My Hustler*; Joe Spencer trying on bathing trunks and Ingrid Superstar taking off her blouse in *Bike Boy*; the entire cast of *Horse* playing strip poker; Eric Emerson stripping in *The Chelsea Girls*. I think we might even include the final reel of *Blow Job*, in which, if you pay close attention to his facial expressions and upper-body language, you can figure out that DeVerne Bookwalter is zipping up his pants and buckling his belt.

When Tally Brown says in *Camp*, "We're all just doing ourselves," she alludes to what had become by late 1964 the cinéma vérité quality of Warhol's films—even those with scripted lines written by Ronald Tavel. The onstage or on-camera costume change can stand as a perfect figure for the blurred line between performing a character and performing oneself, between being, say, Mario Montez and being Mario Montez being Lana Turner, or between being Paul Swan and being Paul Swan being Paul Swan. *Camp* stages this phenomenon by having each participant "perform" in turn to the assembled group, acting as audience, as well as to the camera: Paul dances *To Heroes Slain*, Jodie Babs sings "Let Me Entertain You," Gerard recites a poem called "Camp," and so forth. Warhol wrote of this approach to performance in his reflections on *The Chelsea Girls* in *Popism*: "Everybody went right on doing what they'd always done—being themselves (or doing one of their routines, which was usually the same thing) in front of the camera."[16] There is a slight distinction in *Camp* between each performance *as performance* and the ongoing performance of the entire scene of performance in front of Warhol's camera, such as whether or not the performer stands, in his or her turn, before the microphone. The distinction between the performer as "doing" him- or herself and the performer as performing his or her routine is then more thoroughly confounded in Jack's routine with the closet. Jack does Jack, and Jack also does a number with a shrunken head that he's clearly worked out in advance with Tally, and Jack needles Andy about the abandoned *Batman Dracula* footage, and Jack directs the crew to get the lighting and camera distance the way he wants it, and Jack—being and doing Jack—improvises lines in his inimitable fashion.

Paul is less comfortable with improvising lines. He's used to a long career of recitation. Many of his dances are recitations accompanied by mimed or otherwise symbolic gestures. Indeed, most of Paul's dancing seems to consist of "showing" in gestural movements the scenario of a work. In the second, fire section of *The Elements*, as he performs it in *Paul Swan*, for example, he waves his hands in flamelike motions, then puts his head near the ground and blows, as if to ignite embers. He gradually stands up, and his body and hands swirl together. He flames. He is—I'll risk making the comparison to Smith obvious—a flaming creature. In *To Heroes Slain*, he marches onto the stage, shouldering his sword, then mimes leading his troops forward, alternating with thrusting and parrying the sword. He lays down the sword and bows over it in grief; he gets up, points at the sword (now standing for a dead soldier), and gestures as if beseeching "Why, oh why?" A few hand movements to suggest covering the buried body with dirt complete the ritual. He stands and mournfully moves off the stage, only to quickly return, retrieve the sword, and bear it above his head as he retreats a final time.

The second of *Paul Swan*'s two reels starts with Paul dancing his "Oriental numbers," and Warhol shifts from a completely stationary to a highly mobile camera and from medium shot to tight close-ups—on Paul's face and details of his costume. The film is color (together with *Lupe*, it's one of the first of Warhol's films shot with the Auricon camera to be in color), so we see very clearly Paul's aging pink flesh and his smeared-on black shoe-polish eye makeup. Is Warhol making fun of this old man? Is Paul Swan camp to Warhol? Angell answers both questions:

> Warhol's interest in Paul Swan seems to have been based on the observation that, in his unswerving dedication to his increasingly anachronistic art form, Swan had become the living embodiment of camp, which had been defined by Susan Sontag: "In naïve, or pure Camp, the essential element is seriousness, a seriousness that fails. Of course, not all seriousness that fails can be redeemed as Camp. Only that which has the proper mixture of the exaggerated, the fantastic, the passionate, and the naïve."[17]

And: "Warhol's film *Paul Swan*, while often hilarious, does not really make fun of its subject: instead, the seriousness with which Swan restages his antique performances ... becomes oddly impressive after a while." (It is here that Angell goes on to connect Swan to Smith.) A comparison of *Paul Swan* with two other films is my speculative way of addressing these questions further.

Warhol cast very few old people in his films. The middle-aged Marie Menken appeared in *The Life of Juanita Castro* and *The Chelsea Girls*. But otherwise, apart from a few *Screen Test* subjects—Salvador Dalí, Edwin Denby, and Marcel Duchamp were old in the mid-1960s; Charles Henri Ford, Ruth Ford, Willard Maas, Menken, Henry Rago, and Zackary Scott were middle-aged—there is only *Mrs. Warhol*, a film made the year following *Paul Swan* and one in some ways very much like it. *Mrs. Warhol* is also a two-reel portrait film shot in color.[18] (See plate 7.) And the subject of the film, Warhol's mother, also moves from performing herself to performing her role, that of an aging movie star apparently based on an amalgamation of Gloria Swanson's character in *Sunset Boulevard* and Hedy Lamarr's in *White Cargo*. Her current-in-a-long-line of husbands is played by Warhol's then boyfriend Richard Rheem, and it is more from Richard's dialogue than Julia Warhola's that we can figure this out: "When were you a Max Sennett baby?" he asks, and "For what movie did you win the Academy Award?" or "Are you going to kill me like all the rest?" "How many of them were there, fifteen?" Julia's dialogue suggests little familiarity with Hollywood: "You're just keeping me for cook," she mock-complains, or "I'm going to take a broom on you." The real story of the film is the bond between these two performers, whose affectionately teasing relationship makes domesticity look almost appealing. "You're sweet," Richard tells Julia, and she replies, "You're sweet yourself." They look into each other's eyes. Like Paul Swan, Julia Warhola is a bit daffy in her old age, but she also seems extraordinarily self-aware and able to laugh at herself. The steady gaze of Warhol's camera lets self-awareness seep into these old people's self-portrayals—I'd almost like to say, contradictorily, in spite of themselves—*self-aware in spite of themselves*. Perhaps, then, cinéma vérité is a designation that isn't entirely wrong as applied to Warhol's filmmaking. (When Jonas Mekas applied it to Warhol, he preferred the term "direct cinema.")[19]

Finally, I want to suggest the possibility of self-styled cinéma vérité *as unintentional camp* in another film portrait of a dancer made just a few years after *Paul Swan*.[20] The film, *Man Who Dances*, was made by Drew Associates, the company founded by Robert Drew to make the documentary *Primary*, about the 1960 primary election campaign of John F. Kennedy against Hubert Humphrey in Wisconsin. *Primary*, which Drew claimed was the first film made with sync-sound camera that moved freely among the characters of a breaking story, was made with a team that included D. A. Pennebaker, Richard Leacock, and Albert Maysles.[21] In 1968, Drew Associates made *Man Who Dances* for NBC television's Bell Telephone Hour. As the film's title and subtitle appear on the screen, a voice-over narrator speaks them—"Man who dances, Edward Villella"—and then continues over footage of Villella rehearsing: "He was the welterweight boxing champion of the New York Maritime Academy. Now he's a star of the new generation of male dancers that is exciting the world of ballet with breathtaking speed, power, and manly art." The particular veritas that this vérité work intended to reveal is that a dancer can indeed be a man. And what better man than Villella, who had appeared ten years earlier in another NBC television special, this one directed by Gene Kelly, called *Dancing Is a Man's Game*. Kelly put Villella in the company of Mickey Mantle, Sugar Ray Robinson, and Johnny Unitas to draw parallels between the prowess and grace of dancers and that of athletes. *Man Who Dances* includes a heartwarming sequence in which Villella gives a lecture-demonstration on ballet at Canarsie High School, located in a working-class district of Brooklyn whose population shifted over the years from Jewish and Italian to primarily African-American and Latino.[22] Convincing these tough high school boys that dancing can be a man's game wouldn't be easy, but Villella had the credentials to do it: He went to Canarsie High himself, where he lettered in baseball, and, of course, he was a boxing champ. To clarify the difference in the games of sports and ballet, he begins by explaining that when an outfielder catches a fly ball, he runs the best way he can and jumps the best way he can to make the catch. Catching the ball makes the moves beautiful. But in dancing, the interest is in the form and the line that the body displays when it moves. "I can't just stick my hand out, like that," he says as he thrusts his arm straight out. "There has to be a form. There has to be a line. How am I going to do it? Well, I can't hold it like that. That's too rigid. I can't hold it like that"—he makes an exaggerated limp-wrist gesture—"that's a little, uh, overly poetic. I take a line form the top of my head, right down the side, the shoulder, the elbow, straight to the tips. And this is how I would stand onstage in this particular position." He assumes his port de bras in second position.

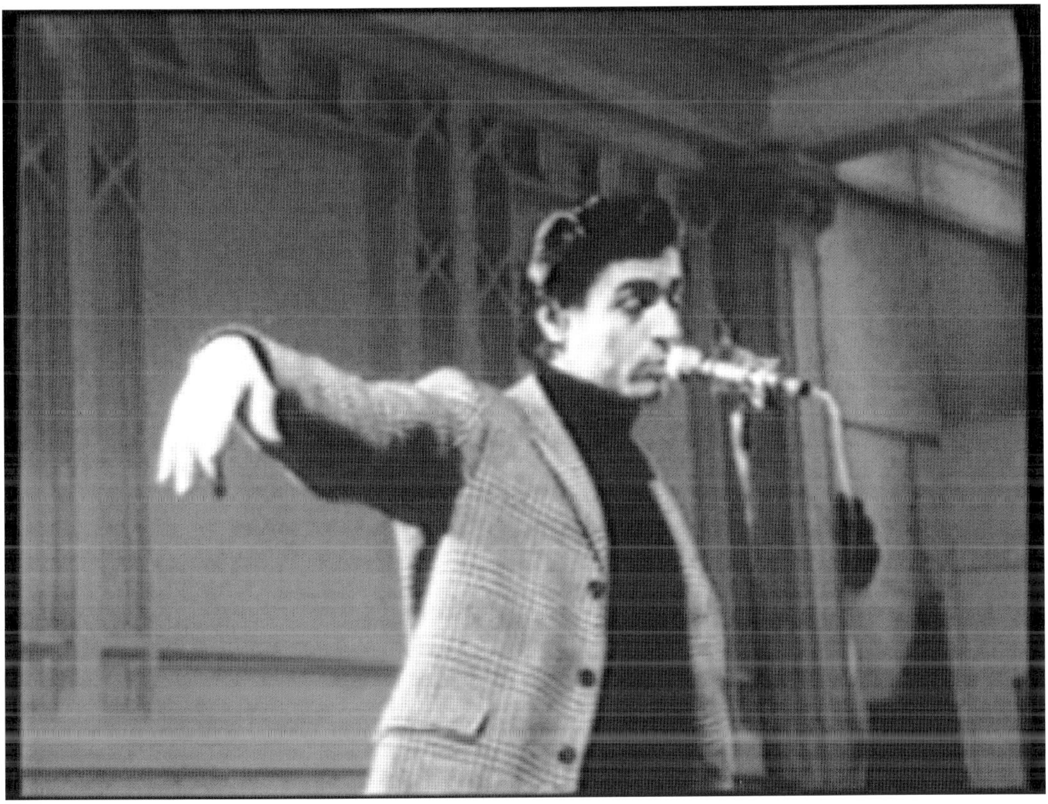

Robert Drew, Drew Associates for the Bell Telephone Hour, *Man Who Dances: Edward Villella*, 1968.

This must have been a fairly standard lecture-demonstration shtick for Villella, because several years earlier he seems to have performed it for Warhol in a photobooth, substituting for the usual face shot a series of arm positions for three out of the four exposures on each strip. The limp wrist isn't a prominent pose, but it's one of the ones he plays with. Villella seems an unlikely subject for Warhol's photobooth procedure; after all, Warhol had to persuade his sitters to meet him for the shooting session in Times Square, where the photobooth he used was located. But Villella was clearly game to be part of *Harper's Bazaar*'s "New Faces, New Forces, New Names in the Arts" feature, for which an editor at the magazine had commissioned Warhol to take the photographs: Twenty-two strips of photobooth photos of Villella were found in Time Capsule Twenty-One at the Andy Warhol Museum in Pittsburgh.[23]

Man Who Dances is a narrative about a particular weekend during which Villella had to dance a number of punishingly difficult roles. In the matinee performance of *Raymonda Variations*, he had fallen onstage after his muscles cramped, so the question is whether he can do the evening performance of *Rubies*, a ballet Balanchine made for him to display his special qualities as an all-American tough guy from Queens. But the real drama isn't about whether Villella will get through *Rubies*; it's about how a dancer can be made to look like a man. How this may be accomplished becomes obvious early on in a scene shot in Villella's dressing room after his fall in *Raymonda*, where we see the dancer massaging his sore body while explaining the problem with his muscles: "Muscles don't know anything about emotion or the mind or how tired your being is," he says. "All they know is the amount of lactic acid in the muscles, which slows them down, makes the cramps, and doesn't let the blood get out. That's all muscles know." Explaining how muscles work, displaying them, showing how ballet taxes them—this is how to make a dancer masculine. It can't be done when the muscles are simply doing their job, when the dancer is onstage, dancing. It is done when he's offstage, or behind the curtain, where the muscles, too full of lactic acid, preventing the blood from replenishing them, are aching, tightening, cramping. In *Man Who Dances*, onstage and offstage are strictly separate spaces. Only offstage can a man show the reality of his muscles, and that reality is not pretty. In the performance of *Rubies* around which the narrative of *Man Who Dances* revolves, every time Villella comes offstage, he collapses, out of breath and in excruciating pain. Somehow, of course, he manages to pull himself together for the next entrance and, in the end, to get through the ballet. But even as he finishes *Rubies* in triumph, he collapses in pain as soon as the curtain comes down. He's still a real man, with real muscles.[24]

In *Man Who Dances*, the terrible strain on Villella's muscles finds its perfect counterpart in the strain exerted by Drew Associates to represent the masculinity of a man who dances. Clearly Warhol didn't think "the most beautiful man in the world" required so much effort—remember, Swan, too, had the temerity to be a man who dances. Nor

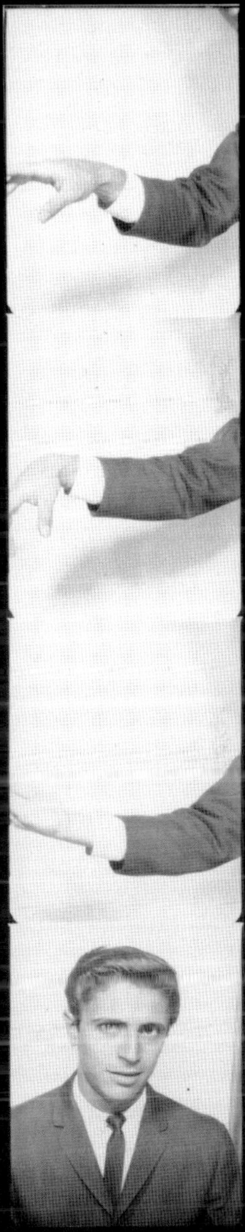

Andy Warhol, *Edward Villella*, 1963. Photobooth photograph. Collection of the Andy Warhol Museum, Pittsburgh, PA.

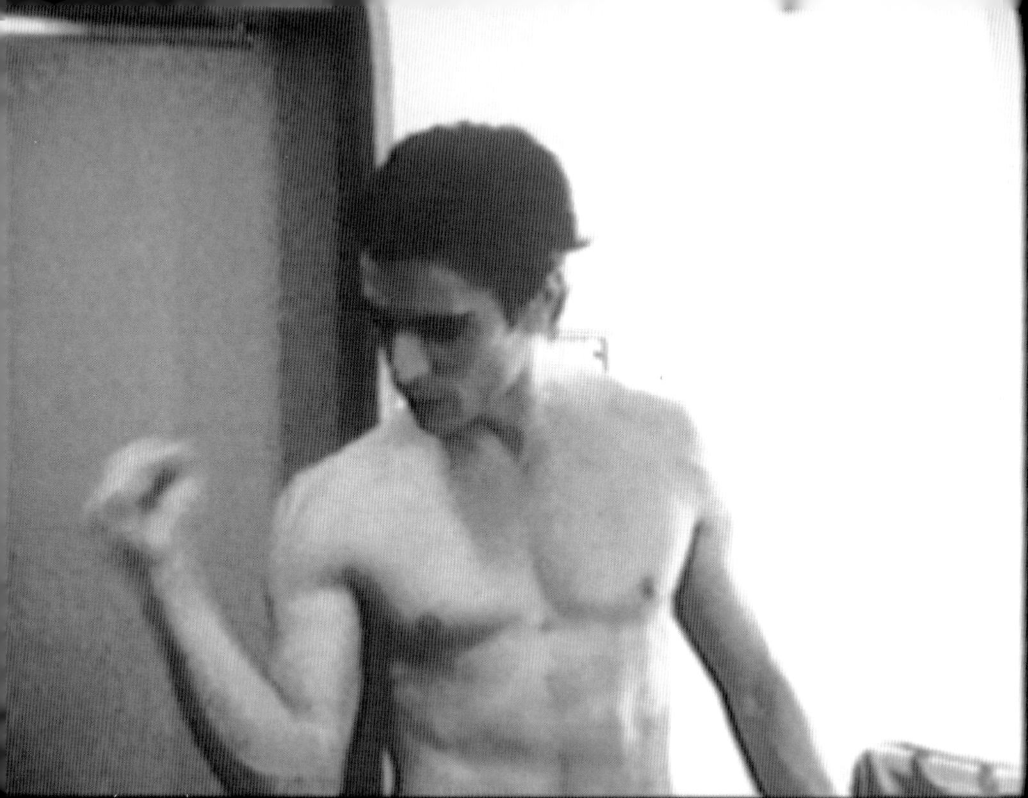

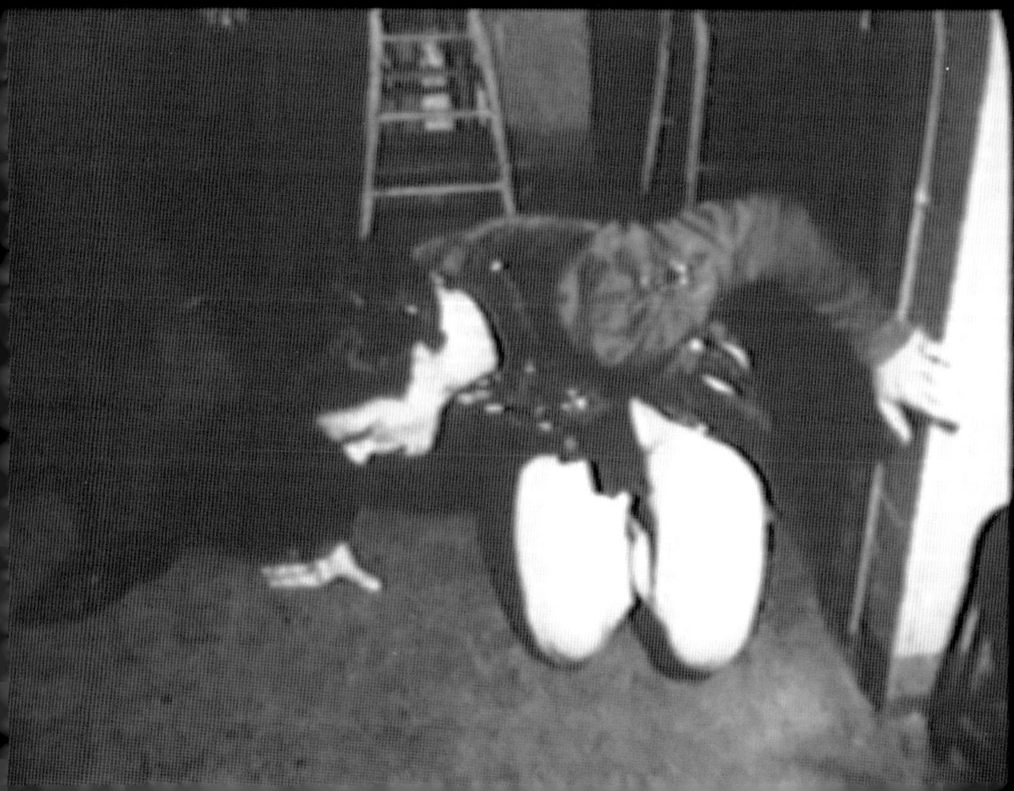

did Warhol feel the need to draw such a distinction between onstage and off. Swan himself took a philosophical view of dancing. A 1944 *Dance Magazine* piece on him reports: "With Swan, dancing is a way of life. He advises people to go home after the day's work, take off their heavy drab clothing, get into something light and colorful, turn on the radio and dance."[25]

Robert Drew, Drew Associates for the Bell Telephone Hour, *Man Who Dances: Edward Villella*, 1968.

ADDENDUM: BORING CAMP

Andy Warhol made seven *Screen Tests* of Susan Sontag, one of which he noted "might be okay" for inclusion in his prospective compilation *The Thirteen Most Beautiful Women.*[1] Callie Angell writes of this particular one: "She seems tired and perhaps a little bored, but gives the camera an entirely serious look, as if it were her equal."[2] In another of them, Sontag camps it up, alternating between the motionless look Warhol generally asked for and a Cheshire-cat grin, produced, it appears, by saying "cheese" over and over again. "The relation between boredom and camp taste cannot be overestimated," Sontag wrote in her famous essay "Notes on 'Camp.'"[3] Warhol's name doesn't appear in the essay (although pop art does), and Sontag would soon come to disdain both camp—"I don't like it very much anymore. It's a big bore: hearing about it all the time"[4]—and Warhol's aesthetic, which, she claimed in *On Photography*, "defines itself between the twin poles of boringness and freakishness."[5] In her comparison of Diane Arbus with Warhol, Sontag returned to her earlier contrast of Jews and (gentile?) homosexuals in "Notes on 'Camp'"—"The two pioneering forces of modern sensibility are Jewish moral seriousness and homosexual aestheticism and irony":

> Arbus had neither Warhol's narcissism and genius for publicity nor the self-protective blandness with which he insulates himself from the freaky nor his sentimentality.... To someone raised a Catholic, like Warhol (and virtually everyone in his gang), a fascination with evil comes much more genuinely than it does to someone from a Jewish background. Compared with Warhol, Arbus seems strikingly vulnerable, innocent—and certainly more pessimistic. Her Dantesque vision of the city (and the suburbs) has no reserves of irony. Although much of Arbus's material is the same as that depicted in, say, Warhol's *Chelsea Girls* (1966), her photographs never play with horror, milking it for laughs; they offer no opening to mockery, and no possibility of finding freaks endearing, as do the films of Warhol and Paul Morrissey.[6]

Sontag first expressed her disaffection with camp in response to a *New York Times* Sunday magazine piece by Thomas Meehan, "Not Good Taste, Not Bad Taste—It's 'Camp.'"[7] Like Sontag, Meehan defined camp by citing examples of it; his list includes, together with Busby Berkeley's *Gold Diggers of 1933* and Troy Donahue in *Parrish*, "Andy Warhol's eight-hour-long film, 'Sleep.'" It's hard to imagine what definition of camp Meehan thought his readers might deduce from this list. "So bad, it's good," I suppose, but does this also apply to such other things that are "generally agreed to be Pure Camp" as "Monopoly games (in Italian)" and stereoscopes? Sontag's lists are just as hard to fathom, including as they do Caravaggio and "much of Mozart," Tiffany lamps and the Brown Derby restaurant, *Swan Lake* and *The Maltese Falcon*, Henry James and Antonio Gaudí. Sontag's boredom with camp, sparked by Meehan's article listing the notoriously boring *Sleep* (boring especially, it seems, to those who haven't seen it, who routinely add three hours to its length), reminds me of a memorable Eve

Arden line from her 1950s television show *Our Miss Brooks*. On a blind date that's going nowhere, the sardonic Miss Brooks's male companion concedes that the two of them are incompatible. "Oh, I think we're made for each other," Arden replies, "You're boring and I'm bored."

Just what is the relation between boredom and camp taste? Sontag explains that camp wards off "the threat of boredom." "Camp taste is by its nature possible only in affluent societies, in societies or circles capable of experiencing the psychopathology of affluence." It is at this point in "Notes on 'Camp'" that she introduces the subject of a "self-elected class, mainly homosexuals, who constitute themselves as aristocrats of taste,"[8] thus suggesting that affluence brings with it not only the threat of boredom but also the threat of homosexuality, a not unusual homophobic correlation of the era of Sontag's essay (although Sontag had reason to know better).

Sontag's other famous "queer" essay dating from 1964 and reprinted in *Against Interpretation* is "Jack Smith's *Flaming Creatures*." It, too, discusses pop art and camp; Smith's film is taken to be exemplary of both. I juxtapose two lengthy passages that might help answer the question, What is Warhol's relation to camp? First:

> *Flaming Creatures* is a lovely specimen of what currently, in one genre, goes by the flippant name of "pop art." Smith's film has the sloppiness, the arbitrariness, the looseness of pop art. It also has pop art's gaiety, its ingenuousness, its exhilarating freedom from moralism. One great virtue of the pop-art movement is the way it blasts through the old imperative about taking a *position* toward one's subject matter. . . .The best works among those that are called pop art intend, precisely, that we abandon the old task of always either approving or disapproving of what is depicted in art—or, by extension, experienced in life. (This is why those who dismiss pop art as a symptom of a new conformism, a cult of acceptance of the artifacts of mass civilization, are being obtuse.)[9]

And:

> The texture of *Flaming Creatures* is made up of a rich collage of "camp" lore: a woman in white (a transvestite) with drooping head holding a stalk of lilies; a gaunt woman seen emerging from a coffin, who turns out to be a vampire and, eventually, male; a marvelous Spanish dancer (also a transvestite [Mario Montez]) with huge dark eyes, black lace mantilla and fan; a tableau from the *Sheik of Araby*, with reclining men in burnooses and an Arab temptress stolidly exposing one breast; a scene between two women, reclining on flowers and rags, which recalls the dense, crowded texture of the movies in which Sternberg directed Dietrich in the early thirties. The vocabulary of images and textures on which Smith draws includes pre-Raphaelite languidness; Art Nouveau; the great exotica styles of the twenties, the Spanish and the Arab; and the modern "camp" way of relishing mass culture.[10]

Pop art and camp seem to come together in these two passages in their connection to mass culture: freedom from moralizing about it, a means of appreciating it. "It's liking things," Warhol famously said of pop art in an interview that dates from 1963, the year he began making films, the year he made *Sleep*.[11] But this raises more questions than it answers. If the camp way of appreciating mass culture is ironic, putting everything in quotation marks ("it's not a lamp, but a 'lamp'; not a woman, but a 'woman'"[12]), can this escape a sense of superiority that is in fact a kind of moralizing?[13] Did Warhol see Campbell's soup cans, Marilyn Monroe, or a sleeping John Giorno ironically? Do his paintings and films put his subjects in quotation marks? On the contrary, Warhol really did seem to *like* these things. And what of Smith? Did Smith love Maria Montez ironically? Was she, for Smith, so bad she was good? Certainly not, if we are to take him at his word. Marc Siegel has argued persuasively for reading Smith's Montez worship not as camp but as belief—indeed as belief in belief. "At least in America," Smith began his essay "The Perfect Filmic Appositeness of Maria Montez," "a Maria Montez could believe she was the Cobra woman, the Siren of Atlantis, Scheherazade, etc. She believed and therefore made the people who went to her movies believe. Those who could believe, did. Those who saw the World's Worst Actress just couldn't and they missed the magic. Too bad—their loss."[14] Siegel glosses Smith's statement:

> What interested Smith ... were those moments when Montez's assumption of her role seemed motivated by the strength of her belief in the fantasy figures she embodied and in the papier-mâché sets of the fantasy world of her films; when her movements, facial expressions, and gestures exposed the complexity of that belief in fantasy as a belief in her own beauty, her own distinctiveness, her own fabulousness. In the belief that motivated the fantastic excesses of Montez's films, Smith saw the heterogeneous signs of the complexity of human desire and fantasy, heterogeneous (and possibly incoherent) signs suggesting that there are different kinds of people and desires to be found in one's world. Believing Montez meant believing in the possibility of thinking differently not only about performance and image-making but also about the world one lives in and the worlds one could live in.[15]

"I hope it is plain that Camp and Jack Smith are two things apart," Ronald Tavel wrote in 1966. "As a matter of fact, using materials natal to Camp, Smith is at the opposite pole. He is all belief."[16]

Maria Montez's contagious belief in herself is all-too-perfectly encapsulated in her rapturous statement, made to an interviewer, "When I see myself on the screen, I look so beautiful I want to scream with joy." The statement might be taken as an example of what Sontag called pure camp, with just the right "mixture of the exaggerated, the fantastic, the passionate, and the naïve." This is the Sontag definition of camp that Callie Angell found appropriate to Warhol's appreciation of Paul Swan and that led her also to link Swan's performances with Smith's. Another Sontag phrase about camp—this one from the essay on *Flaming Creatures*—also seems to link the two performers: "the great exotica styles of the twenties, the Spanish and the Arab": Swan was certainly a proponent of cultural exoticism, which has its origins well before the 1920s in both European and American colonialism. Swan seems to have followed the lead in this respect of his contemporary dancer Ruth St. Denis (whose Orientalism was famously inspired by seeing a poster in a Buffalo, New York, drugstore advertising Egyptian Deities, a brand of cigarettes),[17] whereas the attraction to "the Spanish and the Arab" in Smith is mediated through the Hollywood of a different era, the Montez vehicles of the 1940s. Links can be drawn between the two periods: Michael Moon drew them brilliantly in his essay on Nijinsky and Smith, "Flaming Closets."[18] Another intriguing link connects the earlier moment of American Orientalist dance (Swan's moment) and the camp classic *Cobra Woman*, starring Montez as the twin sisters Naja, the evil one, and Tollea, the good one. The central camp episode of *Cobra Woman* comes when Tollea must pose as her evil twin and convincingly dance the cobra dance, during which her followers show their fealty to her by making "cobras" of their arms and hands, a gesture often mimicked by knowing members of the movie audience. In his study of Ruth St. Denis's "Cycle of Oriental Dances," St. Denis's partner, Ted Shawn, wrote of the dance called *The Cobras*, first performed in 1906 as part of her East Indian or "Hindu" cycle:

> A small platform is brought out, on which [St. Denis] seats herself, cross-legged. Up to this time her arms have been folded, with each hand over the opposite shoulder. But now they come into play. The index and the little fingers are adorned with huge emerald rings which give the hands the appearance of two cobra heads. Then she—herself the snake-charmer; her hands the cobras—begins her dance. The snakes coil, writhe, hiss, intertwine, and strike. One becomes fascinated to the point of believing it all real. When the dance reaches a climax with both cobras striking together, she coils them again about her shoulders and, with her attendants, slouches off, the bazaar life continuing for a few moments until the curtain.[19]

Can we assume that Swan's Orientialism, like St. Denis's, was "naive," whereas Smith's was knowing, "mocking"? Juan Suárez makes a different and more persuasive case in his essay "Jack Smith, Hélio Oiticica, Tropicalism."[20] For Suárez, Smith's exoticism leads us both "out of this world"—to an "enchanted, impossible geography" where difference reigns free—and "deeper into it"—toward the "more socially locatable strands of difference" in the world Smith actually inhabited. Thus, to take but one of Suárez's examples, Smith's earliest completed film, *Scotch Tape*, shot in the rubble of New York City's San Juan Hill, is an elegy to the neighborhood's evicted "exotic" residents—the mostly Puerto Ricans and African Americans who had been displaced to make way for Lincoln Center.[21] Suárez quotes Smith's "Perfect Filmic Appositeness": "What is it we want from Film? ... *Contact with something we are not, know not, think not, feel not, understand not, therefore: An expansion.*"[22]

Warhol had no comparable interest in the exotic. He sought expansion—"liking things"—not by constructing fantasy worlds but through a single-minded attentiveness to the world as he found it. To this extent, his film aesthetic differed markedly from Smith's. Perhaps this explains why Warhol left his film *Batman Dracula* unfinished. The fantasy narrative, shot partly on rooftop locations with characters in elaborate costumes, partly in interiors with dramatic chiaroscuro lighting, might well have seemed to him too camp.

EPILOGUE: WARHOL'S TIME

WHERE ARE YOU RUNNING? AWAY FROM YOURSELF? TO WHAT EXCITEMENT? IF ALL PEOPLE COULD SIT AND WATCH THE EMPIRE STATE BUILDING FOR EIGHT HOURS AND MEDITATE UPON IT, THERE WOULD BE NO MORE WARS, NO HATE, NO TERROR—THERE WOULD BE HAPPINESS REGAINED UPON EARTH.

JONAS MEKAS, *MOVIE JOURNAL*

Empire's first forty-eight-minute reel contains the film's full range of light-to-dark progress, as well as the dramatic moment of the floodlights coming on at the top of the Empire State Building. The film starts with a bright white screen with no image at all, since the camera's aperture is wide open and the sun hasn't yet set. Very soon, though, the familiar silhouette of the Empire State Building begins to be discernible, and from then on the building becomes clearer and clearer, as if in a photograph slowly developing before your eyes in a darkroom. You see the architecture's shape, then its form, then its details. Since you're seeing it from an angle, you see a sliver of the west facade. (*Empire* was shot from a forty-first-floor office of the Time-Life Building in Rockefeller Center, on the northeast corner of Fifty-First Street and Sixth Avenue, and the Empire State Building occupies half the block from Fifth Avenue toward Sixth between Thirty-Third and Thirty-Fourth Streets. The other two buildings' crowns that figure prominently in the film are the New York Life Insurance Company Building at Madison Avenue and Twenty-Sixth Street and the Metropolitan Life Insurance Company Tower at Madison and Twenty-Third. The latter plays a crucial role in all ten of the film's reels.) No sooner has the Empire State Building become fully visible than it begins fading into darkness as the sun sets completely. Then—whang—the floodlights go on, and by the time the reel ends the flood lights are all you see: That is, you see no architectural details or forms or shapes that are not solely configured as light. If what happened forty minutes earlier seemed like an image in a photochemical bath emerging into visibility, what you see now is the purest high-contrast photographic image—swaths and streaks and dots of light on a dark field. You know these patches of light delineate the top of the Empire State Building, since they restore to visibility what had slowly been fading from view. But as time goes on, reel after reel for the next eight reels, what these light splotches denote can be almost forgotten. Of course, you always *know* what it is you're looking at, but your perceptual experience doesn't hold steady over such a long time, just as when you hear a word repeated again and again, its meaning becomes destabilized. Watching

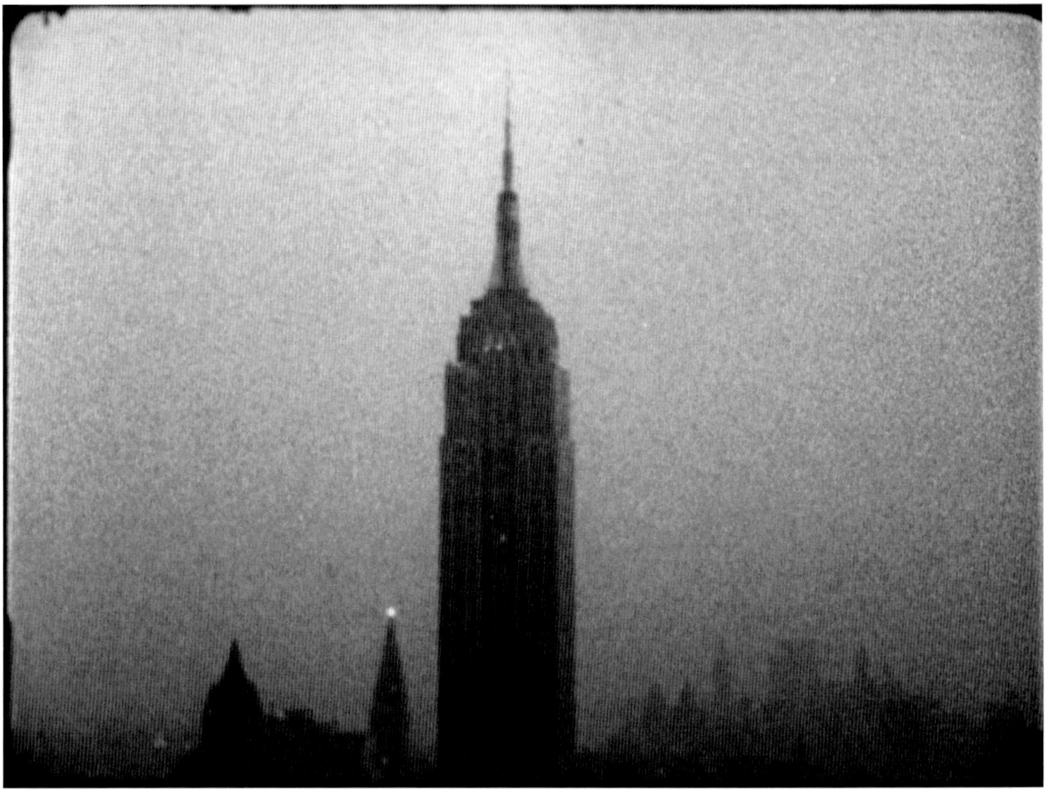

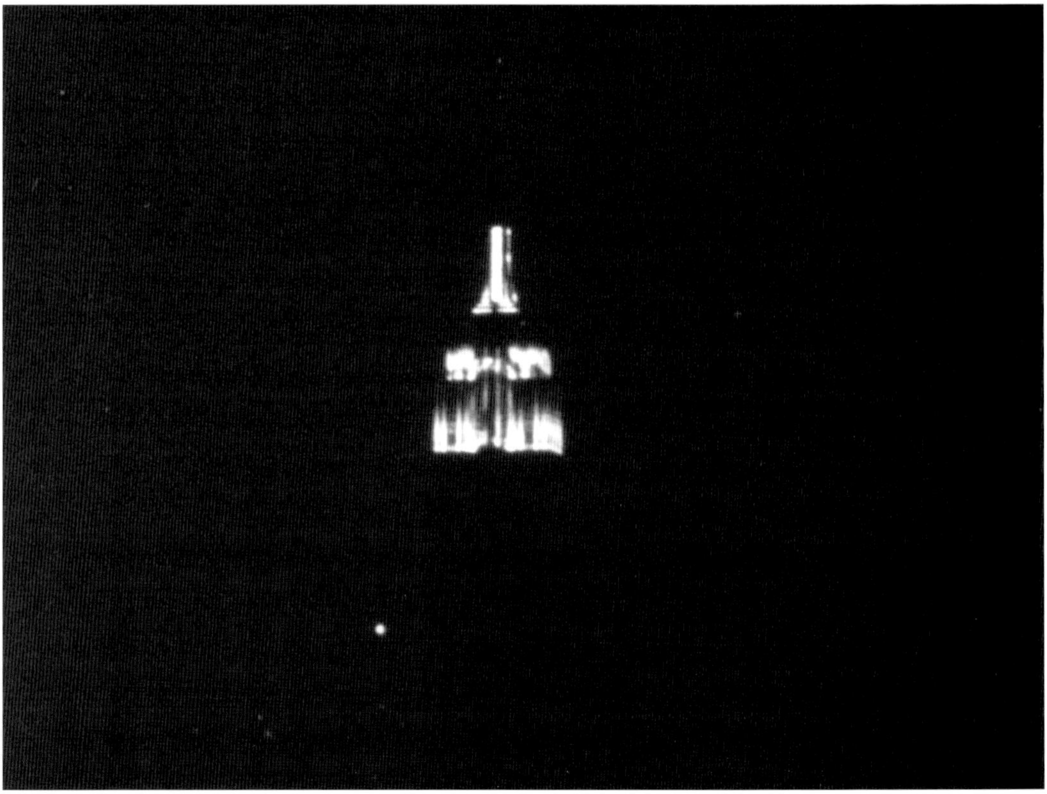

Andy Warhol, *Empire*, 1964. 16mm film, b/w,
silent, 8 hours and 5 minutes at 16 fps.
Film stills courtesy of The Andy Warhol Museum.

Empire, what I found happened most was that the perspective of the building kept reversing itself, so that instead of a solid contour I seemed to be looking at a hollowed-out volume, as if I were seeing a cutaway of interior space. When that happened, I would try in vain to turn concave back to convex, to get the building to become a solid exterior again. I'd stare at the lights on the right side of the image, the ones whose bottom edge, in correct perspective, should be moving away from me, into space, to delineate the west side of the tower. But when that edge appeared to move toward me, making me look *into* the shape, I couldn't trick my eye into correcting the image to get it to read again as the solid form of the familiar building.

The image eventually becomes so abstract that you begin to want to read it like a Rorschach test. In this regard, *Empire* is comparable to Warhol's late abstract paintings, among them the *Rorschachs*, but most of all the *Shadows*, which presumably show shadows of actual solid objects even if thus far no one has determined what those objects are. You do know what *Empire*'s abstract image is, but staring at it for such a long time makes it possible literally to lose sight of it.

In the ninth of *Empire*'s ten reels, the building's floodlights go off, and then for an hour or so more of viewing time there is no image at all, or no image but for a few small dots of light. The brightest of these—which is not on the Empire State Building—is familiar to us from its initial appearance in reel one. It is the top of the Metropolitan Life Insurance Company Tower, whose shape we could still make out at the moment the Empire State Building lights went on. As I said, it plays a role throughout *Empire*: Every quarter hour the light blinks off for about twenty seconds—in real time, not the sixteen-frames-per-second silent-speed projection time, and not accounting for the time it took Warhol and his crew to change film magazines. The light also marks full hours by blinking the appropriate number of times.[1] Otherwise, what we see in the final reels are just some smaller points of light. Five of the lights are on the television-broadcasting antenna at the top of the Empire State Building. The top one blinks regularly every second. A few others must be in other buildings within the camera's view. These become fewer as the film proceeds, as they are turned off during the night.

There are three further "events" in *Empire*. At the beginning of reels five, seven, and ten, we momentarily see someone reflected in the window of the office from which the film was shot; they are, respectively, Jonas Mekas, Warhol, and John Palmer, all of whom were shooting the film.[2] When *Empire* was made, each time the film in the magazine ran out, the crew would reload the film and start the filming again. Once the camera had been reloaded and filming began again, the lights in the office that had been turned on for reloading were switched off, but in these three instances the lights remained on for a few seconds, long enough for the ghostly presences of the filmmakers to be captured.

What else do we see in *Empire*'s eight hours and five minutes?[3] Like the structural films of which it is a precursor, we see the materiality of film as such. Most dramatically, we see a number of light flares that result in a graying of the otherwise black field that also reveals the grain of the film. The floodlit image of the Empire State Building's summit at these moments appears to dim, insofar as the high contrast we've grown used to is reduced by the lightening of the image as a whole. Although these flares are technically mistakes, the result of relatively crude laboratory conditions under which the highly light-sensitive film was push-processed to compensate for underexposure of film shot in the dark, they are perfectly commensurate with Warhol's film aesthetic, not unlike the white flares at the end of each of the spliced-together Bolex reels in *Kiss* and *Blow Job* or the flickering fade-out of the image followed by film-stock-identifier punch holes at the end of each reel of the sound films made in 1965–1966.[4] They are among the many ways in which we see film *as film* in Warhol's cinema, just as we see silkscreen ink *as ink* in Warhol's paintings. This celluloid materiality is one of the several reasons why it is crucial to see Warhol's films projected in analog format rather than digital transfers, which have lamentably become standard in museum exhibitions of the films over the past several years.

The most egregious case to date is the Museum of Modern Art's 2011 exhibition *Andy Warhol: Motion Pictures*, which critic Amy Taubin rightly called "a disgrace to an institution that has played a major role in the preservation of Warhol's films." "It is astonishing," Taubin went on to say, "that a major museum devoted to the art of the modernist era would countenance an exhibition that so blithely disregards one of the signal concerns of modernist aesthetics: medium specificity (a concern that was, one hastens to add, absolutely central to Warhol's engagement with cinema)."[5] The MoMA exhibition included a selection of Warhol's *Screen Tests*, together, confusingly, with *Blow Job*, projected digitally onto framed surfaces as if they were still pictures. Although Warhol referred to the *Screen Tests* as "stillies," they are not, of course, still. In most cases, the subjects were asked to hold still for the duration of the 100-foot Bolex reel, refraining, if possible, even from blinking; but to do so instructed for three minutes while staring at Warhol's camera proved impossible for even the most intrepid of sitters. "What you get," Callie Angell wrote of the *Screen Tests*, "are some very intense performances, performances which emerge from the tension that is created when people are asked to behave as if they were their own image."[6] The gradual defeat of the sitter's facial composure—whether through increasing numbers of blinks, twitching around the mouth, or, in the astonishing case of a *Screen Test* of Ann Buchanan, tears streaming down her cheeks from her successfully unblinking eyes—constitutes much of the interest of these films. Seeing them shown digitally on monitors or flat screens in museum galleries, however, you have to be conscious of this fact in advance and determined to stand in front of each one, *start to finish*, for the full four minutes (the films gain a minute through projection at sixteen frames per second) to appreciate them fully. What generally happens instead, in my experience, is that viewers scan the gallery quickly, see who is pictured in each *Screen Test*—There's Lou Reed. Oh, look, it's Susan Sontag. Isn't Edie Sedgwick beautiful!—and move on. This tendency is only increased by the fact that museum curators often select *Screen Tests* of the most recognizable celebrities to project digitally onto their gallery walls, even though famous faces comprise a very small percentage of the 472 works.[7]

The experience of time is perhaps the most consistent feature of Warhol's cinema throughout its many permutations. In the case of the silent films, the silent-speed projection of film shot at sound speed slows them down by one-third and creates their dreamlike quality. It is not immediately obvious slow motion, but neither, perceptibly, is it real time. This slowed speed also reinforces our awareness of the films' materiality in the *Screen Tests*: "The almost complete absence of camera movement and editing and the minimal movement of the subjects mean that the pulse of the films comes from the flicker of the film projector, which effectively lays down a beat—sixteen per second—that organizes the movement of the grain from frame to frame. When this movement is lost or mucked up, the films become dead things."[8] Thus, in these deceptively simple films, time is decisive in at least four ways: the rhythm of the film frames passing through the projector's gate, the demands exerted by actual time on the sitter facing the camera, the projection speed that stretches that time and makes it uncanny, and the linear time in which the drama of the face unfolds. We may add to these four, protracted duration (even the four minutes of the one-reel *Screen Tests* are a long time to look at a basically unmoving close-up of a face).

There is no question but that Warhol was interested in extended length as such in his films; after all, in addition to *Empire*, he famously made the five-hour-and-twenty-one-minute *Sleep*, the three-and-a-half-hour *The Chelsea Girls*, and the twenty-five-hour ★★★★ (*Four Stars*). He also intended a nearly fourteen-hour film called *Six Months*, for which he proposed shooting a *Screen Test* of his boyfriend Philip Fagan every day for half a year; although Warhol and Fagan's relationship deteriorated after only three months, the existing ninety-six reels make up a film lasting longer than *Sleep*.[9]

Henry Geldzahler is something of an extended *Screen Test*, an eighty-eight-minute silent portrait film in which Warhol's curator pal is defeated by the camera's relentless stare over much too long a time for him to handle comfortably or even gracefully. (If you see *Henry Geldzahler* projected digitally on a museum wall, as it was in the Whitney Museum of American Art's exhibition *Off the Wall: Part 1—Thirty Performative Actions*, 2010, how likely are you to stand in front of it long enough to comprehend its durational demands, on both sitter and viewer?) *Henry Geldzahler* is a companion film to *Empire*: It was made with the same rented Auricon camera the day after *Empire* was shot, using two leftover reels of film. One way of characterizing the difference between the two is that Geldzahler's encounter with extended time in front of the camera is shared by the audience's encounter with Geldzahler as depicted in slowed-down time, whereas the encounter is ours alone when we watch *Empire*, since in that case what we see is, as Gregory Battcock says to make the point, "simply, a big nothing."[10] Battcock writes, "Warhol's decision to show the slow passing of dusk and night emphasizes the importance that the artist gives to the time element. In commercial films, events seldom are presented in their full time span. Time is distorted in such films—usually by compression. The time is distorted in *Empire* in a different way. It is distorted perhaps, simply by not being distorted when one would reasonably expect it to be."[11]

Of course, Battcock is wrong: Time *is* distorted in *Empire* by the slower projection speed. Nevertheless, the gist of his argument is right: To varying degrees we always experience time in Warhol's films as, among other things, duration. The mistake of thinking *Empire* shows real time is perpetuated by John Bernard Myers in his response to Battcock, which he intended as a critique not only of *Empire* but of underground film more generally. For Myers, the essence of cinema is not time as such but montage, which reconfigures real time as filmic time. "In a way," Myers writes,

> one must praise Warhol for raising the question, "What do you mean by time in a movie?" He places the camera before the Empire State Building for several hours. The time in [*sic*] which it took to make the film is the time it also takes to unreel it. This supposedly is real time, not a depiction of time. To him it would seem, in other words, that time is exactly like the unreeling of a film; for me, a highly simplistic concept. If I were the camera, I would faint with boredom, staring that long at one thing, the Empire State Building. Two hours would seem like two years.... I have always believed that the experience of time—whether in a kiss or the drilling of a tooth—is primarily psychological and that the passage of time in human affairs is immeasurable except in subjective terms.[12]

Plainly, time in human affairs is also measurable in *objective* terms, whether by the clocks that organize our working days or the number of feet on a reel of film that determines how long we will have to stay in our theater seats to watch a movie from beginning to end. What Meyers means, I suppose, is that we are variously affected psychologically in our experience of time, depending on the circumstance, which is just what interests Warhol, albeit *differently*. "'My time is not your time' is the message of the silent films," asserts Taubin:

> By being shot at sound speed and projected at silent speed ... the films unwind at a pace that is out of sync with the rhythms of the viewer. This disjunction—between the body clock of the person *as image* and the person watching heightens the viewer's alienation from the image. It makes us aware of the image as "other" and therefore unknowable. Hollywood codes of realism elide the gap between seeing and knowing. Warhol's films reinforce it.[13]

But they do even more with time. Perhaps I can suggest what Warhol's time accomplishes anecdotally. I saw *Empire* at an Anthology Film Archives screening one summer Saturday afternoon and evening in the company of my friend and fellow Warhol film devotee and scholar Juan Suárez. For the following week, another friend-devotee-scholar, Jonathan Flatley, had booked three days at the MoMA Film Study Center to look at Warhol films, and I took the opportunity to see a number of them with him, including *Kiss*, *Soap Opera*, *Henry Geldzahler*, *Horse*, *More Milk Yvette*, *Eating Too Fast*, *Since*, *Sunset*, and *Imitation of Christ*—thus, in one week, I saw more than eighteen hours of Warhol's films (still seven hours less than the twenty-five hours of ★★★★). Jonathan and I remarked to each other after our final day's screenings that our sense of time had been utterly altered by the experience. On the simplest level, we had become completely relaxed about how much time was passing and not at all impatient at the films' usually long-seeming duration. We felt at that moment as if we could go on watching Warhol films for days on end and continue to enjoy the experience thoroughly. Our time, to reverse-paraphrase Taubin, had become Warhol's time.

When *Film Culture* gave the Sixth Independent Film Award to Warhol in 1964, the citation read, in part:

> We watch a Warhol movie with no hurry. The first thing he does is that he stops us from running. His camera rarely moves. It stays fixed on the subject like there was nothing more beautiful and no thing more important than that subject. It stays there longer than we are used to. Long enough for us to begin to free ourselves from all that we thought about haircutting or eating or the Empire State Building; or, for that matter, about cinema. We begin to realize that we have never really seen haircutting or eating. We have cut our hair, we have eaten, but we have never really seen those actions. The whole reality around us becomes *differently* interesting, and we feel like we have to begin filming everything anew. A new way of looking at things and the screen is given through the personal vision of Andy Warhol.[14]

How willing are we these days to spend time in this way? Has digital culture irrevocably changed time? Certainly. And yet just how it has changed time and how we respond to changed time is not obvious. For some of us, it has made Warhol's time newly pertinent—and I mean "Warhol's time" both in the sense of the historical moment that Warhol made his films and in the senses of time that those films deliver. When Juan and I decided to go to Anthology Film Archives that Saturday afternoon to see *Empire*, we conjectured about how large the audience would be and how long any of us would stay. It was announced that whoever stayed for the entire length of the film would be rewarded with a prize. Approximately thirty people gathered at Anthology's Maya Deren Theater, and the great majority, about twenty-five of us, stayed for the entire film (but for occasional bathroom breaks).[15] The age demographic was what most surprised and delighted me: Most people were under thirty-five. I should have predicted it: *The Chelsea Girls* sold out a weeklong run at the 200-seat movie theater at MoMA in June 2007, and many of the audience members at those screenings, too, were likely not yet born until after Warhol stopped making films. Perhaps we are coming around to Warhol's time. Ronald Tavel told David James that Warhol

> would sit and watch [his own films] for endless hours with one leg crossed over the other and his face in his hands and his elbows on his knees, with absolute fascination and he was puzzled why the public wasn't equally fascinated. When we stopped off at a screening of *Empire* to see how it was doing, and there were six people in the theater, he said, "Well, look at that. They'll just pile in to see"—and he referred to some Hollywood blockbuster, you know—"and nobody comes to see *Empire*." It was a genuine remark, he was not dissembling. He said to me, "Why don't they come in droves to see *Empire*?" So we should not think that these films were not interesting to him or that he didn't want them to be interesting. As with any visual artist, the entire visual world was fascinating to him, and he did behave rather traditionally in that sense. I mean, after watching a face for three hours in a Warhol movie, you never look at faces again in the same way.[16]

We'll have to wait for the preservation of *Six Months* to watch a Warhol film of a face for three hours and more, but in the meantime there are all those four-minute *Screen Tests*; even watching them—properly projected in a movie theater—changes the way we look at faces. And not only faces.

NOTES

PREFACE

1. This project is hinted at in my essay "Getting the Warhol We Deserve," *Social Text* 59 (summer 1999): 49–66.

2. According to the Berlin project group, which included, in addition to Diederichsen, Haase, and Rebentisch, Christoph Gurk, Martin Saar, and Ruth Sonderegger, "The focus [of *Cross Gender/Cross Genre*] is on a critical reconstruction of the period between 1966 and 1974 that saw the aesthetic subversion and destabilization of prevailing orders of gender beyond the borders of traditional disciplines of art, be it the activities of film-maker Jack Smith, John Vaccaro's 'Playhouse of the Ridiculous,' or Andy Warhol's Factory—a development that was later to lead to the formation of the phenomenon known as 'Glam' and which today could prove to be productive for the gender-political discussion concerning the relation between the concepts of 'performance' and 'performativity'" (*Remake/Re-model* program brochure, Steirischer Herbst 99).

3. Papers related to *Remake/Re-model* were published in *Golden Years: Materialien und Positionen zu queerer Subkultur und Avantgarde zwischen 1959 und 1974*, ed. Diedrich Diederichsen et al. (Graz: Camera Austria, 2006).

4. For an account of Mario Montez's contributions to New York underground culture, see Juan A. Suárez, "The Puerto Rican Lower East Side and the Queer Underground," *Grey Room* 32 (summer 2008): 6–37.

5. By that time the Whitney Museum had completed its two Warhol exhibitions, comprising about half of the films that would eventually be preserved by the Museum of Modern Art in the first round of planned restorations, now completed. See *The Films of Andy Warhol: An Introduction* (New York: Whitney Museum of American Art, 1988) and Callie Angell, *The Films of Andy Warhol: Part II* (New York: Whitney Museum of American Art, 1994).

6. For my introduction to the film program and the program itself, see *Dia's Andy* (New York: Dia Art Foundation, 2005), 72–75.

7. Two monographic studies of *Blow Job* were published after "Face Value" was written; neither discusses *Eating Too Fast*; see Roy Grundmann, *Andy Warhol's Blow Job* (Philadelphia: Temple University Press, 2003); and Peter Gidal, *Andy Warhol: Blow Job* (London: Afterall Books, 2000).

8. Leo Bersani, preface to *Is the Rectum a Grave? and Other Essays* (Chicago: University of Chicago Press, 2010), ix–x.

9. Leo Bersani, *Homos* (Cambridge, MA: Harvard University Press, 1995), 7.

FACE VALUE

1. Stephen Koch, *Stargazer: The Life, World, and Films of Andy Warhol*, revised edition (New York: Marion Boyars, 1991), 48.

2. On silent-film projection speeds, see the technical notes in Callie Angell, *The Films of Andy Warhol: Part II* (New York: Whitney Museum of American Art, 1994), 9.

3. Angell, *The Films of Andy Warhol*, 10.

4. Callie Angell, *Something Secret: Portraiture in Warhol's Films* (Sydney: Museum of Contemporary Art, 1994), 8.

5. Koch, *Stargazer*, 47.

6. Ibid., 50.

7. Ibid., 48.

8. Ibid., 35.

9. Ibid., 48.

10. Ibid., 42.

11. David E. James, *Allegories of Cinema: American Film in the Sixties* (Princeton: Princeton University Press, 1989), 67.

12. Koch, *Stargazer*, 44.

13. There are a few exceptional color *Screen Tests*. For the *Screen Tests*, see Callie Angell, *Andy Warhol Screen Tests: The Films of Andy Warhol Catalogue Raisonné*, vol. 1 (New York: Abrams, 2006). Angell notes that among Warhol's first *Screen Tests* are two of Kelly Edey, who made a diary entry for January 20, 1964, that read, "Andy Warhol wants to make a movie called *Sex* starring Avery and me." One of the *Screen Tests* of Edey, Angell goes on to say, "appears to have been shot from below, with Edey's head tilted back and somewhat foreshortened. Subtle changes in his expression—twitching an eyebrow, closing his eyes, furrowing his brow, parting his lips, and swallowing repeatedly—suggest that this may indeed be a sex film, perhaps the precursor of Warhol's better-known Minimalist work *Blow Job*" (Angell, *Andy Warhol Screen Tests*, 70).

14. Jonathan Flatley, "Warhol Gives Good Face: Publicity and the Politics of Prosopopoeia," in *Pop Out: Queer Warhol*, ed. Jennifer Doyle, Jonathan Flatley, and José Esteban Muñoz (Durham: Duke University Press, 1996), 112. Flatley's essay has been crucial for my own thinking about Warhol, and the title of my essay pays homage to Flatley's by appropriating the section heading from which the quoted passage is taken. In his essay's final section, "Giving Face as Giving Head," Flatley's short discussion of *Blow Job* begins the contestation of voyeurism that I seek to elaborate here.

15. James, *Allegories of Cinema*, 69.

16. Ibid., 67.

17. Ronald Tavel, "The Banana Diary (The Story of Andy Warhol's 'Harlot')," *Film Culture* 40 (spring 1966): 44.

18. Ibid., 84. Tavel is alluding to Jack Smith's "The Perfect Filmic Appositeness of Maria Montez," in *Wait for Me at the Bottom of the Pool: The Writings of Jack Smith*, ed. J. Hoberman and Edward Leffingwell (New York: High Risk Books, 1997) (first published in *Film Culture* 27 [winter 1962–63]).

19. Andy Warhol and Pat Hackett, *Popism: The Warhol Sixties* (New York: Harcourt Brace, 1980), 91.

20. James, *Allegories of Cinema*, 67.

21. In this regard, see Marc Siegel, "Documentary That Dare/Not Speak Its Name: Jack Smith's *Flaming Creatures*," in *Between the Sheets, in the Streets: Queer, Lesbian, Gay Documentary*, ed. Chris Holmlund and Cynthia Fuchs (Minneapolis: University of Minnesota Press, 1997), 91–106.

22. Thomas Waugh, "Cockteaser," in Doyle et al., *Pop Out: Queer Warhol*, 54.

23. James, *Allegories of Cinema*, 67.

24. Pier Paolo Pasolini, *Lutheran Letters*, trans. Stuart Hood (Manchester: Carcanet New Press, 1983), 58.

25. Eve Kosofsky Sedgwick, *Epistemology of the Closet* (Berkeley: University of California Press, 1990), 22.

26. Gretchen Berg, "Nothing to Lose: An Interview with Andy Warhol," in *Andy Warhol: Film Factory*, ed. Michael O'Pray (London: British Film Institute, 1989), 60 (first published in *Cahiers du Cinéma in English* 10 [1967]).

27. Warhol and Hackett, *Popism*, 51.

28. John Giorno, *You've Got to Burn to Shine* (New York: High Risk Books, 1994), 146.

29. DeVerne Bookwalter appears in a *Screen Test* shot at about the same time as *Blow Job* and did, in fact, appear in a Shakespeare in the Park production of *Macbeth* in 1963 and a Clint Eastwood movie in 1976. See Angell, *Andy Warhol Screen Tests*, 41.

30. Koch, *Stargazer*, 122. For a more interesting analysis of the relations among Warhol, passivity, and hustling, see Jennifer Doyle, "Tricks of the Trade: Pop Art/Pop Sex," in Doyle et al., *Pop Out: Queer Warhol*, 191–209.

31. Koch, *Stargazer*, 79.

32. Tony Rayns, "Death at Work: Evolution and Entropy in Factory Films," in *Andy Warhol: Film Factory*, 165.

33. Ibid., 169.

34. It is not clear that the changes Rayns attributes to Morrissey are really the result of Morrissey's contribution to *My Hustler*. Chuck Wein is credited as codirector with Warhol; Morrissey is credited only with sound.

35. Emmanuel Levinas, *Ethics and Infinity: Conversations with Phillippe Nemo*, trans. Richard A. Cohen (Pittsburgh: Duquesne University Press, 1985), 86–87.

ADDENDUM: *EATING TOO FAST*

1. E-mail from Callie Angell, May 21, 1999.

2. This was Callie Angell's view of a number of films from this period, including *Paul Swan*, 1965; *More Milk Yvette*, 1965; and *Mrs. Warhol*, 1966. *Outer and Inner Space*, 1965, was Warhol's first experiment with double-screen projection; *Lupe*, 1965, and *The Chelsea Girls*, 1966, are the best-known uses of this technique. For the suggestion that *Eating Too Fast* might have been intended for this manner of projection, see *The Films of Andy Warhol* (brochure) (New York: Museum of Modern Art Circulating Film Library, n.d.).

3. When Patrick Smith asked Battcock, "I understand that the sound version of *Blow Job* was filmed in your apartment. What happened during the filming of it?" Battcock replied, "That was my apartment when I lived in the Village. Lou Reed was there, and Andy was there.... The dialogue was just whatever happened to come up. You know? Sometimes Warhol or somebody would set up provocations, which *might* stimulate dialogue in one way or another but not really direct it" (Gregory Battcock interview, October 15, 1978, in Patrick S. Smith, *Andy Warhol's Art and Films* [Ann Arbor, MI: UMI Research Press, 1986], 214). Since dialogue is almost entirely absent from the film and largely irrelevant to "what happened during the filming of it," Battcock appears to be evading the question.

4. Gregory Battcock, "Notes on 'Blow Job': A Film by Andy Warhol," *Film Culture* 37 (summer 1965): 20–21.

MARIO MONTEZ, FOR SHAME

1. Eve Kosofsky Sedgwick, "Queer Performativity, Warhol's Shyness, Warhol's Whiteness," in *Pop Out: Queer Warhol*, ed. Jennifer Doyle, Jonathan Flatley, and José Esteban Muñoz (Durham: Duke University Press, 1996), 135.

2. Warhol withdrew his films from circulation in the beginning of the 1970s. After his agreement in 1982 to allow the Whitney Museum of American Art to research and present the films, the museum began showing them in installments, the first in 1988, the second in 1994. See *The Films of Andy Warhol: An Introduction* (New York: Whitney Museum of American Art, 1988) and Callie Angell, *The Films of Andy Warhol: Part II* (New York: Whitney Museum of American Art, 1994). *Screen Test No. 2*, the film discussed here, was restored in 1995 and screened in 1998.

3. The stakes of such a project comprise a portion of my argument in "Getting the Warhol We Deserve," *Social Text* 59 (summer 1999): 49–66.

4. Eve Kosofsky Sedgwick, *Epistemology of the Closet* (Berkeley: University of California Press, 1990), 23.

5. Andy Warhol and Pat Hackett, *Popism: The Warhol Sixties* (New York: Harcourt Brace, 1980), 181.

6. Ibid., 91. Hedy Lamarr was notoriously litigious; thus, since Warhol's film, with a script by Ronald Tavel, was inspired by a real-life incident in 1966 in which Lamarr was charged with shoplifting (charges of which she was later cleared), the title was variously obfuscated. Lamarr was arrested at least twice more for shoplifting.

7. Warhol and Hackett, *Popism*, 91.

8. Ibid., 124.

9. *Andy Warhol's Exposures* (New York: Andy Warhol Books/Grosset & Dunlap, 1979).

10. Stefan Brecht, *Queer Theatre* (New York: Methuen, 1986), 113–114 (the idiosyncrasies of spelling and syntax are Brecht's). It should be said that among Warhol's superstars Mario Montez was exceptional in *not* being sycophantic toward Warhol; if anything, the reverse was true. Gregory Battcock writes of Montez's exposure in *Screen Test No. 2* as "self-exposure": "Mario Montez is certainly at his best, as he seems utterly to expose himself in this new revelation of the gulf between acting and experience. In effect, this gulf has been closed, the experience cannot be separated from the acting and the question of determining whether Mario is acting or not is thrust upon the audience" (Battcock, "Notes on 'Screen Test': A Film by Andy Warhol," *Film Culture* 38 [fall 1965]: 62).

11. "In 1965, Tavel was the Warhol dramatist in residence. He did the scenarios for what were, except for *Harlot* and *Drunk*, Warhol's first sound movies: *Screen Test Number One, Screen Test Number Two, Life of Juanita Castro, Vinyl, Suicide, Horse, Bitch, Kitchen.* His Warhol scripts, directed by John Vaccaro 1965–7, also became the first plays of the Playhouse of the Ridiculous" (Brecht, *Queer Theatre*, 107; see also the footnote on page 29).

12. There was no scenario for *Harlot*. The soundtrack consists of an off-screen conversation improvised on the spot by Tavel, Billy Name, and Harry Fainlight. The conversation is reproduced in Ronald Tavel, "The Banana Diary (The Story of Andy Warhol's 'Harlot')," *Film Culture* 40 (spring 1966): 43–66.

13. See *Wait for Me at the Bottom of the Pool: The Writings of Jack Smith*, ed. J. Hoberman and Edward Leffingwell (New York: High Risk Books, 1997), 25–35. Originally published in *Film Culture* 27 (winter 1962–63).

14. "Warhol's films are about being unfit to star, and how inadvertently that can make one a star nonetheless" (Matthew Tinkcom, *Working Like a Homosexual: Camp, Capital, Cinema* [Durham: Duke University Press, 2002], 89).

15. This moment of *Screen Test No. 2* suggests that the tour-de-force scene of Paul Morrissey's *Trash*—Holly Woodlawn's Coke-bottle masturbation scene—was a reused Tavel idea. For all that Morrissey professed to find Warhol's early films self-indulgent, dull, and pretentious, he nevertheless made much use of them for his own filmmaking.

16. Warhol and Hackett, *Popism*, 91. Warhol is here paraphrasing Mario Montez's interview in *Film Culture*, in which he replies to the question "Do you think the Lord is upset with you?" "I know He's probably upset about what I'm doing ... but if He didn't want me to do it he'd take my life. I worry about it once in a while ... but not too often" (Gary McColgen, "The Superstar: An Interview with Mario Montez," *Film Culture* 45 [summer 1967]: 18).

17. See Stephen Koch's brilliant analysis of this sequence of *The Chelsea Girls* in *Stargazer: The Life, World, and Films of Andy Warhol*, revised edition (New York: Marion Boyars, 1991), 94–97.

18. Warhol and Hackett, *Popism*, 181. Warhol writes that "Ondine slapped 'Pepper,'" misremembering Angelina "Pepper" Davis in place of Ronna Paige.

19. *Edie: American Girl*, ed. Jean Stein, with George Plimpton (New York: Grove Press, 1994), 242.

20. "Stonewall, Then and Now," *New York Times*, June 29, 1999, A18.

21. Eve Kosofsky Sedgwick, "Queer Performativity: Henry James's *The Art of the Novel*, *GLQ* 1, no. 1 (1993): 1–16. All subsequent quotations from Sedgwick in this section are taken from this essay.

22. As Sedgwick writes, "Readers who have paid attention to the recent, meteoric rise of shame to its present housewife-megastar status in the firmament of self-help and popular psychology ... may be feeling a bit uneasy at this point. So, for that matter, may those used to reading about shame in the neo-conservative framework that treasures shame along with guilt as, precisely, an adjunct of repression and an enforcer of proper behavior. In the ways that I want to be thinking about shame, the widespread moral valuation of this powerful affect as *good* or *bad*, *to be mandated* or *to be excised*, according to how one plots it along a notional axis of prohibition/permission/requirement, seems distinctly beside the point" (ibid., 6).

23. Michael Warner, *The Trouble with Normal: Sex, Politics, and the Ethics of Queer Life* (New York: Free Press, 1999), 3.

24. Ibid., 35–36.

25. "[T]he universal humiliation of all characters in this [ridiculous, queer] theatre gives it a repulsive air of viciousness, even cruelty, because it is absolute: the victims are accorded no basic dignity, no saving graces. We are not reassured of worthy or innocent motives of underlying rational seriousness. The characters are not just clownish or foolish but clowns and fools. They are not exactly funny. Isolated clown scenes, jokes and parodies that at first seem pure fun trouble us by their implications of profound ridiculousness. Some important, often protracted, actions are specifically and formally cruel humiliations. Bajazelli's enslavement in [*When*] *Queens* [*Collide*]/*Conquest* [*of the Universe*], the entire action of *Screen Test*, Lady Godiva's undressing (according to [John] Vaccaro), in *Lady Godiva*, Victor's re-education in *Vinyl* These humiliations bring this close to a theatre of the terrible. It takes a strong stomach to participate in their fun" (Brecht, *Queer Theater*, p. 36). *Screen Test* and *Vinyl* are both films by Warhol whose scenarios by Tavel became plays performed by the Play-House of the Ridiculous.

26. Warhol and Hackett, *Popism*, 91.

27. Tavel, "The Banana Diary," 51.

28. Ibid., 56.

29. "Mario, who appears in 'The Chelsea Girls,' 'Flaming Creatures,' and at least 10 other Underground epics, has a divinity achieved by no Hollywood goddess. With that eternal feminine gesture of pushing the hair of his-her rat's nest wig from a pancaked cheek, and pouring from the depths of his-her liquid dark eyes a painful sweetness that passeth understanding, he-she

projects a vision of androgyne mysteries, a glimpse of the *unio mystica*, the blessed union of all striving opposites" (Rosalyn Regelson, "Where Are 'The Chelsea Girls' Taking Us?" *New York Times*, September 24, 1967).

ADDENDUM: MOTHER CAMP

1. Esther Newton, *Mother Camp: Female Impersonators in America* (Chicago: University of Chicago Press, 1979), xx.

2. Stefan Brecht, *Queer Theatre* (New York: Methuen, 1986), 80.

3. Donald Newlove, "Prothalamion for Wet Harmonica and Johnny Stompanato," *Realist* 68 (August 1966): 19.

COMING TOGETHER TO STAY APART

1. Tavel wrote screenplays for the following completed Warhol films: *Screen Test No. 1*, *Screen Test No. 2*, *Suicide*, *The Life of Juanita Castro*, *Horse*, *Vinyl*, *Kitchen*, *Space*, *Hedy*, and the "Hanoi Hanna" and "Their Town" sequences of *The Chelsea Girls*. He also wrote a number of screenplays never produced as films, including *Withering Sights*, *Jane Eyre Bare*, and *Shower*, the last of which was produced as a play. *Screen Test No. 2*, *The Life of Juanita Castro*, and *Vinyl* were also done as plays. "And then what could be more blatant than [Warhol's] telling me to establish my own theater. This is all the more remarkable since people think Jack Smith had something to do with it, but he was only peripherally involved, with the costumes and sets and the logo and the program for the initial thing. But it was Warhol. It's one of his children, the Theater of the Ridiculous" (Ronald Tavel, quoted in David E. James, "The Warhol Screenplays: An Interview with Ronald Tavel," *Persistence of Vision* 11 [1995]: 59).

2. In fact, it was de Antonio who set up the shot, although it was Warhol's idea to add Brigid Berlin (also known as Brigid Polk); see Branden W. Joseph, "1962," *October* 132 (spring 2010): 132. Nevertheless, since the setup is unique among all those in the film, it seems plausible to credit Warhol: de Antonio was clearly forced to think differently about how he would interview Warhol on camera.

3. For the Theater of the Ridiculous, see Ronald Tavel, "The Theatre of the Ridiculous," *Tri-Quarterly* 6 (1966): 93–109; Peter Michelson, "The Pop Scene and the Theater of the Ridiculous," *Tri-Quarterly* 6 (1966): 111–117; Stefan Brecht, *Queer Theatre* (New York: Methuen, 1986); *Theatre of the Ridiculous*, ed. Bonnie Marranca and Gautam Dasgupta (Baltimore: The Johns Hopkins University Press, 1998). For Tavel, see Dan Isaac, "Ronald Tavel: Ridiculous Playwright," *Drama Review* 13, no. 1 (fall 1968): 106–115.

4. Comparing the commercial success of *Hair* with Charles Ludlam's underground *Conquest of the Universe*, Warhol wrote in *Popism*, "Now it was clear that there were two types of people doing underground-type things—the ones who wanted to become commercial and successful and move right up into the mainstream of society with their stuff, and the ones who wanted to stay where they were, outside society. The way to be counterculture and have mass commercial success was to say and do radical things in a conservative format.... The other people—the ones who didn't care at all about mass commercial success—did radical things in a radical format, and if the audience didn't happen to get the content or the form, then that was that" (Andy Warhol and Pat Hackett, *Popism: The Warhol Sixties* [New York: Harcourt Brace, 1980], 250).

5. Michel Foucault, "What Is an Author?" in *Michel Foucault: Aesthetics, Method, and Epistemology*, ed. James D. Faubion (New York: New Press, 1998), 205–222.

6. In one of the most often-cited interviews given by Warhol, he says, "I'm working principally with Ronald Tavel, a playwright, who's written about ten movies for me; he writes the script and I sort of give him an idea of what I want and now he's doing the films as off-Broadway plays" ("Andy Warhol: My True Story," in *I'll Be Your Mirror: The Selected Andy Warhol Interviews*, ed.

Kenneth Goldsmith [New York: Carroll & Graf, 2004], 91). This interview, conducted by Gretchen Berg in the summer of 1966, was initially published in the *East Village Other*, November 1, 1966. The only other writer to contribute scenarios for Warhol's films was playwright Robert Heide, whose play *The Bed* was filmed for a double-screen film of the same title and used, uncredited, for two reels of *The Chelsea Girls*. Heide also wrote a short scenario for *Lupe*. See Debra Miller, *Billy Name: Stills from the Warhol Films* (Munich: Prestel Verlag, 1994), 32, 64; and Callie Angell, "Doubling the Screen: Andy Warhol's *Outer and Inner Space*," *Millennium Film Journal* 38 (spring 2002): 25.

7. Gary McColgen, "The Superstar: An Interview with Mario Montez," *Film Culture* 45 (summer 1967): 19.

8. David E. James, *Allegories of Cinema: American Film in the Sixties* (Princeton: Princeton University Press, 1989), 69. Jack Smith, who acted in a number of Warhol's films, said something startlingly similar: Asked in an interview by Gerard Malanga what pleasure he took from performing in front of the camera, Smith replied, "I don't know. It's—I could never afford psychoanalysis, and so it is—that's what it—actually this turned out to be—but it's a little—It was very brave of me to take psychoanalysis in that form" (Gerard Malanga, "Interview with Jack Smith," *Film Culture* 45 [summer 1967]: 15).

9. Ronald Tavel, "You Can't Be Too Excessive: Interview von Matthias Haase und Marc Siegel," in *Golden Years—Materalien und Positionen zur queeren Subkulturen 1959–1974*, ed. Diedrich Diederichsen et al. (Graz: Camera Austria, 2006), 149; quotation from the English transcript of the interview.

10. Montez finally relented and performed Juanita Castro in a staged version during *Live Film! Jack Smith! Five Flaming Days in a Rented World* in Berlin in October 2009. Montez said that he felt relations with Cuba had sufficiently thawed at that point for him to be able to perform the part.

11. Ronald Tavel, *The Complete In-Facsimile Warhol Shooting Scripts*, manuscript. All following quotations from Ronald Tavel are taken from this manuscript.

12. This blasé attitude is differently belied in the stationary-shot films by the care required to achieve the studied casualness of the shot.

13. "Last year several of Warhol's films were shot from scripts by Ronald Tavel … with people who had not rehearsed their lines. By reading them for the first time before the camera, an odd off-balance effect of notoriously bad acting was arrived at. What seemed like bad acting was really an indication of the person's truer character coming forward under the conditions of having to read a script sight unseen" (Toby Mussman, "The Chelsea Girls," *Film Culture* 45 [summer 1967]: 44).

14. A few years later, in *Performance Demonstration* (1968), choreographer Yvonne Rainer would introduce rehearsal into her dance performances.

15. Leo Bersani, "Sociability and Cruising," in *Is the Rectum a Grave? and Other Essays* (Chicago: University of Chicago Press, 2010), 57.

16. Of course, narcissism means much more than this in psychoanalytic theory; Freud alone continually revised his ideas about narcissism.

17. Bersani has proposed these new forms of relationality in his writings since *Homos* (Cambridge, MA: Harvard University Press, 1995), which include *Caravaggio's Secrets*, with Ulysse Dutoit (Cambridge, MA: MIT Press, 1998); *Forms of Being*, with Ulysse Dutoit (London: British Film Institute, 2004); *Intimacies*, with Adam Phillips (Chicago: University of Chicago Press, 2008); and *Is the Rectum a Grave? and Other Essays*.

18. In the staged version of *Screen Test*, John Vaccaro, the play's director, played the director.

19. Like the screen-test films, *Suicide* is based on real-life episodes and facts of the life of the "tested" subject, but in this case notes transcribed and edited for a prefilm interview constitute the film's text. Rock Bradett's task as an actor, whose scarred wrists provide the screen image, was to read his own words from the script in front of him while the camera rolled. What made this particularly disconcerting for him was the fact that his confessions of homosexual liaisons and suicide attempts took place in front of not only the camera but also a crowd of journalists and Factory denizens who had gathered for the film shoot.

20. As Tavel puts it, "*Horse*'s lines imply ... an outlook and literary themes ... which, ideally, should demythologize the Western novel and film and introduce the hidden in the anthropometric image and stale ethnography of cowboys: their phallic worship, Levi competition, homosexuality, bestiality, onanism, racism, and institutionalized ignorance" (Tavel, *The Complete In-Facsimile Warhol Shooting Scripts*).

21. "This movie, more directly than any other experience, identifies my later formulating and naming a Theater of the Ridiculous" (ibid.).

22. James, *Allegories of Cinema*, 71.

SPACIOUS

1. Callie Angell identified the children as Darius de Poleon and Sean Bolger; see Callie Angell, *Andy Warhol Screen Tests: The Films of Andy Warhol Catalogue Raisonné*, vol. 1 (New York: Abrams, 2006), 141.

2. Gretchen Berg, "Andy Warhol: My True Story," in *I'll Be Your Mirror: The Selected Andy Warhol Interviews*, ed. Kenneth Goldsmith (New York: Carroll & Graf, 2004), 90.

3. Stephen Koch describes this moment in his chapter on *Haircut* in *Stargazer: The Life, World, and Films of Andy Warhol*, revised edition (New York: Marion Boyars, 1991), 54. Koch mistakenly refers to Billy Linich (Billy Name) as the person getting, not giving, the haircut. More irresponsibly, he identifies Freddy Herko not by name, but with a description even more distasteful than the one of DeVerne Bookwalter that I criticize in "Face Value": "Nearest the camera ... is a very nasty-looking type posing without a shirt. He wears exhibitionistically tight, and very dirty, white jeans that glare a bit in the lens. Both he and his clothes look as badly scuffed as the loft itself. Bluntly, he looks like he knows 42nd Street as well as or better than the protagonist (antagonist?) of *Blow-Job*. His face and body have the strung-out wiriness, the tough, undernourished gracelessness of a slum escapee who survives on street food, on sausage sandwiches bought at greasy open-air stands, hot dogs, Pepsis, and amphetamines. His chest and arms swarm with matted masses of black hair, but whatever vitality he has seems deflected into a loveless, hollow-eyed preening over the groin that his (otherwise carelessly worn) jeans force into high relief. Close to the camera, he preens and postures in a laconic, faintly nasty way" (53).

4. Ronald Tavel, *The Complete In-Facsimile Warhol Shooting Scripts*, manuscript.

5. Ibid.

6. Callie Angell, "Andy Warhol: *Outer and Inner Space*," in *From Stills to Motion and Back Again: Texts on Andy Warhol's "Screen Tests" and "Outer and Inner Space"* (Vancouver: Presentation House Gallery), 14; see also Callie Angell, "Doubling the Screen: Andy Warhol's *Outer and Inner Space*," *Millennium Film Journal* 38 (spring 2002): 19–33.

7. A transcript of the sound of *Outer and Inner Space* was prepared by a lip-reader; see "What Edie Said in *Outer and Inner Space*," in *From Stills to Motion and Back Again*, 27–39.

8. That Warhol's films are nearly always concerned with portraiture is the point of Callie Angell's *Something Secret: Portraiture in Warhol's Films* (Sydney: Museum of Contemporary Art, 1994); Stephen Koch writes that Warhol's films "are, to a degree unknown to any other modern director,

portrait films" (Koch, *Stargazer*, 29). See also *About Face: Andy Warhol Portraits*, ed. Nicholas Baume (Hartford: Wadsworth Atheneum; Cambridge, MA: MIT Press, 1999).

9. Viva writes of Nico, whom she calls Olga, in *Viva Superstar*, "Olga hated sex except with 'yoooooooooung boys.' 'I only like yoooooooooung boys,' she'd say, sounding like growling" (*Viva Superstar* [New York: G. P. Putnam, 1970], 104).

10. Parker Tyler, "Drugtime and Dragtime or, Film à la Warhol" (1967), in *Andy Warhol Film Factory*, ed. Michael O'Pray (London: BFI, 1989), 102.

11. In his nasty portrayal of Dorothy Dean, which employs every cliché about "fag hags," Hilton Als writes that "Warhol treated Dean's performance as marginal; the film literally runs out while she is still speaking, most of the time in underexposed darkness" (Hilton Als, *The Women* [New York: Farrar, Straus, Giroux, 1996], 102). Dean is indeed a marginal figure in the film, but she has in fact stopped speaking, at least momentarily, when the film runs out. In any case, it is characteristic of Warhol's films that they end when the reel runs out. The film is not underexposed during Dean's appearance. Like the two actors who precede her in propositioning Paul America, she is silhouetted and backlit from within the space of the bathroom. For a more complex reading of Dean's "shadowy" appearance in *My Hustler*, see Taro Nettleton, "White-on-White: The Overbearing Whiteness of Warhol Being," *Art Journal* 62, no. 1 (spring 2003): 15–23.

12. In this respect, *yaoi*, the term of ironic self-derogation that fans have invented for the genre of Japanese manga aimed at teenaged girls and involving romances between beautiful boys, seems apt for Warhol's cinema. *Yaoi* derives from the words meaning "no climax" (*yama-nashi*), "no punchline" (*ochi-nashi*), "no meaning" (*imi-nashi*). I thank Akiko Mizoguchi for this information.

MISFITTING TOGETHER

1. Jack Kroll, "Underground in Hell," *Newsweek*, November 14, 1966, 109.

2. Brian O'Doherty, "Narcissus in Hades," *Art and Artists* 1, no. 11 (February 1967): 13–15.

3. Toby Mussman, "The Chelsea Girls," *Film Culture* 45 (summer 1967): 42.

4. "Andy Warhol has produced a film that is half Bosch and half bosh" (Dan Sullivan, "Andy Warhol's 'Chelsea Girls' at the Cinema Rendezvous," *New York Times*, December 2, 1966). "'The Chelsea Girls' has a classical grandeur about it, something from Victor Hugo" (Jonas Mekas, "Movie Journal," *Village Voice*, September 29, 1966). Joyce, Dante, Dickens, and D. W. Griffith are all cited as comparisons previously made for *The Chelsea Girls* by Rosalyn Regelson ("Where are 'The Chelsea Girls' Taking Us?" *New York Times*, September 24, 1967), and Caravaggio is cited in the same way by Gregory Battcock ("Notes on *The Chelsea Girls*: A Film by Andy Warhol," *Art Journal* 26, no. 4 [summer 1967]: 364, fn. 4). In "'Chelsea Girls' in Midtown West" (*New York Times*, December 1, 1966), Vincent Canby writes that "The Film-Makers' Distribution Center … has apparently found its 'Sound of Music" in Andy Warhol's new production, 'The Chelsea Girls.'" In two later articles, "Coast Will See Warhol Film" (*New York Times*, January 19, 1967) and "Cannes Will See Warhol Picture" (*New York Times*, April 25, 1967), he claims that *The Chelsea Girls* has been called "'The Sound of Music' of the Avant-Garde" and "'The Sound of Music' of the underground cinema," respectively (but doesn't say that it was he who suggested the comparison in the first place); it was also Canby who said, in "Coast Will See Warhol Film," that "Mr. Mekas … is beginning to sound like Darryl F. Zanuck." Warhol himself said of *The Chelsea Girls*, "There are no other similar films except *Who's Afraid of Virginia Woolf?* and *Tom Jones*" (in *I'll Be Your Mirror: The Selected Andy Warhol Interviews 1962–1987*, ed. Kenneth Goldsmith [New York: Carroll & Graf, 2004], 129).

5. Nam June Paik, "Expanded Education for the Paper-less Society" (1971), reprinted in *Video 'n' Videology: Nam June Paik, 1959–1973*, ed. Judson Rosebush (Syracuse: Everson Museum of Art, 1974).

6. Benjamin H. D. Buchloh, "An Interview with Andy Warhol," in *Andy Warhol*, ed. Annette Michelson (Cambridge, MA: MIT Press, 2001), 119.

7. *The Chelsea Girls* was one of four films seized in Boston during a six-month period under Massachusetts obscenity laws, and was the only one of the four in which the theater was found guilty as charged. The other three were Swedish films, *My Sister, My Love*; *Night Games*; and *I, a Woman* (whose title Warhol would parody the following year with *I a Man*). See "Exhibitor of 'Chelsea Girls' in Boston Is Fined $2,000" (*New York Times*, June 9, 1967).

8. Rex Reed, *Big Screen, Little Screen* (New York: Macmillan, 1971), 193.

9. Bosley Crowther, "The Underground Overflows," *New York Times*, December 11, 1966.

10. Andrew Sarris, "The Sub-New York Sensibility," *Cahiers du Cinema in English* 10 (May 1967): 43.

11. See J. Hoberman, *On Jack Smith's "Flaming Creatures" (and Other Secret-Flix of Cinemaroc)* (New York: Granary Books, 2001), 42–49.

12. Jonas Mekas's early Warhol filmography includes the following note: "The Program of September 15, 1966, lists: Room 732—*The Pope Ondine Story*; Room 422—*The Gerard Malanga Story*; Room 946—*George's Room*; Room 116—*Hanoi Hanna*; Room 202—*Afternoon*; Room 632—*The John*; Room 416—*The Trip*; Room 822—*The Closet*" (Jonas Mekas, "The Filmography of Andy Warhol," in John Coplans, *Andy Warhol* [Greenwich, CT: New York Graphic Society, 1970], 153).

13. Stephen Koch's description of *The Chelsea Girls* uses a different sequencing of reels from the one that is now standard. See Stephen Koch, *Stargazer: The Life, World, and Films of Andy Warhol*, revised edition (New York: Marion Boyars, 1991), 86–97.

14. The projection instructions for *The Chelsea Girls* include the following note: "As soon as a reel ends, it should be replaced immediately by the next one scheduled for that projector; in this way, the five minute difference between the two projectors which was established at reel #2 will be maintained throughout the entire film. *The Chelsea Girls* is intended to be slightly different each time it is projected, so timing is approximate" ("*The Chelsea Girls*: Instructions for Split-Screen Projection," in *The Films of Andy Warhol* (brochure) (New York: Museum of Modern Art Circulating Library, n.d.).

15. Andy Warhol and Pat Hackett, *Popism: The Warhol Sixties* (New York: Harcourt Brace, 1980), 185.

16. I employ the titles for the reels of the "definitive" *Chelsea Girls* given by Warhol and his colleagues at the Factory and, according to Callie Angell, written on the film cans.

17. Yvonne Rainer, "Don't Give the Game Away," *Arts Magazine* 41, no. 6 (April 1967): 45.

18. Ibid., 45–46. Susan Pile writes, similarly, "They [the 'actors'] are not acting, merely pretending, but the airs they assume and the people they imagine themselves to be become so overwhelming that they forget that they *know* they are only playing a game" (Susan Pile, "The Chelsea Girls," *Film Culture* 45 [summer 1967]: 46).

19. Rosalyn Regelson, "Where Are 'The Chelsea Girls' Taking Us?" *New York Times*, September 24, 1967, 131.

20. Rosalyn Regelson, "'Not a Boy, Not a Girl, Just Me,'" *New York Times*, November 2, 1969, D1.

21. Rosalyn Regelson, "Is Motherhood Holy? Not Any More," *New York Times*, May 18, 1969, D1.

22. Rosalyn Regelson, "Up the Camp Staircase," *New York Times*, March 3, 1968, D1. Regelson continues: "Miss Sontag's bourgeoisified version of Camp is indeed trivial, and it was natural that Madison Avenue and the merchandisers should have latched on to her essay like manna. They have put their heavy guns behind Pop-Camp, using the suggestion of homosexuality to give their products and their ads a frisson of the forbidden, catering to a new class of culture consumer who sought in art and fashion the veneer of the new and odd. Feeling insecure and inauthentic, they sensed that the homosexual had a special knowledge about these things and, stealing his tight pants, unpadded shoulders, and manicured sideburns, they tried to take up his knowledge with his clothing. They pursued him into his longstanding private retreats and stole his vocabulary. Having invaded the homosexual's world as far as possible, they then started talking of conspiracies of homosexuals to take over their world."

23. According to an entry for "Gay Studies" in *Gay Histories and Cultures: An Encyclopedia* (ed. George E. Haggerty [New York: Garland, 2000], 389), "The first regular college courses to adopt an approach sympathetic to homosexuality and uphold scholarly aspirations seem to have been offered by Rosalind [*sic*] Regelson at New York and Yale Universities in the late 1960s."

24. *I'll Be Your Mirror*, 193–194.

25. Ibid., 166.

26. Carrie Lambert discusses the relation of contingent and rationalized time in her chapter on Yvonne Rainer's *Parts of Some Sextets* in *Being Watched: Yvonne Rainer and the 1960s* (Cambridge, MA: MIT Press, 2008), 75–125.

27. "[Warhol] took a napkin, and said, 'I want . . .,' and drew a line right down the center, and he put the capital letter 'B' and the capital letter 'W.' And he said, 'I want two energies . . . I want black and white, at the same time.' He said, 'Do you understand?' And I said, 'Yes.' And that was it. That was the discussion for *Chelsea Girls*" (Ronald Tavel, quoted in David E. James, "The Warhol Screenplays: An Interview with Ronald Tavel," *Persistence of Vision* 11 [1995]: 57).

28. A transcript of Eric Emerson's monologue from *The Chelsea Girls* is published in *Little Caesar* 7 (ca. 1978): 49–52.

29. "I was reflecting that most people thought the Factory was a place where everybody had the same attitudes about everything; the truth was, we were all odds-and-ends misfits, somehow misfitting together" (Warhol and Hackett, *Popism*, 219).

MOST BEAUTIFUL

1. "Society: Edie & Andy," *Time*, August 27, 1965, 66–67.

2. I was unable to determine what the Latin dance rhythm was, so I asked Mario Montez just after he'd seen *Camp* again at the *Live Film! Jack Smith! Five Flaming Days in a Rented World!* festival in Berlin in October 2009. He said he was combining merengue, pachanga, and calypso.

3. Malanga announces in *Camp* that his poem called "Camp" is based on John Wieners's "Memories of You," and indeed it follows that poem's subject and cadences very closely.

4. Among the many commentators on camp in the wake of Susan Sontag's 1964 *Partisan Review* essay "Notes on 'Camp,'" one in the *New York Times* Sunday magazine section singled out Batman comic books as "low camp" (Thomas Meehan, "Not Good Taste, Not Bad Taste—It's 'Camp,'" *New York Times*, March 21, 1965). A year later, a *New York Times* piece by Judy Stone on the Batman television series was entitled "The Caped Crusader of Camp" (see Sasha Torres, "Caped Crusader of Camp," in *Pop Out: Queer Warhol*, ed. Jennifer Doyle, Jonathan Flatley, and José Esteban Muños [Durham: Duke University Press, 1996], 238–255).

5. In an interview with Smith in *Film Culture*, Gerard Malanga asks, "You certainly are always asked about it—your portrayal of Dracula. How did it evolve? How did you feel?" Smith replies,

"But nobody has ever asked me that. But I thought it was forgotten. When is Andy going to release it in fact?" At the end of the interview Smith repeats, "Yes, and what I'm trying to think of is DRACULA. When will that ever be released, do you think?" ("Interview with Jack Smith by Gerard Malanga," *Film Culture* 45 [summer 1967]: 13, 14).

6. My discussion of Swan's career is drawn primarily from Janis Londraville and Richard Londraville, *The Most Beautiful Man in the World: Paul Swan, from Wilde to Warhol* (Lincoln: University of Nebraska Press, 2006).

7. Directed by Charles Allen and Francis Trevelyan Miller, the film was reviewed in the *New York Times* on June 19, 1916, upon its release at the Strand Theater.

8. For an over-the-top biography of Pavley, which is at the same time an autobiography of the author, see Arthur Corey, *Danse Macabre: The Life and Death of Andreas Pavley* (Dallas: Southern Methodist University, Bridwell Library, 1977).

9. Quoted in Londraville and Londraville, *The Most Beautiful Man in the World*, 91, 93.

10. Ibid., 112.

11. Ibid., 157.

12. Ibid., 165.

13. Ibid., 213.

14. Callie Angell, *The Films of Andy Warhol: Part II* (New York: Whitney Museum of American Art, 1994), 23.

15. Stefan Brecht, *Queer Theatre* (New York: Methuen, 1986), 160.

16. Andy Warhol and Pat Hackett, *Popism: The Warhol Sixties* (New York: Harcourt Brace, 1980), 180.

17. Angell, *The Films of Andy Warhol*, 23.

18. Callie Angell informed me that a number of two-reel films made in 1965–1966, especially including those with one static reel and one shot with a highly mobile camera, were screened as double-screen projections.

19. See Jonas Mekas, "On Cinéma Vérité, Ricky Leacock, and Warhol," in *Movie Journal: The Rise of the New American Cinema 1959–1971* (New York: Macmillan, 1972), 153–155.

20. For a discussion of documentary—but pointedly *not* cinéma vérité—and camp in a related context, see Branden W. Joseph's discussion of Susan Sontag's review of Emile de Antonio's *Point of Order* in "1962," *October* 132 (spring 2010): 121–123.

21. Interestingly, *Film Culture* gave its 1961 Independent Film Award to Leacock–Maysles for *Primary* and its 1964 award to Andy Warhol for *Sleep*, *Haircut*, *Eat*, *Kiss*, and *Empire*. The award's citation of Warhol's cinema for its purity of representing unadorned the world as it is includes the following parenthetical statement: "(even Cinema Veritè [*sic*] did not escape this subjection of the objective reality to ideas)" ("Sixth Independent Film Award," *Film Culture* 33 [summer 1964]: 1). For Drew Associates, see P. J. O'Connell, *Robert Drew and the Development of Cinema Verité in America* (Carbondale: Southern Illinois University Press, 1992).

22. In 2007, Canarsie High School was slated to be closed because of poor class performance and violence.

23. "New Faces, New Forces, New Names in the Arts," *Harper's Bazaar*, June 1963, 64–67. The Villella photobooth photos are reproduced in *Andy Warhol's Time Capsule 21* (Pittsburgh: The Andy Warhol Museum; Frankfurt: Museum für Moderner Kunst, 2003), 179.

24. Villella writes in his autobiography, "Backstage everyone was fraught with anxiety. We all held our breath as the ballet got under way. I felt stimulated, turned on by the excitement. I get off on risks and high stakes. I have a taste for drama. That night I took one of the biggest risks of my life. I could have sustained a serious injury that might have had dire consequences for my career, but luck was with me, and even though I kept crashing breathless into the wings, the performance passed without a hitch. I'd do it again in a minute—just for the rush" (Edward Villella, *Prodigal Son: Dancing for Balanchine in a World of Pain and Magic* [New York: Simon & Schuster, 1992], 196).

25. "The Dance as a Way of Life," *Dance Magazine*, November 1944, 9, 25.

ADDENDUM: BORING CAMP

1. See Callie Angell, *Andy Warhol Screen Tests: The Films of Andy Warhol Catalogue Raissoné*, vol. 1 (New York: Abrams, vol. 1, 2006), 190.

2. Ibid.

3. Susan Sontag, *Against Interpretation and Other Essays* (New York: Dell, 1979), 289.

4. Henry Luhrman, "A Bored Susan Sontag: 'I Think Camp Should Be Retired,'" *Columbia Owl*, March 23, 1966, 11.

5. Susan Sontag, *On Photography* (New York: Farrar, Straus & Giroux, 1977), 44.

6. Ibid., 44–45.

7. Thomas Meehan, "Not Good Taste, Not Bad Taste—It's 'Camp,'" *New York Times*, March 21, 1965.

8. Sontag, *Against Interpretation*, 289–290.

9. Ibid, 229–230.

10. Ibid., 231.

11. G. R. Swenson, "What Is Pop Art?" *Art News* 62, no. 7 (November 1963): 26. For an extended analysis of Warhol's "liking" see Jonathan Flatley, "Like: Collecting and Collectivity," *October* 132 (spring 2010): 71–98. Flatley is currently completing a book in the subject of likeness and liking in Warhol.

12. Sontag, *Against Interpretation*, 280.

13. Marcie Frank argues persuasively that Sontag's distancing herself from camp in her own essay about it already exhibits the moralism that would come to characterize her critical perspective beginning with "Fascinating Fascism" (see Marcie Frank, "The Critic as Performance Artist: Susan Sontag's Writing and Gay Cultures," in *Camp Grounds: Style and Homosexuality*, ed. David Bergman [Amherst: University of Massachusetts Press, 1993], 173–184).

14. Jack Smith, "The Perfect Filmic Appositeness of Maria Montez," in *Wait for Me at the Bottom of the Pool: The Writings of Jack Smith*, ed. J. Hoberman and Edward Leffingwell (New York: High Risk Books, 1997), 25.

15. Marc Siegel, "A Gossip of Images: Hollywood Star Images and Queer Counterpublics" (dissertation, University of California, Los Angeles, 2010), 160.

16. Ronald Tavel, "The Theatre of the Ridiculous," *Tri-Quarterly* 6 (1966): 104. Quoted in Siegel, "A Gossip of Images," 164.

17. Interestingly, when St. Denis married Ted Shawn, a newspaper reporter confused Shawn with Swan and thus appeared the newspaper headline "RUTH ST. DENIS MARRIES TED SHAWN, THE MOST BEAUTIFUL MAN IN THE WORLD" (see Walter Terry, *Miss Ruth: The "More Living Life" of Ruth St. Denis* [New York: Dodd, Mead, 1969], 107–108).

18. Michael Moon, "Flaming Closets," *October* 51 (spring 1989): 19–54.

19. Ted Shawn, *Ruth St. Denis: Pioneer and Prophet—Being a History of Her Cycle of Oriental Dances* (Breinigsville, PA: Yokai Publishing, 2011), 36.

20. Juan Suárez, "Jack Smith, Hélio Oiticica, Tropicalism," expanded version of paper presented at *Live Film! Jack Smith! Five Flaming Days in a Rented World*, Berlin, October 2009, forthcoming in *Criticism: A Quarterly for Literature and the Arts*. Suárez first made this argument in "City Films, Modern Spatiality, and the End of the World Trade Center," in *Film and Television after 9/11*, ed. W. Wheeler Dixon (Carbondale: Southern Illinois University Press, 2004).

21. Suárez's argument about *Scotch Tape* is similar to one made by Jennifer's Doyle in her paper, "Like the Weather and Flowers and Stuff: Poetry, Correspondence, and *Scotch Tape*," also presented at *Live Film! Jack Smith! Five Flaming Days in a Rented World.* A revised version of Doyle's presentation, titled "New Jersey Junkyard," will appear in *Criticism: A Quarterly for Literature and the Arts*.

22. Smith, "The Perfect Filmic Appositeness of Maria Montez," 34.

EPILOGUE: WARHOL'S TIME

1. For a chart detailing the events in *Empire*, see Callie Angell, "Guide to EMPIRE," in *The Films of Andy Warhol: Part II* (New York: Whitney Museum of American Art, 1994), 18.

2. According to Gerard Malanga, the camera crew that shot *Empire* included, in addition to Warhol and Malanga, Jonas Mekas, Marie Desert, and John Palmer, with Henry Romney of the Rockefeller Foundation also present (see Gerard Malanga, *Archiving Warhol: An Illustrated History* [New York: Creation Books, 2002], 85).

3. It is increasingly difficult to find projectors that project at 16 frames per second (fps), the silent speed used by Warhol in the 1960s. Projected at 18 fps the film lasts slightly less than seven hours and eleven minutes.

4. "On the reversal original (that is, the film that was in the camera), the dots are actually perforations punched into the film. If you looked at the film on an editing bench, rather than on screen, you would see that the dots 'spell' out a number several digits in length across multiple frames. When the exposed-but-undeveloped reversal original was sent to the lab in its original box, the lab technician punched the same number on both the box flap and end of the film roll. After development, the roll was matched to the box with this number and sent back to Warhol. Because this footage comes at the end of the roll, there is an almost-certain possibility of light leakage during handling, which accounts for the exposure fluctuations. This affects the beginning of rolls as well. Even though film is supposed to be loaded and unloaded in absolute darkness, even a dark room won't be as dark as the interior of the camera, where the supermajority of the film will not receive any incidental exposure. Suffice it to say, for almost any other filmmaker, the impulse would be to trim out this material. An industrial filmmaker working in 16mm would automatically assume that the first and last ten feet of a roll will be unusable; most avant-garde filmmakers would take the same stance. It is a measure of Warhol's integrity as a filmmaker that he left all these artifacts in the final film—a demonstration that nothing has been trimmed out, nothing finessed. You are seeing the very first frame to the very last" (e-mail from Kyle Westphal, chief projectionist, George Eastman House, March 5, 2011).

5. Amy Taubin, "Andy Warhol: Motion Pictures," *Artforum* 49, no. 7 (March 2011): 261, 262.

6. Callie Angell, "Doubling the Screen: Andy Warhol's *Outer and Inner Space*," *Millennium Film Journal* 38 (spring 2002): 27.

7. This is the number of individual *Screen Tests* cataloged in Callie Angell, *Andy Warhol Screen Tests: The Films of Andy Warhol Catalogue Raissoné,* vol. 1 (New York: Abrams, 2006).

8. Taubin, "Andy Warhol: Motion Pictures," 261.

9. For *Six Months*, see Angell, *Andy Warhol Screen Tests*, chapter 3, "Six Months," 217–241. There were other (possibly fanciful) projects of extreme length—twenty-four hours in the life of Edie Sedgwick and a twenty-four-hour film of Marcel Duchamp; see Callie Angell, *The Films of Andy Warhol: Part II* (New York: Whitney Museum of American Art, 1994), 15.

10. "The decision to film *an object* allowed for the presentation of the full range of tones from black to white.... The choice of the Empire State Building seems a logical one. It's not some faceless building in Queens that demands identification or clarification, nor is it a building from which any aesthetic pleasure or stimulation can be gained (at least at this time). It is, simply, a big nothing" (Gregory Battcock, "Notes on *Empire*: A Film by Andy Warhol," *Film Culture* 40 [spring 1966]: 39). Callie Angell suggests, on the contrary, that Warhol would have been especially intrigued by the Empire State Building at the time of filming *Empire* because the exterior flood lights had recently been installed on the building for the opening of the New York World's Fair (Angell, "Guide to EMPIRE," 16). Warhol famously remarked, "The Empire State Building is a star"; see Jonas Mekas, *Movie Journal* (New York: MacMillan, 1972), 151.

11. Battcock, "Notes on *Empire*," 39–40.

12. John Bernard Myers, "A Letter to Gregory Battcock," in *The New American Cinema*, ed. Gregory Battcock (New York: Dutton, 1967), 139–140.

13. Amy Taubin, "My Time Is Not Your Time," *Sight and Sound* 4 (June 1994): 21.

14. "Sixth Independent Film Award," *Film Culture* 33 (summer 1964): 1. Stan Brakhage was famously outraged. He resigned from the Film-Makers' Co-op and wrote to Jonas Mekas, "I cannot in good conscience continue to accept the help of institutions which have come to propagate advertisements for forces which I recognize as among the most destructive in the world today: 'dope,' self-centered Love, unqualified Hatred, Nihilism, violence to self and society" (quoted in Victor Bockris, *The Life and Death of Andy Warhol* [New York: Bantam Books, 1989], 159).

15. Because only one of Anthology's projectors in the Maya Deren Theater has 16 fps capacity, on this occasion half the reels were screened at 18 fps, resulting in a total time length of seven and a half hours rather than the correct eight hours and five minutes. "The Empire screening was a little sketchy in terms of who stayed. The official statement was that twenty-five people stayed through the screening. I think half of the people were mostly in and out, especially the crowd in the back. They returned about forty-five minutes before the end to be in the count. The folks in the front and around our rows were probably a little more serious about the screening" (e-mail from Thomas Kiedrowski, March 9, 2011).

16. Ronald Tavel, quoted in David E. James, "The Warhol Screenplays: An Interview with Ronald Tavel," *Persistence of Vision* 11 (1995): 51.

INDEX

Note: Page numbers in italics refer to illustrations.